# DAVID POWNALL

*The Composer Plays*

## MASTER CLASS
## MUSIC TO MURDER BY
## ELGAR'S RONDO
## ELGAR'S THIRD

Oberon Books
London

First published in this collection in Great Britain by Oberon Books Limited, 521 Caledonian Road, London N7 9RH.

Tel: 071 607 3637/ Fax: 071 607 3629

Printed by The Chameleon Press Limited, London.

Cover design: Andrzej Klimowski

ISBN 1 870259 41 6

# CONTENTS

# PREFACE

I was not in Britain during the Sixties - that crucible of divine discontent between Kennedy's assassination and the Apollo landing on the moon - so the impact of the Theatre of Cruelty, the Absurd and Ritual, which so pulverised, mocked and ceremoniously dumped the ideal of freedom, was merely tangential. Although we produced the new crop of plays in the Zambian copperbelt mining towns where I worked, the audience related to the politics of a newly independent African state where freedom was not a target to be shot at, but a shibboleth between all citizens who carried the right party card.

Had I been more perceptive and in less of a rush to start a new life as a writer upon my return to Britain in 1970, I might have better interpreted, and more sympathetically, the weird, aggressive orthodoxy prevalent in British theatre at the time, viewing it in a rosier light - as an attempt not to discard, but to reconstruct the ideal of freedom.

Perhaps Bernard Levin ought to have been working in the provinces with the new generation of theatre practitioners in 1970; then he would never have described Britain in that year as "a nation undecided whether to go backwards or forwards." For many directors, actors and writers the move was sideways into a glazed Sovietism within which liberty was preserved like a 1917 foetus, yellowing in formalin.

Although music has stringent inner laws, it is also invested with a mystery of meaning and animal evasiveness that enables a writer to escape from even the most subtle and seemingly consensual forms of censorship. From the first play that I wrote upon my return to the present, music has always been a strong, sustaining accomplice. During this time Political Correctness has emerged as a force in the whole of society, not only in the theatre, and its threatening self-righteousness is difficult to combat with words alone.

Meaning in music cannot be nailed down. Pure sound cannot be a signed confession of anything. Music shares the original unmeaningness of existence that theatre challenges, but never conquers. We need not have taken the message of the Sixties so seriously as to concede victory to the idea that freedom was done for, and to stand by while the theatre was drafted into political journalism.

Paradoxically, my first contact with music as a function of freedom came within the discipline of attending church - Sunday after Sunday spent as a boy treble in a cold chancel, watching the sexton pump the organ, listening to Reverend Quick meandering through incoherent sermons. When we stood up to sing it was always a moment of liberation. However, even as a twelve-year old, I knew that without tempo, clarity, control and guidance, the music went nowhere and became nothing.

★

Two years after my return to England I became resident playwright at the new Duke's Playhouse in Lancaster. For five years I wrote non-stop for the company - everything from large-scale folk epics to pub shows, pantomimes, revues, anything that could be used to bring the audiences in. Eventually all was done, the theatre regularly filled, and it was the moment to step outside.

Of the full-length plays that mattered to me, one was based on an horrific double murder committed by a local Parsee Indian doctor in 1936; the second on John of Gaunt in Purgatory; the third on the linoleum millionaire who had run the town; and the last a municipal comedy. I used music in all of them - working with Stephen Boxer the theatre composer - but I had not written about music. This I turned to at the point of imminent departure from my long apprenticeship at Lancaster. It was the means of getting out and getting in to myself. Fortunately, I had worked with a number of actors who were also musicians and singers - this was the director, Peter Oyston's style - and to make use of all these skills was a natural choice.

First, I wrote a one-act play for the Duke's Playhouse, called *The Pro*, built around the making of a new folk-song in a traditional mode. In the cast was Harriet Walter with her flute, Stephen Boxer with his guitar, Noreen Kershaw as the singer who can't get it right, and Will Tacey as the despairing roadie. After playing it at Lancaster, we took it to a fringe venue in London. When Paines Plough was founded in 1975, all the ingredients of that first little play were present - actors I could write for who could play instruments and sing, and a free company, not tied to any function other than theatre itself. There was also the advantage of having John Adams as Director, a very playful, Houdini-like man of enviable taste, and gifted with a revelatory understanding of how music and theatre can spark off each other.

Another musical influence coincided with John's at that time - the arrival of Julian Leigh in Lancaster from Canada. He was, by then, an ex-composer by his own confession. As the son of Walter Leigh, he had struggled with the patrimony and rejected his musical genes. Yet his knowledge was as fascinating as his fierce character in those days, and he sat me down and taught me music with a drink, a sceptical laugh, and a considerable amount of arm-twisting.

It was Julian who slipped me a copy of *Gesualdo, Musician and Murderer* by Philip Heseltine [later Peter Warlock] and Cecil Gray, published in 1926. I read it on a train journey from Lancaster to London. Before reaching Euston I had finished it and was already wondering how to make a play from the diabolical connection between the book and Warlock as the writer of the book.

*Music to Murder By* was the result. In it themes from *The Pro* re-emerged - the cost of getting the music right and the expense of a creative self - freedom as a form of slavery - and the imperative to write outside all social and political limits. It was the most demanding play I had made so far. The way that it worked surprised me. At the heart of it was that strong feeling, so marked in those days, that things kept apart were edging back together. With the theatre in the right hand and music in the left, a balance other than that between heavy relevance and avoirdupois political was now possible. All the other parts of the mind and spirit could return to the mystery on the stage.

★

*Music to Murder By* was written for five actors and a set that would go into a transit van for touring. *Master Class* was even more parsimonious - four actors and a piano. These were the circumscriptions drawn by the theatre of British subsidised poverty, and the means of getting round them were not only frugal but fugal. Apologists can be heard for keeping the arts short on rations - as they can for the benevolent effects of totalitarianism on creative minds - but these are arguments for another day. I mention them because it was music that gave these plays an extra dimension for me, making them feel bigger, more capable of stretching out beyond controls and restrictions.

*Master Class* was born out of an extremely minor political decision. The Drama Panel of the Arts Council - made up of fellow workers - refused a grant to Paines Plough for the production of *Music to Murder By* on the grounds that it was élitist theatre, being about two obscure composers, rather than an issue of the day. The play went on to be a success of a sort and this decision was reversed, but the damage was done. At a point when

I wished to jettison a lot of the thought-baggage about how Britain had changed in the Sixties, and simply get on with writing from imagination, up jumps a company of commissars cursing dead composers for not being Beethoven. The situation was laughable, but grim in its implications. These were not bureaucrats who had taken this decision, but actors, directors, maybe even playwrights!

Enter, once again, Julian Leigh - with sardonic stealth the minutes of the Conference of Musicians at the Central Committee of the All-Union Communist Party held in Moscow in January 1948 were slid under my door. This ironic gift arrived in 1977, made in the full knowledge of what I still felt on the subject of music and democratic despotism. The effect of reading the minutes was the same as I had felt upon hearing the Arts Council decision on *Music to Murder By*. A chill down the back that induced a special kind of laughter.

The following year I went to Moscow, knowing that there was a play to be written, but unable to shape the size of the story to fit into a transit van.

In Russia no-one wanted to talk about Stalin, or his hatchet-man, Zhdanov, but there was the winter, the Kremlin, and huge occasions of institutional art. Yet no key was turned until I sat next to an old English diplomat on the flight home who told me that he had been in Moscow in 1948 and had heard a rumour that Stalin had offered to give Prokofiev a piano lesson.

Suddenly there was a room, a piano, two men, and a mad sort of teaching taking place. Before the plane reached England, both Shostakovich and Zhdanov had also entered and some very strange sounds were coming from the piano. As it happened, when I finished the play in 1981, Paines Plough was so broke that it could not even afford the four actors.

When the play opened at the Leicester Haymarket theatre the transit van scale of the setting had gone and had been replaced by a great, golden room in the Old Kremlin. During the last twelve years I have seen productions of the play all over the world, but it was only last year in Paris, at the Théatre de la Commune Pandora that I encountered a production with the severity and simplicity originally envisaged.

★

While writing plays for the theatre about music one encounters a paradox; that music is freedom to the listener but slavery to the composer. The deeper one investigates this most evanescent of all the arts, the more it vanishes into the authority of an inhuman universe. The laws are there, still intact as they were in Pythagoras's day, proof of a harmonious construct without a purpose, unless God is called in as musician for composers to imitate and interpret.

Because I write plays about composers I am often asked: "Is that what you would really like to be?" The answer is - certainly not. I don't envy composers at all. But I do feel for their seriousness, their acceptance of this inarticulate dictation from a source outside themselves. More than any other artist they must live in a landscape that is desolate, until sound saves them. With writers, painters, sculptors, it is people who offer redemption. But the composer has to make do with the vibration of an unknowable mind, the beginning, the maker of meanings as yet unloosed.

This takes them closer to the pre-human world. Now when we are so inclined to doubt the authenticity and value of language, it is the composers who offer an alternative. It is no accident that the explosion in music that has taken place since the last war only scraped the surface of the world inhabited by Gesualdo, Shostakovich and Elgar, or that contemporary music has been driven into such a hole. It is a retreat from the knowledge that the impulse towards music, rather than the word, will bring us into collision with a primitive force that we would rather not embrace. Until now protection has been available through religion. But, as those absurdities slip away, and the world of images rusts in its own inanities, the composers are the only ones left who can enter the cave where the truth lies.

This paradox, I believe, lies at the root of Elgar, that arch-conservative, that parody of an Edwardian squire and nationalist. Like Dostoevsky, his sheer power as a creator eclipsed his proud prejudices but, unlike the author of *Crime and Punishment*, he could not go through with the sufferings and dangers that being a great composer exposed him to. He wanted to be himself first and a servant of music's terrible duty second. Taking this choice, he hoped to be free. But I am certain that if he could speak now he would admit that his barren years were spent in the Siberia of silence.

I had taken only an unthinking interest in Elgar's music until an accidental encounter while doing research for a play on the Chamberlain dynasty commissioned by Birmingham Rep. Elgar hated academics and what they had done to English music. But this did not prevent him appearing in the robes of a Cambridge Doctor of Music to give his inaugural lecture as a professor at Birmingham University. It was a betrayal that Elgar understood and had taken upon himself in order to belong to what he instinctively rejected. In the audience was Neville Chamberlain, a pianist of mild ability, engendering another betrayal within his own love of music and the dominance of his nationalistic *Land of Hope and Glory* father. Fanciful - undeniably. Over-heated hindsight, perhaps. But from the flash between two characters that have walked onto the stage in one's mind comes the impulse for a play. In this case, music was the reason why the two men were in the same room and also the medium through which the impulse came to write *Elgar's Rondo*.

Elgar's abiding melancholy was caused by late recognition and the compromises he had to make. As a composer he was self-taught, but Edwardian society finally shaped him more than any conservatoire could have done. When he submitted to inertia and neglect after the Great War it was as if he had arrived at a place where he did not want to be, but could find no way out that would not lead him back there again.

Although there was no ironical purpose behind the BBC's commission for the 75-year old Elgar to compose a new symphony fourteen years late - the subject of *Elgar's Third* - it is difficult not to feel that edge. At the start of a new age of mass radio communication, when strident voices in Germany and Italy, those great musical nations, were already making use of the medium, Elgar was invited to emerge from his slumber, full of regrets and nostalgia, and stir the nation again.

If the new symphony had been finished, rather than left in tiny fragments, what would have been Elgar's musical message? Another enigma perhaps?

DAVID POWNALL
*1994*

# MASTER CLASS

*For Andrew Leigh*

*Master Class* was first performed at the Haymarket Theatre, Leicester, on 27 January, 1983, with the following cast:

ZHDANOV, *Jonathan Adams*
PROKOFIEV,  *Peter Kelly*
SHOSTAKOVICH,  *David Bamber*
STALIN,  *Timothy West*

Directed by Justin Greene
Designed by Martin Johns
Composer and Musical Director, John White

The production transferred to the Old Vic Theatre, London, with the same cast, on 18 January, 1984.

# ACT ONE

*A richly decorated reception room in the old Kremlin with a grand piano. A washroom and toilet stand adjacent right. The walls of both rooms are open. The entrance to the sitting room is from upstage. The door adjoining it with the washroom is from the right.*

*[Lights up on ZHDANOV washing his hands in the washroom. As he is drying his hands he suffers a pain in his chest and sucks in his breath. In some haste he takes a small bottle of pills out of his pocket, swallows two and drinks from the cold water tap to wash them down. Pause. He looks at himself in the mirror and grimaces. He combs his hair, adjusts his suit, walks through to the sitting room. He puts a record on a gramophone. It is a jazz cornet piece. ZHDANOV looks at his watch, sits down, lights a cigarette and listens to the music. He concentrates hard, frowning, puffing on his cigarette. PROKOFIEV arrives at the door to the sitting room. He is using a stick and is obviously in some distress. He is beautifully and correctly dressed. Steadying himself, he pauses, listening to the music which he can hear through the door. He smiles as he recognizes it. He waits, then shrugs and knocks at the door. ZHDANOV does not hear the knock above the music. PROKOFIEV knocks on the door with the handle of his stick]*

ZHDANOV: Enter!

*[PROKOFIEV straightens himself up, opens the door and enters, closing the door behind him. ZHDANOV looks at him but says nothing. PROKOFIEV stands in front of ZHDANOV like a soldier before his commanding officer, not daring to move. He leans heavily on his stick. He looks at ZHDANOV half enquiringly, half pityingly, as if trying to guess the reason for ZHDANOV'S bad manners. ZHDANOV suddenly gets up and takes the needle off the gramophone]*

ZHDANOV: So much for your reputation as a punctual man, Prokofiev.

PROKOFIEV: I arrived on time but I managed to get lost in the building. There are a lot of stairs.

ZHDANOV: I left instruction for you to be taken to the lift. No matter. You're here. That music mean anything to you?

PROKOFIEV: Bix Beiderbecke, I think.

ZHDANOV: [*Looking at the record*] Leon Bismark Beiderbecke according
   to this. Not very Germanic in tone. Obviously a man who has betrayed
   his origins.
PROKOFIEV: May I sit down?
ZHDANOV: Yes.
[*PROKOFIEV sits down. Pause. ZHDANOV looks at his watch again*]
ZHDANOV: Someone told me that you'd had a bad fall.
PROKOFIEV: That is correct.
ZHDANOV: You should look where you're going.
PROKOFIEV: I blacked out, actually.
ZHDANOV: It's a wonder I don't black out being stuck at the Musi-
   cians' Union Conference for days on end. Can you imagine what
   it's like suffocating in a room with hundreds of bloody musicians
   and composers, trying to get some sense out of them. What a time
   I've had.
PROKOFIEV: I'm sorry that I cannot join you.
ZHDANOV: Can't or won't?
PROKOFIEV: It would be my duty to be there if I were capable of making
   a contribution.
[*SHOSTAKOVICH arrives at the door and knocks immediately*]
ZHDANOV: Enter!
[*SHOSTAKOVICH enters and closes the door behind him. He appears anxious
   and slightly pugnacious as though expecting to fend off an attack*]
ZHDANOV: The least that we might expect from a musician is that he
   should keep good time.
SHOSTAKOVICH: This place is a warren.
ZHDANOV: Not full of rabbits though.
SHOSTAKOVICH: Sergei, how are you? Don't get up.
PROKOFIEV: Much better, thank you.
ZHDANOV: Well, Comrade Shostakovich, you can fill in your colleague
   about what progress we are making at the conference. That shouldn't
   take long, should it?
PROKOFIEV: That would be useful if I'm to understand the basis for
   this evening's discussion.
ZHDANOV: Discussion? [*Laughs*] I like that. Discussion. Go on,
   Shostakovich. Shoot! We have a few moments to spare before he
   comes.
SHOSTAKOVICH: Well, let's see. We have spent a lot of time on
   Muradeli's opera, *The Great Fellowship*. Comrade Zhdanov, as the

chairman of the conference you may see it differently but I would say that we are using Muradeli's work as a test case, analysing it...

ZHDANOV: Not by itself. It has been coupled with your own masterpiece, *Lady Macbeth of Mtensk*, these two works being the most unpopular operas written in Russia for fifty years.

SHOSTAKOVICH: I didn't hear anyone making that observation.

ZHDANOV: Didn't you? Well, I'm making it now.

SHOSTAKOVICH: [*To PROKOFIEV*] Did you hear Muradeli's opera when it was first produced?

PROKOFIEV: No, I missed it, unfortunately. What is it about?

SHOSTAKOVICH: Where shall I start? It's set in Georgia up in the mountains. It's about the period when the Soviet Government was being established there.

PROKOFIEV: I see.

SHOSTAKOVICH: The Party's land reform programme is opposed by some wealthy farmers...

ZHDANOV: At unexpected moments the whole orchestra starts blaring! During lyrical interludes the drums suddenly burst in! In the middle of heroic passages he plants sad, elegiac, winsome themes. Muradeli is mad. And you're no better.

PROKOFIEV: I would like to have heard this discussion. Did the conference come up with any answers?

SHOSTAKOVICH: The Art Committee and its chairman, Comrade Khrapchenko, were partly blamed. Muradeli blamed himself and his musical education. Some interesting facts emerged. I didn't know, for instance, that three hundred operas have been written in the Soviet Union in the last thirty years. Nor that the price of harps was so outrageous.

ZHDANOV: You and your friends have confused the entire music brotherhood of the Soviet Union. Only one man can sort it out now. But, I ask you, should we be wasting his time?

SHOSTAKOVICH: At least we will find out what he thinks.

ZHDANOV: I've been telling you what he thinks! I am his spokesman on all cultural matters!

SHOSTAKOVICH: Do you know what he actually thinks of my work, himself?

ZHDANOV: You're going to find out shortly.

SHOSTAKOVICH: Has he any respect for it?

ZHDANOV: Have you?

SHOSTAKOVICH: Have I? I have to live with it.

ZHDANOV: [*To PROKOFIEV*] Do you respect his work?

PROKOFIEV: I know that he is always interested in constructive criticism. When and if I am in a position to provide some I will make it available in a serious, respectful way.

ZHDANOV: You talk like you write music - backwards!

[*Pause. ZHDANOV looks at his watch. He is getting even more irritable with anxiety. He lights another cigarette*]

PROKOFIEV: Is there anything we should know before he arrives? I have never met Comrade Stalin. I am not even sure of the correct way to address him.

[*STALIN enters the washroom through a hidden door. He is carrying a flat, rectangular parcel. He closes the door and goes through to the toilet. Putting the lid down on the pedestal he sits on it. For a moment he looks very tired. Leaning the parcel against the pedestal he gets to his feet and looks in the mirror. Taking a small comb from his pocket he combs his moustache, his eyebrows and his hair. There is something almost womanly about the way he does this*]

ZHDANOV: His official titles are: Father of the People; the Greatest Genius in History; Friend and Teacher of all Toilers; Shining Sun of Humanity; and Life-Giving Force of Socialism - but you say what you like. Why not call him Cloth-Ears?

PROKOFIEV: I would appreciate your advice. What is the proper form?

ZHDANOV: Comrade Stalin is the form. The same as anyone else. Kiss his big toe if you want to.

PROKOFIEV: All this trouble over a little music. It is shameful that we have to bother him about it.

[*STALIN starts singing in the washroom as he combs his thick, black hair. Its colour has a hard, unnatural gloss to it*]

STALIN: [*Singing*] He who clothes himself with light as with a garment, stood naked at the judgment. On his cheek he received blows from the hands which he had formed. The lawless multitude nailed to the Cross the Lord of glory.

[*As soon as ZHDANOV hears the first bars of the song he leaps to his feet and listens*]

ZHDANOV: That's him! He's coming.

[*Pause. The three of them look at the upstage door. SHOSTAKOVICH and PROKOFIEV realize that the sound is coming from elsewhere and look at the other door which leads to the washroom. ZHDANOV follows suit*]

ZHDANOV: How did he get in there?

SHOSTAKOVICH: What's in that room?

ZHDANOV: A lavatory. He's in the lavatory. What the hell is he singing about?

PROKOFIEV: It's the old Easter hymn. Don't you recognize it?

[*The singing stops. Pause. STALIN sits on the pedestal again, picks up the parcel and clutches it to his chest. Pause. ZHDANOV listens intently. STALIN reaches up and pulls the chain. ZHDANOV smiles, relaxes a little*]

ZHDANOV: Sounds like one of your string quartets.

[*STALIN gets up and leaves the washroom, turning the light out as he goes*]

ZHDANOV: Look lively now.

[*STALIN enters. He goes straight to the mantelshelf and props the parcel up on it. PROKOFIEV is struggling to get out of his chair. STALIN presses him back*]

STALIN: Sit down before you fall down. You don't look well. What's your doctor like?

PROKOFIEV: Good evening, sir. My doctor is competent, I believe.

STALIN: I doubt it.

PROKOFIEV: I hope, for my sake, you are wrong.

STALIN: Oh, I can be wrong. Health is a very personal matter. The foundations of a sound constitution are laid in childhood - the air we breathe, the environment. Andrei here had a bad doctor. He wasn't helping him at all, was he?

ZHDANOV: No.

STALIN: He was killing him - neglect, ignorance. So Andrei is now being treated by my doctors - all seven of them. I'm so healthy that they've got nothing to do so they're keeping their hand in with Andrei. He's a real challenge to them. A very complicated case, aren't you?

[*He goes to a painted wall and opens up a hidden cupboard that is packed with bottles of vodka of different colours*]

STALIN: Who's drinking? Not much food here. A few nuts and biscuits. I would have invited you to dinner but I had another engagement. Are you hungry? You look well fed. [*He roots in the drinks cupboard looking at the bottles*] It's years since I was in this room. Who was I with last time? Can't remember. What shall we try tonight? Ah, there's more of this than the others. The yellow one. Is yellow our colour, Comrades?

[*He holds up a bottle of zubrovka-flavour vodka. Idly he tosses it to*

ZHDANOV *who is very nearly caught off guard. He immediately starts to open it*]

STALIN: You like the smell of grass in your vodka? No, you two are more for pepper, I should think. Or big, fat, glossy plums. But we can start off with the zubrovka. The flavour of horse fodder.

ZHDANOV: I don't think I'll have any. It's bad for my heart.

[*Pause. STALIN pours himself a glass of vodka and knocks it back. Pause. He looks meaningfully at ZHDANOV*]

STALIN: I don't want any nonsense from you, Andrei.

ZHDANOV: Your doctors say I shouldn't.

STALIN: What do they know about it? Doctors think everything is bad for you. Do you know how I've stayed so fit? Ignoring doctors and eating gooseberries. Are you drinking, Shostakovich?

SHOSTAKOVICH: Yes, please.

STALIN: And you, my well-travelled man?

[*PROKOFIEV smiles uncertainly*]

PROKOFIEV: I am forbidden alcohol.

STALIN: The bottle is here if you change your mind. This is very pure, you know? The best. What can we give you? I'll get some tea later. You like tea, don't you?

PROKOFIEV: Please don't go to any trouble. I dined before I came here.

STALIN: Very cold. Not a night to be out. I hope you wrapped up well. Always protect the throat. That is a crucial area. And wear a good hat. Well, this is very pleasant. My dinner was good fun.

[*STALIN sits down. ZHDANOV follows suit. SHOSTAKOVICH sits down*]

STALIN: Old friends. We reminisced. Old friends are the best. We were at school together. The laughs we had in those days. It is good to share food with old companions, maybe cry a little. We sang a few songs from the old days. I wonder if you'd know them? [*Pause. He looks at SHOSTAKOVICH, then at PROKOFIEV*] Did you have a good Christmas?

SHOSTAKOVICH: Quiet.

STALIN: My old friends brought me a present. I haven't opened it yet.

[*ZHDANOV pours out three glasses of vodka and hands one to STALIN who takes it and stands by the mantelshelf. ZHDANOV looks at SHOSTAKOVICH, then at the glass of vodka. He has no intention of serving him with it. SHOSTAKOVICH takes the glass*]

STALIN: Let's guess what it is. You first.

[*He nods at SHOSTAKOVICH*]

SHOSTAKOVICH: May I pick it up?

STALIN: Why not?

[*SHOSTAKOVICH picks up the parcel and weighs it in his hands*]

SHOSTAKOVICH: Reasonably heavy.

STALIN: Reasonably heavy. Not metal?

SHOSTAKOVICH: No. Too light for metal. Maybe wood.

STALIN: What about you, Prokofiev?

PROKOFIEV: Could it be a book?

STALIN: Imagination at work. A book. What do you say, Andrei?

ZHDANOV: Has it been examined?

STALIN: Don't be so officious, man! This was a Christmas present! Old
friends bought it with their own money, carried it all the way to
Moscow.

ZHDANOV: It should have been examined.

[*Pause. STALIN takes the parcel off SHOSTAKOVICH and walks
purposefully over to PROKOFIEV, putting the parcel into his hands, then
retreating a few paces*]

STALIN: Open it for me.

[*Pause. PROKOFIEV smiles. STALIN moves to the other side of the room*]

PROKOFIEV: Don't you like opening presents? I love it. It's the antici-
pation. What can it be? Something I've always wanted or... handker-
chiefs, socks, an awful tie...

[*PROKOFIEV unwraps the parcel. It is an icon. He holds it up. Pause.
STALIN smiles, nods, goes over to PROKOFIEV and tenderly takes the
icon out of his hands. He laughs out loud*]

STALIN: Fancy them knowing that I needed an icon. A very thoughtful
present. [*He gives it to ZHDANOV to look at*] What do you think?

ZHDANOV: Seventeenth-century Georgian. Excellent workmanship. A
very true, firm style. Simple but effective.

STALIN: Do you see the artist there? No. Not a trace. He has submerged
himself in his work. No individual screaming to get out. What is the
subject?

SHOSTAKOVICH: Christ in glory.

PROKOFIEV: Or Christ in judgment. Perhaps they are the same thing.
I can't remember.

STALIN: Keep the difference in mind. You'll find that it helps. Now, the
men who brought me this beautiful gift all the way from Tiflis are all
well over a hundred years old. They are my old tutors from the

seminary. I thought they'd all be dead but no. Relics from the nine-
teenth century. Saints in the making.

PROKOFIEV: That is remarkable.

STALIN: I thought so. Those three old men to take that terrible journey
in winter! Astonishing. I didn't even know they were coming. I find
that very touching. To go to such trouble for a boy who failed to do
what they wanted him to. That is truly noble.

[*He throws back his vodka and gives his glass to ZHDANOV who refills it.
STALIN takes it and nods to ZHDANOV to drink his own. ZHDANOV
unwillingly obeys. To SHOSTAKOVICH:*]

STALIN: Play me the best thing you've ever written.

SHOSTAKOVICH: I'm not sure what that is.

STALIN: Have another drink first.

[*STALIN fills SHOSTAKOVICH's glass, then stands by the piano.
SHOSTAKOVICH goes across, frowning apprehensively*]

SHOSTAKOVICH: Much of my best work is symphonic in form, I'm
afraid.

STALIN: Scale it down.

SHOSTAKOVICH: Well, that would take time...

STALIN: A tune! Play me a tune! Don't quibble.

SHOSTAKOVICH: I'm not quibbling. I'm just trying to explain.

STALIN: You're as nervous as a girl on her wedding night. What's the
matter with you? I thought this was your profession. You just stroke
the keys with your fingers. [*He plays a few notes*] Is this thing in tune?

SHOSTAKOVICH: Near enough.

STALIN: Andrei!

SHOSTAKOVICH: It's all right.

ZHDANOV: The central heating affects the wires.

STALIN: And what a rubbishy old piano. Can't we afford something
better than this? I'm sorry, Shostakovich. I'm asking you to perform
on an inferior instrument. A genius of your calibre should have a
Steinway. This isn't good enough for you. No tone. No style. No
resonance. [*He plays a run of notes. One of them is a thud*] What's that
note? [*Plays it again and again*] Sounds like something very avant-
garde. [*Opens up the piano and looks down. Putting in his hand he pulls out
a letter*] Someone has been using our piano as a post-box. [*He reads the
address on the letter, than hands it to ZHDANOV*]

STALIN:Who is it addressed to?

ZHDANOV: Someone's wife. I think I remember his face.

STALIN: It must be a farewell letter. See that the wife gets it. Better late than never. Now, let us enjoy some beautiful, soul-stirring music. I feel ready for that. [*He takes SHOSTAKOVICH by the shoulders and firmly pressed him down on the piano stool*] Only a little tune. Show me what you can do.

SHOSTAKOVICH: Don't you laugh, Sergei.

STALIN: He won't. He's next. Come, we have a lot to get through. Wait. Wait. I want to ask someone for something. [*He goes over to the icon*] Let this boy pass his examinations. He has worked hard. We have paid for lessons for him, made sacrifices. People have gone without food or shelter so this boy can learn his music. The whole family has done without so young Dmitri can be a great composer and make us proud.

[*Pause. STALIN looks at SHOSTAKOVICH who remains still and quiet at the piano, waiting. Pause. SHOSTAKOVICH makes a false start then sits back*]

SHOSTAKOVICH: Sorry.

STALIN: Don't worry. Nerves. Pretend that never happened. Start again. [*SHOSTAKOVICH plays the trombone theme from the adagio of The Golden Age, opus 22. STALIN pours himself another drink. ZHDANOV is getting very angry, glaring at SHOSTAKOVICH. STALIN puts a hand on his arm and indicates that he should remain cool. PROKOFIEV leans his forehead on the knob of his stick as if listening, or praying. SHOSTAKOVICH builds up his piece from a lulling, slow movement into a tremendous finale and finishes. Pause. STALIN blows an enormous raspberry*]

STALIN: Thought you'd like an extra instrument at the end.

SHOSTAKOVICH: I did score a trombone in the piece itself. You instinctively recognized the need for it.

STALIN: When did you write that?

SHOSTAKOVICH: Ten years ago.

ZHDANOV: It's an insult.

STALIN: Don't be so emotional, Andrei. Ten years ago. Another age. Before the war. I can hardly remember what it was like to be alive then, so much has happened. What did you think of that piece, Prokofiev?

PROKOFIEV: There was a certain tension in the playing that I found worrying.

STALIN: Not the playing. The piece.

PROKOFIEV: It is part of a larger work.

ZHDANOV: You know that work as well as I do. You've had to sit through it. Come on, you're a man, aren't you? You've got a mind of your own. What did you think of it? [*Pause*] I'll say one thing. The members of the Musicians' Union certainly stick together.

PROKOFIEV: We were well taught. In unity is strength.

[*STALIN chuckles. Pause. SHOSTAKOVICH rises hesitantly from the piano stool, hoping his ordeal is over. STALIN stares at him and he subsides. STALIN grins, then beckons him to get up. SHOSTAKOVICH leaves the piano*]

STALIN: Now, I'm ignorant about some music. You three are all from good, solid, bourgeois backgrounds. You should understand that kind of tricksy, intellectual creation we've just heard. What did it mean?

ZHDANOV: It didn't mean anything.

STALIN: Andrei gives in straight away. Come on, you can do better than that. You must have spent hours on a Sunday in the front parlour listening to bourgeois music, making bourgeois music. This is very much your field.

ZHDANOV: We never listened to shit like that.

STALIN: What did you listen to?

ZHDANOV: Er... I don't know... my father wasn't all that musical...

STALIN: A Tsarist Inspector of Schools not musical? [*He taps out a rhythm on the piano top with his glass*] Know what this is?

PROKOFIEV: Two four time.

STALIN: My father was a shoemaker. [*Pause. STALIN pours himself another drink*] When he was drunk, which was often, he used to amuse himself playing different rhythms on his last as he repaired the shoes of the bourgeoisie. And he'd sing as he worked well into the night. I used to lie in my bed under his bench listening. I can still sing all those old songs. But no matter how long I listened to your music, Shostakovich, I would never remember the melody. Do you know why?

ZHDANOV: Melody? He's never heard of it. There is no melody.

STALIN: Let him answer.

ZHDANOV: We've been through all this at the conference. Everyone has condemned his kind of formalist, progressive crap.

STALIN: In his greatest moments Shostakovich writes music which we accept as the emotional language of Soviet reality.

[*Pause. SHOSTAKOVICH smiles a wintry smile. ZHDANOV is puzzled. PROKOFIEV can hardly suppress a laugh*]

STALIN: One cannot but be proud of a talent so unique, so original, so universally significant.

ZHDANOV: Ha! That sly, boot-licking critic, Asafiev. [*To SHOSTAK-OVICH*] How much did you pay him?

STALIN: You don't get out of it that easily, Andrei. In September 1944, The Central Committee of the Party - on which you sit - proclaimed this young man's *Leningrad Symphony* to be a work of genius of the first magnitude. As you were the commander of our forces at Leningrad, Andrei, perhaps you felt grateful that Shostakovich had made you immortal?

ZHDANOV: No one can think straight in wartime. We've had a chance to consider it since. I'll say one thing. He did write quite a good tune for that symphony. And do you know what he did? He gave it to the German army. It was their theme. Bam-bam-bam as they hammered on the gates of Leningrad.

PROKOFIEV: If one had been a cat in the siege of Leningrad, one would have been eaten, so I hear.

ZHDANOV: You weren't there, of course. What were you doing in the war, comrade? Building barricades across the door of your salon?
[*Pause. STALIN sits at the piano*]

STALIN: You know that your friend, the critic Asafiev who wrote such a glowing tribute to your work, is in the process of changing his mind about it?

PROKOFIEV: Will you excuse me for a moment?
[*PROKOFIEV struggles to his feet. No one goes to help him. He leans heavily on his stick and crosses to the washroom door. STALIN plays a theme on the piano. PROKOFIEV goes into the washroom and shuts the door, locking it. Leaning on the basin he shakes his head, then runs cold water into it and splashes his face*]

STALIN: [*To SHOSTAKOVICH*] You are in very serious trouble.

SHOSTAKOVICH: What have I done?

STALIN: You are in more trouble than any of the others - more than poor, old Prokofiev, Khachaturyan, Miaskovsky and that lot. Do you know why?

SHOSTAKOVICH: I have no idea.

STALIN: Because you are younger. You are the future.
[*PROKOFIEV is suddenly violently sick*]

SHOSTAKOVICH: Please do not think me impertinent, but every one of the composers you have mentioned, including myself, have been showered with Stalin Prizes year after year. There is no more room on my mantelpiece.

STALIN: Do you believe in prizes? Do you believe in all that fawning? How many members of the Stalin Prize Committee do you still see in high office? Or any office. What do you think of this theme?

[*STALIN plays it again. PROKOFIEV sits down on the lid of the pedestal, his head in his hands. After a while he lights a cigarette*]

SHOSTAKOVICH: What is it?

ZHDANOV: I thought you knew everything about music. The darling of the Conservatoire.

STALIN: Haunting, isn't it?

SHOSTAKOVICH: Prokofiev is a long time in the washroom.

[*STALIN slams the lid of the piano down and stalks away. PROKOFIEV hears the crash and reacts*]

STALIN: That was insulting, Shostakovich, very insulting!

SHOSTAKOVICH: I'm sorry. I don't know the piece.

STALIN: It's mine. I just made it up. I looked at that beautiful
icon with all its memories, its history of suffering, and that music came into my head. I saw old Hermogenes, the principal of the seminary, a very stiff, stern old man, and I wondered what had happened to him.

[*Pause, SHOSTAKOVICH pours himself another vodka. He knocks it back. STALIN smiles*]

STALIN: I'm sorry. No man should think that he can do everything. Look at Andrei. He has too many jobs to do. He is crippled with overwork. I feel for him. Chairman of the Foreign Affairs Committee, chief of the Propaganda and Agitation Department, military councillor for the Red Navy... and culture? He is the supremo, the top man. The Inspector of Schools rides again.

[*PROKOFIEV finishes his cigarette and throws the butt down the pan. He flushes it away*]

ZHDANOV: A lot of thinking has been going on in there. Let's hope he's got rid of all the shit he was going to write during the next few years.

STALIN: How is your wife, Irina? Your son, Maxim? Your daughter, Galya? All well?

SHOSTAKOVICH: Yes.

STALIN: There is too much sickness around. Naturally we are healthy animals. I'm tired of ill people. I would like to see everyone with bright eyes and rosy cheeks.

[*PROKOFIEV enters. He looks very shaky*]

STALIN: Help him.

[*SHOSTAKOVICH goes to support PROKOFIEV*]

STALIN: Not you.

[*ZHDANOV helps PROKOFIEV to a chair*]

ZHDANOV: He's been sick. I can smell it on his breath.

PROKOFIEV: I'm sorry.

STALIN: Where did you eat dinner?

PROKOFIEV: At home.

STALIN: No one would want to poison you, would they? Perhaps the meat was off. Did you have meat?

PROKOFIEV: I am very nervous.

STALIN: No matter what happens, a person should have control of his eating. The stomach and the mind are strongly interconnected. You are an emotional man. That is a good quality.

PROKOFIEV: Thank you.

STALIN: Why did you refuse to attend the Musicians' Union Conference?

PROKOFIEV: I didn't refuse. My doctor said that it would not be advisable.

STALIN: What's the matter with you, anyway?

PROKOFIEV: A stroke. I am still recovering. It is a nuisance.

STALIN: But you are here. If you can come here, why can't you attend the conference?

PROKOFIEV: I was not given an option.

STALIN: That's right. And Comrade Zhdanov was wrong to give you an option not to attend the conference. I'd have had you carried in on a stretcher. You're a very important man. The conference is crippled because you're not there. How can they take a decision of any sort without the senior Soviet composer? You will go tomorrow.

PROKOFIEV: You flatter me, sir.

STALIN: Andrei, I want to be notified the moment this man enters the conference chamber tomorrow morning. If he needs an ambulance, send one. Give him a sedan chair if he wants one. Rig up a cable car!

PROKOFIEV: I'm very tired.

STALIN: I'm older than you, and look at me. People live a long time where I come from. We have sound, peasant constitutions - clean, wholesome food, fresh air. You spent too much time in Paris and New

York as a young man. Your liver is wrecked. [*Pause*] Here, you might as well drink. It will keep you going. It's as good as medicine any day. [*He puts a glass of vodka in PROKOFIEV's hand and stands over him*]

PROKOFIEV: I would rather not.

STALIN: It will do you no harm.

PROKOFIEV: I'm not allowed stimulants.

STALIN: Don't lie to me. The truth is that you don't drink vodka. Your preference is for French and German wines. I hear that you have a special affection for champagne.

PROKOFIEV: I've been drinking vodka all my life.

STALIN: Let's see you drink it now then.

[*PROKOFIEV sips the vodka. He smiles up at STALIN*]

PROKOFIEV: Excellent quality.

STALIN: Only the best. I'll give you a toast. To the power of the human heart. [*He clinks his glass with PROKOFIEV and beams down at him*] I am very disappointed in the work of the Musicians' Union Conference so far. All we have had is back-biting, book-licking. ancient professors covering their tracks, everyone sucking up to the Chairman and the Central Committee, saying what they think I want to hear. It has been a travesty of open, democratic discussion. No one will take the plunge. All they're good for is following the Party line. That's no use to me. I thought, in my innocence, if all those creative people are stuffed into one room and made to think hard, they'll come up with some new ideas for Soviet music, some useful ideas. How wrong I was. They hadn't got the guts to reach out and claim what was theirs. Now I've got to do it for them.

ZHDANOV: Many of the delegates said...

STALIN: I don't want to hear any more sycophantic drivelling!

ZHDANOV: All I was going to say is that everyone is grateful for the time and trouble that the Central Committee is taking over music - not the most obvious of our priorities.

STALIN: Good of them. To me music is as important as heavy industry or agriculture. It has got to work.

SHOSTAKOVICH: I think some good things have come out of the conference...

STALIN: Confessions, complaints, throat-cutting. I've read the transcripts each day.

SHOSTAKOVICH: I thought that the point about the peoples of the Soviet Union having more than a hundred languages and nearly as many musical styles was a good one; we have the four-voice music of the Ukrainians, the seven-note scale of Azerbaijan, the five-note scale of the Tartars and the Buriat Mongols... the variety is enormous. How do we forge one national music out of all these without destroying something?

STALIN: Your musical hearing will have to become as acute as my political hearing.

ZHDANOV: I think the conference has also agreed that bad, disharmonious music undoubtedly has a damaging effect on the psycho-physiological activity of the brain. The part of the brain that controls hearing also controls balance and vomiting. So, you two are making everyone physically sick as well as mentally ill. You probably brought on that stroke yourself, Prokofiev - listening to your own music.

PROKOFIEV: My own doctor has said that if I keep on composing music it will kill me. I wonder if he meant the same thing?

STALIN: When the conference is over, the Central Committee is going to issue a decree. The decree, in itself, will be a piece of paper if I don't get the support of men like yourselves.

PROKOFIEV: We are both loyal citizens.

STALIN: But not loyal composers. Read them the decree.

ZHDANOV: [*Taking a paper out of his pocket*] This will be issued in the second week of February. [*Reads*] The Central Committee of the Communist Party decrees that: One, the formalist tendency in Soviet music is anti-people and is leading to the liquidation of music. Two, Soviet composers must become more conscious of their duties to the People and stimulate the kind of creative activity that will lead to higher quality works being composed which will be worthy of the Soviet people. Three, a proposal should go forward to the Propaganda and Agitation Department of the Central Committee and the Government Arts Committee that the state of affairs in Soviet music must be improved and its present faults liquidated.

PROKOFIEV: Am I a present fault?

ZHDANOV: You are. And a formalist tendency.

SHOSTAKOVICH: I would like to study that document closely. Some of the ideas are quite complex... [*He gets agitated*] Well, I can't say that I understand what it's getting at! Have you any idea what it means? May I have a good look at it? I honestly want to be... clear. Comrade Stalin... was that anything to do with me? I'm mystified. Conscious of my duties? I've never been anything else.

STALIN: Let me see that.

[*ZHDANOV hands him the decree*]

STALIN: How many times have you drafted this?

ZHDANOV: Ten, at least.

STALIN: It still sounds very clumsy, Andrei, very clumsy. It's jargon. You know how I feel about language. You mustn't mangle it.

SHOSTAKOVICH: And aren't you jumping to conclusions if you've written that before the conference is over? I thought that's what we were supposed to be discussing. We haven't made any recommendations yet.

ZHDANOV: [*In a fury*] D'you think we're going to wait until you bloody idiots make up your minds? That could take till doomsday!

[*Pause. SHOSTAKOVICH looks hurt and puzzled*]

SHOSTAKOVICH: Well, all I can say is that it won't be worth us reporting our findings to the Central Committee if you've already made up your minds.

ZHDANOV: [*Trying to keep his temper*] The conference has been a bloody calamity from beginning to end! It's been going round in circles!

STALIN: [*Gently*] This is just a short cut, Shostakovich - a technique that statesmen must use when they're under pressure. I agree with you that it goes against the grain but there we are. Time is precious.

SHOSTAKOVICH: Well, I suppose you know best. I was just thinking of all the hard work we've put in at the conference. Never mind. Will we still be allowed to make our report?

STALIN: Of course. It will be read with great interest, I assure you.

SHOSTAKOVICH: Good. You never know, we might come up with something.

ZHDANOV: And pigs might fly. This decree will have the same force as law, Shostakovich. Anyone who goes against it will be punished.

PROKOFIEV: How will we know when we are writing works not worthy of the Soviet people?

STALIN: Well, have you got an answer to that? It's a fair question.

ZHDANOV: [*Pause*] When you don't live up to...

PROKOFIEV: Expectations? Aspirations?

ZHDANOV: Don't put words in my mouth!

PROKOFIEV: In practice people tell us what they think of our work by coming to hear it or staying away. Even that is not completely reliable, however. People are not always right.

ZHDANOV: The People aren't always right? Go on, go on.

PROKOFIEV: That may sound like heresy but many great works were very unpopular when first performed. People were hostile to them for decades. Some composers have to wait a hundred years or more while the public comes round to giving them recognition. By then, of course, the poor fellows are dead and gone.

STALIN: That's worth thinking about. Even the greatest lives are snuffed out, made into total failures. It's hard, very hard. And its so random. How d'you feel about it?

PROKOFIEV: One has to be fatalistic.

STALIN: Do you worry that there remains much of your best work left undone? Perhaps that preys on your mind? You must sit at home, looking into the future. Doesn't it get you into a grim kind of mood? You stop. You disintegrate. Everything melts away. What could be left is nothing but lies. Have you spent your life well?

PROKOFIEV: A lot of time has been wasted. As a young man I got side-tracked quite a lot. However, there were compensations. [*Pause*] Life isn't over yet.

STALIN: Surely you don't think that you're going to get better? Once you've had one stroke...

PROKOFIEV: [*Sharply interrupting STALIN*] I will deal with that myself, thank you!

STALIN: You're right. With will-power anything is possible. You want to carry on, staggering along?

PROKOFIEV: I can't think what else I'd like to do. Somehow it remains entertaining.

STALIN: Shostakovich has his best years ahead of him, and his health. There's hope for him. But what about you?

ZHDANOV: You must have had many moments of despair. I would in your position. Nothing to look forward to. You're probably drying up.

SHOSTAKOVICH: That's no so, he's just written...

ZHDANOV: I don't know why you bother to hang around.

STALIN: Leave him alone.

[*Pause. PROKOFIEV stares ZHDANOV out*]

STALIN: Andrei's had an uphill fight with culture. It enrages him sometimes. Don't forget, he is a dedicated man. If he feels antagonism towards you it will be on a matter of principle, not personal.

[*Pause. He looks at the decree again*] This is an admission of defeat, really. That aspect of it offends me. But you have to feel for them, Andrei. Music is not an exact science. [*He continues examining the decree*]

ZHDANOV: Don't tell me. [*Pause*] I don't think we need to take up too much of your time tonight. It is my opinion, and the feeling of the conference, that all that is needed is a purposeful, practical approach based on our success in re-orientating other areas of the arts. First, we'll have to have a complete clean-out...

SHOSTAKOVICH: May I ask when this was discussed at the conference? I've been there all the time but I've never heard anyone bring that up.

ZHDANOV: I said that was the feeling of the conference! [*Pause*] We did it with literature. We did it with painting. Film. Even poetry. There are no problems left in those areas. Only music is holding us up. [*Pause*] Delegates have come to me privately and said that the influence of Prokofiev and Shostakovich is too great for any other composer to take a new step forward. They hold people back. In their own way, they are dictators.

PROKOFIEV: That is a ludicrous suggestion!

ZHDANOV: You can appreciate how difficult it is for any other composer at the conference to get up and speak his mind. He feels that he will be jeopardizing his position with Shostakovich and Prokofiev. After the conference is over he still has to earn his living. With the power that these two wield in the music establishment they could destroy him. So, they come to me off-the-record, as it were. They are very disturbed.

PROKOFIEV: May we know who these disturbed people are?

ZHDANOV: They want that kept a secret.

PROKOFIEV: In case we victimize them?

ZHDANOV: Makes sense, doesn't it?

SHOSTAKOVICH: They're mad! If they haven't got the courage to say this to our faces you shouldn't take it into consideration.

ZHDANOV: We take everything into consideration. [*Pause*] Music has to be swept clean if there's to be any real chance of progress. That's what people want. And I think they're right.

STALIN: I must say that I wasn't aware that these two had become so unpopular amongst their own kind. That is worrying. Of course, achievement often excites envy. A very human failing, I'm afraid.

ZHDANOV: They reckon they're untouchable!

STALIN: You don't think you're untouchable, do you?

PROKOFIEV: Only in the Indian sense.

STALIN: Whether you like it or not, these two are the greatest composers in the world! No, it's you I'm disappointed with, Andrei. I want to delegate but people like you let me down. You're supposed to be a well-read, cultured, civilized man but you appear to have no common sense. You can't talk to these men in a language that they understand. Anti-people? What does that mean to them? Have they ever even heard of the Propaganda and Agitation Department? Why should they have? And the liquidation of music! That is a term that is well beyond their comprehension - and mine, incidentally.

ZHDANOV: They know what I'm getting at.

STALIN: Are either of you two paid-up members of the Communist Party?

SHOSTAKOVICH: I didn't think we had to be...

STALIN: Don't get so defensive. I was only asking. Prokofiev?

PROKOFIEV: No, I'm not.

STALIN: Have either of you ever read Marx? Does he mean anything to you?

PROKOFIEV: I tried to read *Das Kapital* when I was a student.

STALIN: But it defeated you. Perfectly natural. Only someone with a truly scientific and philosophical mind of the highest grade can tackle that monster. I have read it from cover to cover. Andrei must have conquered it. Eh?

ZHDANOV: Took me three months. It was worth every minute.

STALIN: They may be the experts on music, you see, Andrei - but we are the philosophers. This is the problem. To get our vision into their heads. Given the choice, Prokofiev would prefer some kind of liberal government, wouldn't you?

PROKOFIEV: I generally restrict my choices to what is available.

STALIN: You can be honest with me. Communism is a scientific creed. We can't expect artists to understand it without our help. That's what I'm trying to do - help you. Tell me what political party you would join if you had the chance, Shostakovich.

SHOSTAKOVICH: I don't think about it much...

ZHDANOV: Best you keep it that way, Josef, you won't get anything out of them on this tack. We know that neither of them have ever been politically active. They're ignoramuses. It wouldn't make a scrap of difference to them if they lived under capitalism or communism. They don't want to serve anyone's ideas but their own. Politically they're made of jelly.

STALIN: If I arranged for special classes - one of our top theoreticians - that might help. Some of them are very good teachers. How about that, Prokofiev? In the time that you've got left on this earth - which can't be long - you could get to grips with the beauties of scientific communism. It's a garden of delights - take my word for it.

ZHDANOV: He'll say yes but he won't mean it. He's a cynic right through to the core. His motivation has always been self, self, self. It's too deeply rooted in his make-up to get it out now. It takes guts to reach down and purify yourself, get all the dirt out...

STALIN: Why can't these two do that? You managed it somehow.

ZHDANOV: Josef, we're talking about being reborn by an effort of will. That's what you have to go through. All your old, false values have to be destroyed. They haven't got the slightest intention of changing. They think they're perfect.

PROKOFIEV: Perhaps Comrade Zhdanov would give us lessons in self-denial?

[*Pause. ZHDANOV stares coldly at PROKOFIEV*]

ZHDANOV: There're quite a few lessons I'd like to give you, Prokofiev. [*Pause*] Don't you realize what you are? Like me you were born into a rotten, decadent class. But I got out. Not you. You still like it. Being a parasite is right up your street.

PROKOFIEV: Is that why I came back to Russia?

ZHDANOV: Parasites need things to live off.

PROKOFIEV: I can assure you that being a parasite is much easier in the West. I could have lived out the rest of my life there on the reputation that I had by 1932. We have heard about your struggle - are you interested in mine?

ZHDANOV: Russia means nothing to you.

PROKOFIEV: [*Angrily*] It is my home!

ZHDANOV: Your home? Your playground, you mean!

PROKOFIEV: What else must I call the place where my family, my friends live? You talk about being reborn. There are personal ways to achieve change in oneself. Some people can do it faster than others. It is not always a straightforward matter.

ZHDANOV: Nothing ever is with you. [*Pause*] A family man, eh? Such devotion. Pity you can't spare some of that for your country.

PROKOFIEV: I am devoted to my country. I always have been.

ZHDANOV: Married a Spaniard. Not important, I suppose. It just demonstrates an attitude of mind. Not surprising though. He's of Polish extraction himself, I've heard. A foreigner. Yes, Prokofiev's almost an immigrant, really. [*Pause*] Give my regards to your mistress. Does she count as family? Or don't I understand bohemian life?

[*PROKOFIEV takes a measured pause to control his anger*]

PROKOFIEV: My wife's father was Spanish. That I confess though I fail to see that it can be held against her, or against me. But I am not in any way Polish. I am pure Russian. All my grandparents were Russian. Also, I am not a bohemian but I do share their views on the need for freedom in one's personal feelings. Do you have such things?

ZHDANOV: That's a crack I'll hold to your account.

PROKOFIEV: Always paid my bills. To honest tradesmen, at least.

ZHDANOV: Say that again!

PROKOFIEV: I try to avoid repeating myself.

STALIN: I think it would help matters if you tried to get on. You must watch your tongue, Prokofiev. Keep to the business in hand.

PROKOFIEV: That is my wish.

STALIN: Come on, this is a professional matter. I don't want any silliness. You were very provocative, Andrei. What do we care about his wretched love life?

[*ZHDANOV refuses to be moved. He glares at PROKOFIEV, then turns away as if preventing himself from making a physical attack on him. STALIN pats him on the shoulder to soothe him down*]

ZHDANOV: The hypocritical, bourgeois bastard is getting at me! I won't have it!

STALIN: Andrei! That's enough now! You're spoiling our evening.

ZHDANOV: I can't stand being the same room as him! Send him out!

PROKOFIEV: Not yet, be fair. I've been quite looking forward to doing my party piece. Dmitri did his stuff at the piano. So should I. You know how vainglorious I am. Any opportunity to show off. Just put me at the centre of attention and I'm happy. Don't you want me to sit my pianoforte examinations?

STALIN: Quite right. [*Pause. He looks at PROKOFIEV with some approval*] You keep your head and remember things. I find that praiseworthy.

SHOSTAKOVICH: Yes, play for us, Sergei. I'd like to hear you. Play a good long piece. Really, I need to get my breath back. I don't know where I am...

PROKOFIEV: I doubt whether I'll be on top form tonight.

STALIN: Don't tell me your hands are shaking. You? Master of the keyboard?

PROKOFIEV: No, no. Just a passing phase. The body letting the mind down. I don't know. Well? Should I play? I'm quite happy to, really. It's up to you.

STALIN: No, I don't think so. My judgment must remain clear. You might make too good an impression on me. [*Pause*] Even I am not impervious to charm, Prokofiev.

ZHDANOV: But I am. We know that you're a dab hand at the keyboard -oh, you're a very polished performer. What I'm interested in is the creature inside the natty suit when everything is quiet. No music. No amusing conversation. Just a little man thinking his thoughts. How about owning up to those?

[*Pause. PROKOFIEV looks straight ahead*]

ZHDANOV: They call me old X-ray Eyes. [*Pause*] Shostakovich was at a friend's apartment last week - funny friends he has, I might add - and someone - it might have been him - called you Genghis Khan the Second, Josef.

STALIN: Did they really?

SHOSTAKOVICH: That simply isn't true. Where do you get such stories from? Somebody must spend a lot of time making them up.

STALIN: Genghis Khan. Hm. Andrei, you mustn't tell me these things. The idea of artists making fun of me behind my back is very painful.

ZHDANOV: They say worse things than that. Little Hitler.

STALIN: Little Hitler? Not even Big Hitler. Now I do feel put out. This is so much tittle-tattle. You don't honestly expect me to take it seriously, do you?

ZHDANOV: You should hear them, Josef. They go at it hammer and tongs. Jokes, stories, we've even found cartoons they've drawn. Look at these.

[*ZHDANOV gives STALIN a piece of paper. He studies it, nods. He keeps a perfectly straight face and shows it first to PROKOFIEV and then to SHOSTAKOVICH. They remain deadpan, immobile, killing all expression in their faces*]

STALIN: Har-har-har. Aren't I funny? Good old Uncle Joe. [*He makes the gesture of wiping his arse on the paper*] Har-har-har.

ZHDANOV: The woman who drew those lived two floors above Shostak-ovich. She was a journalist.

[*STALIN hands the cartoons back to ZHDANOV who puts them away*]

STALIN: Mickey Mouse. Donald Duck. What about Pluto? Why leave him out? Why did they give a stupid dog that name? Do you know who the real Pluto was, Shostakovich? He wasn't a Yankee dog at all, was he?

SHOSTAKOVICH: He was the Greek god of Hell, I think. But he had a dog.

STALIN: Trust the Americans to forget something like that. No sense of what fits, just belittling culture, ridiculing everything that is sacred. They contaminate thought, they poison the world. All they want is money. If I sent you to America on a goodwill mission, would you come back?

SHOSTAKOVICH: Of course... The dog's name was Cerberus, by the way.

STALIN: Andrei, look into the eyes of these men. What do you see? Confusion. Something has been radically wrong with their schooling at all levels. Get me a list of everyone who has been responsible for their education.

SHOSTAKOVICH: Comrade Stalin... I've tried to make my own mind up about things... my teachers can't be held responsible for my failure.

STALIN: I'll decide that.

SHOSTAKOVICH: They did their best. I wasn't the perfect pupil by any means.

STALIN: If we agree - as I think we must - that you have either been corrupted or neglected - someone is to blame. I don't think it's you but you can persuade me otherwise if you wish. We will only ask these people a few questions about the curriculum, their teaching methods, disciplinary problems that they might have had. Andrei can arrange this kind of investigation quite easily, using only skilled people. Rest assured that everyone's feelings will be respected. After all, a teacher can only do so much. What was Lenin's view of the Soviet artist in society?

SHOSTAKOVICH: Lenin's view... ah, it's on the tip of my tongue.

STALIN: Come on, have a go. You remember Lenin. The one with the bald head. Don't say you've forgotten him already.

SHOSTAKOVICH: No... it's just that my mind...

ZHDANOV: My mind. My mind. My this. My that.

SHOSTAKOVICH: Very well. I'll shut up then. I'm lost anyway.

STALIN: You are supposed to be the engineer of the soul. I can just see Prokofiev in his oily overalls with a spanner in his hand. One of the results of our great victory in the war has been that people are discussing the soul a great deal. It is a word on everyone's lips. The reason? We all felt that wonderful joy in victory. We asked ourselves what it was. What organ of the body made the sensation. It was the soul. It is in my mind to create a government department for the soul. [*Pause*] Want the job, Andrei?

ZHDANOV: Not if you make me keep men like this on the books. You've listened to my suggestions before, taken action on them. We've cleaned out Soviet culture from top to bottom and it's ten times better for it. Why won't you listen to me this time?

STALIN: The Department of the Soul. Do you know, I think I'd give up my present responsibilities and take that on if people would leave me in peace. Prokofiev would work there, Shostakovich too. Although I would be their supervisor we would have a very close working relationship. We would lunch together in the canteen of the Department of the Soul. I like them, Andrei. As men, I like them. And they like me, I think. Do you like me?

PROKOFIEV: Yes. Very much.

STALIN: He does. Shostakovich is thinking about it.

PROKOFIEV: Dmitri is trying to do something very difficult.

STALIN: What is that?

PROKOFIEV: To separate the idea of you from the actual man. The awe and respect we feel for our leaders sometimes prevents us from appreciating them as people. But I think Dmitri has made up his mind.

SHOSTAKOVICH: I like you. We get on. That means a lot to me.

STALIN: What a relief. Well, that's three of us who like each other. We haven't involved Andrei yet. Do we like him?

ZHDANOV: Leave me out of it. These two know how I feel about them.

STALIN: Andrei, soften your heart. Tell me, old faithful, have you ever heard of the music of the spheres? Well, here we have two major planets which have fallen out of orbit, that's all. The sun must pull them back.

ZHDANOV: I want these two removed!

STALIN: Andrei!

ZHDANOV: Other composers will come along. Throw these two out! Get rid of them!

STALIN: That would be a waste.

ZHDANOV: If a gun's barrel gets bent you don't bother to try and straighten it out. It will never be the same again no matter what you do. So, melt it down and recast.

STALIN: That's very hard. Who ever bothered to put these two right? I never had the time, you were busy.

ZHDANOV: I'd set fire to their shirt-tails and use the bastards for target practice. I'd strap the sods over a cannon's mouth and blow their balls to Berlin and back!

STALIN: He doesn't mean that!

ZHDANOV: I do! I've given up with them. They're write-offs!

STALIN: Andrei, calm down. You know that artists are prone to suicide. And these are sensitive men.

ZHDANOV: Let them hang themselves. I couldn't care less.

STALIN: Don't be so defeatist. It's not like you. It's our job to make them happy. That's very important. They won't get into that state with old soldiers barking at them.

ZHDANOV: Yes, I'm a soldier, and proud of it. What's the matter with serving your country? Is it a crime?

STALIN: Not at all. But has it occurred to you that our friends here wish to serve their country as well?

ZHDANOV: Don't make me laugh!

STALIN: They do! The problem is - how? [*Pause*] It's not as easy to work out as a soldier's sacrifice. What a genius has got to offer is something very special. Try to understand that.

ZHDANOV: I'll tell you what I understand, Josef! That when you've marched five hundred thousand men into battle you know all about how many beats to the bar. I've stood in flooded trenches with farm boys who'd sing better than opera stars when they could hear themselves above the artillery. That was real music to my ears. And they didn't ask for sympathy. But, I tell you, to me those simple soldiers were special. They had a genius. But what do they get from these two twittering arseholes? Crash! Bang! Wallop! [*Hits the piano keys with his fist*] A din worse than the guns! [*Hits the keys with his elbows*] Any old rubbish! [*Sits on the keyboard*] Crash! Bang! Wallop!

STALIN: I would give a lot to hear, just once, music that transformed our recent history of suffering and heroism into joy. Purge the misery, change pain into delight. Do a job for our souls, boys. Isn't that what you're here for? To do a job for our souls?

ZHDANOV: Music's in the blood! And my blood's red, not dishwater. Yes, and good music makes me want to dance! Come on, we'll show 'em, Josef! We can dance these two lilies into the ground! Rum-ti-tum-tum!

[*ZHDANOV dances around SHOSTAKOVICH and PROKOFIEV*]

STALIN: Andrei, your heart!

ZHDANOV: To hell with my heart!

[*They dance together. It is a cumbersome but impressive routine that suggests years of practice at parties*]

STALIN: What will your doctors say?

ZHDANOV: To hell with my doctors!

[*They dance with linked arms, then ZHDANOV breaks away into a solo performance of a wilder dance. STALIN laughs, clapping and egging ZHDANOV on. ZHDANOV gets carried away by the dance, exultantly showing off. Suddenly he gasps in pain, clutches his chest and stops. STALIN smiles grimly and nods, then walks away from ZHDANOV*]

STALIN: Someone knocking at your door, Andrei? Take a pill.

ZHDANOV: What pill? What pill? I don't take pills. Go on talking without me.

STALIN: Sit down.

ZHDANOV: No, leave me be!

STALIN: You look terrible.

ZHDANOV: Don't go on about it. [*Pause*] It will pass.

[*Beats at his heart*]

Get back in your kennel, you old dog.

[*He encounters PROKOFIEV's eye*]

Well? What's the matter with you? What are you looking at?

PROKOFIEV: Self-destruction has always been a mystery to me.

ZHDANOV: When I die, musician, what I leave behind will be more than a few vibrations.

STALIN: Don't be so morbid, Andrei. Sit quietly for a moment. That's an order. Get your breath back. We'll listen to some gramophone records.

[*ZHDANOV sits down. STALIN goes over to the record cabinet*]

STALIN: What have we got of Prokofiev's in the collection?

ZHDANOV: All his work that's been recorded.

STALIN: That should keep us occupied. [*Looks through the records*] You have been busy.

ZHDANOV: Do we have to? I'm not in the mood for any of that stuff right now.

STALIN: Ah, I see, you have different versions of the same work.

ZHDANOV: Oh, yes - French recordings, British, German, American -and our own. The Soviet ones are much inferior, of course... Feast your eyes, Prokofiev. There's your world-wide reputation.

PROKOFIEV: You do seem to have gone to an awful lot of trouble.

ZHDANOV: The Western record companies are very selective, of course. Unlike us, your devoted Soviet fans, they don't record every piece of nonsense that you write. They only like you in parts. But we love you in toto.

STALIN: Come over here.

[*PROKOFIEV gets up and moves across*]

STALIN: I want you to choose your favourite piece from this lot and put it on the gramophone.

SHOSTAKOVICH: Sergei, if you tell me which piece you want played I'll find it for you and put it on.

STALIN: You stay where you are. Let him come and browse. Surely you've got the strength to put on a gramophone record.

PROKOFIEV: [*Moving across to the gramophone*] Oh, it will be difficult to choose. All my recorded work. Such a plethora.

SHOSTAKOVICH: Have you got a full collection of my work as well?

ZHDANOV: Ah, he's jealous. You artists. So vulnerable. Your pile is much smaller than Prokofiev's. The West has not developed such a taste for your music - yet. But there's time.

[*PROKOFIEV stands at the record cabinet trying to look at the collection. It is very awkward for him*]

PROKOFIEV: I'm sorry to have to be such a nuisance, but I'm not supposed to do any bending over.

ZHDANOV: I thought you queens spent all your time bending over.

[*PROKOFIEV straightens up. He walks towards the door with as much dignity as his body will allow*]

STALIN: Where are you going?

PROKOFIEV: I do not intend to stay here if he speaks to me like that.

STALIN: You are quite right. That remark was most uncalled for. Andrei will apologize.

ZHDANOV: Come on, it was only a joke. You know what they say about artists being pansies.

PROKOFIEV: And you know what they say about soldiers being stupid. May I make a joke about that?

[*Pause. PROKOFIEV eyes ZHDANOV defiantly*]

STALIN: Have the grace to apologize to the man.

ZHDANOV: I'm sorry, Prokofiev. Please forgive me.

PROKOFIEV: Thank you. I would like to go home.

STALIN: No. Choose your record.

PROKOFIEV: It is impossible for me to think clearly under these circumstances!

STALIN: [*Conducting PROKOFIEV back to the record cabinet*] Andrei
will behave himself from now on, I promise you. Now, let's all
have another drink and relax. Listening to music should be a
pleasure.
[*Pause. PROKOFIEV reaches the cabinet. He tries to bend but cannot. He
raps on the floor with his stick in frustration*]
PROKOFIEV: Really, I can't manage this...
STALIN: Why don't you sit on the floor to look at the records? Wouldn't
that be easier?
[*STALIN gives PROKOFIEV his arm. PROKOFIEV bows his head.
STALIN half forces him down as a nurse might do with a recalcitrant patient.
ZHDANOV laughs softly and pours out more vodka. SHOSTAKOVICH
turns away, very upset. STALIN remains standing over PROKOFIEV*]
STALIN: Georgia is the place for artists. You would feel happier
there, Prokofiev. Georgia is our Soviet Mediterranean. As a colo-
nial myself I have to make the point that you Russian men of
culture don't have to go sniffing round the sewers of Rome, Ath-
ens, even Moscow to get the smell of civilization. We have it all
there in my homeland. Balconies with trailing vines. Rolling
wheat fields. The Caucasus mountains. Yes, I'm thinking very
seriously about the idea of a camp for all the artists in the Soviet
Union to be set up in Georgia. You'd enjoy that, wouldn't you?
PROKOFIEV: Sounds lovely. This really is a very good collection,
Dmitri.
[*PROKOFIEV looks through the collection, trying to look as relaxed as
possible. ZHDANOV sits on the piano stool, glaring down at him*]
ZHDANOV: Found anything yet?
PROKOFIEV: It's terribly difficult to choose. I don't play my own music
back on records very much. I feel a little shy.
ZHDANOV: You wrote the stuff. You must have some idea what bits of
it have any value. Does getting your hands on that pile give you a thrill,
Prokofiev? Does anything matter but fame?
PROKOFIEV: It might be more appropriate for you to ask Comrade
Stalin that question.
[*STALIN bursts out laughing and caresses the top of PROKOFIEV's head*]
STALIN: Good boy, you tell him. Always stick up for yourself. Don't let
Andrei bully you around. [*Sits next to PROKOFIEV on the floor*] What
have we got here? *Alexander Nevsky. Ivan the Terrible. War and Peace.*
What a good Russian you are.

ZHDANOV: Know my favourite piece of yours, Prokofiev? *Peter and the Wolf.* It appeals to my childish mind. Da-da-da-da-da-da-da...

STALIN: Romeo and Juliet. Young love. Shakespeare was a randy devil I hear. He went to bed with Queen Elizabeth. Sorry, we're not allowed to mention the word queen. What's this? *The Duenna.* Never heard of that. What's it about?

ZHDANOV: It's based on a play by an English playwright called Sheridan.

STALIN: Another English playwright? Hm.

PROKOFIEV: Irish, actually.

STALIN: Ah, that's different. Obviously he was a revolutionary. Didn't he inspire the Celts to resist British imperialism?

PROKOFIEV: Sheridan lived in London for most of the time. He wrote comedies about eighteenth-century social life.

STALIN: Criticizing the aristocracy and the repressive capitalist regime.

ZHDANOV: Yes, yes, all that kind of thing. Prokofiev wouldn't have decided to adapt it otherwise, would he?

[*PROKOFIEV holds up a record*]

PROKOFIEV: I've made my choice.

STALIN: Let me see.

[*PROKOFIEV hands STALIN the record. He studies it*]

*STALIN: Footsteps of Steel.* Ballet music. Never heard of it. Has it ever been produced?

PROKOFIEV: The subject is the Machine Age. It was first produced in Paris in 1927 by Diaghilev.

[*STALIN is helping PROKOFIEV to his feet. At the mention of Diaghilev they go still. A short, cold pause*]

STALIN: Diaghilev has something to do with this thing?

PROKOFIEV: Yes. We seemed to work quite well together most of the time. We had our differences.

ZHDANOV: I should hope you did. Diaghilev refused to work in Russia. He was a traitor.

PROKOFIEV: As a producer of ballet he had a lot of style.

STALIN: And he betrayed his country with a lot of style.

[*Breaks the record on his knee*]

Sorry we can't play your choice. What else have we got here?

[*He takes another record out of its sleeve*]

Ah, your Fourth Piano Concerto. There must be some merit in that. Let's hear what it sounds like.

[*He smashes it. He takes another record*]

The *Classical Symphony*. What a nice label. His Master's Voice. A little white dog. The English breed good dogs.

[*He smashes it, takes another record*]

Your Second Symphony. Play this one for us, Andrei.

[*STALIN gives the record to ZHDANOV. He looks at it for a moment, smiles at PROKOFIEV, then smashes it against the furniture. STALIN empties the cabinet, handing the records to ZHDANOV who smashes them. They work swiftly, efficiently, like production workers on a machine line of destruction. Shostakovich's drum crescendo from the Eleventh Symphony takes over*]

[*Lights fade to blackout*]

# ACT TWO

*Out of the darkness comes the drum crescendo of Shostakovich's Eleventh Symphony.*

*[Lights swiftly up on STALIN and ZHDANOV smashing records. STALIN hands a record to ZHDANOV who swings back his arm...]*

STALIN: No! We'll play that one.

ZHDANOV: Come on! Let's do the lot!

STALIN: No, we'll play it. We should hear one, at least.

ZHDANOV: Let's finish the job!

STALIN: We'll take it as Prokofiev's choice - blind. He's a gambling man, aren't you?

ZHDANOV: What about Shostakovich's lot? We're going to do them as well, aren't we? It wouldn't be fair otherwise.

STALIN: My arm's aching. *[Takes the record back off ZHDANOV]* Let's see what we've got here.

*[STALIN puts the record on the gramophone. It is Bix Beiderbecke playing Ol' Man River. ZHDANOV looks acutely uncomfortable. STALIN frowns. Shouting:]*

STALIN: You wrote this?

*[PROKOFIEV shakes his head. He cannot help laughing. STALIN takes off the record]*

STALIN: What's going on here? Is somebody playing games with me?

ZHDANOV: I can explain, Josef...

STALIN: Is that someone's idea of a joke? What's that record doing here? How did it get in?

ZHDANOV: I'm trying to keep track of the black market in Western music. This stuff has been smuggled in for years. We're working on a case at the moment... I, er, had it with me when I arrived...

STALIN: And I thought poor old Prokofiev had written it. *[Roars with laughter, then stops. Pause]* Do you listen to that kind of thing?

SHOSTAKOVICH: It is my... business to keep abreast... I mean, it's very difficult to ignore anything... even music from... India or Japan, anywhere... Patagonia!

STALIN: You have to take drugs to listen to jazz. You took drugs?

SHOSTAKOVICH: No. I wouldn't know where to start.

STALIN: So where did you find this record, Andrei? In the shops?

ZHDANOV: In a writer's flat.

[*STALIN hands the record to ZHDANOV*]

STALIN: You'd better take care of it then if it's evidence. But be careful where you leave things like that in future, Andrei. Prokofiev got the shock of his life, didn't you?

[*STALIN laughs and pats PROKOFIEV on the shoulder. Telephone rings. ZHDANOV walks over the broken records to answer the telephone*]

ZHDANOV: Yes? What is it? I said we weren't to be disturbed. [*Pause*] Oh. Not good. [*Pause*] How many? [*Pause*] Hm. That's rough.

STALIN: What is it? Hurry up and get off the line.

ZHDANOV: There's been a mining disaster in the Ukraine. The editor of Pravda wants to publish a message from you to the survivors in tomorrow's issue...

STALIN: Tell him that I'm too busy.

ZHDANOV: Four hundred and twenty dead.

STALIN: I can't deal with it now. Tell him I'm involved with something far more serious. Maybe I'll do a piece for the day after tomorrow. We'll see.

ZHDANOV: Try again tomorrow...

STALIN: Afternoon at the earliest.

ZHDANOV: Late afternoon.

STALIN: Say I'm working on something which is probably going to take all night.

ZHDANOV: It's an all-night session. Make it evening before he tries again.

[*ZHDANOV puts the telephone down. Pause. STALIN pours himself more vodka and takes a handful of nuts. He wanders round the room filling up the other glasses*]

ZHDANOV: That makes me feel sick. Four hundred and twenty dead and we're stuck here yapping about music.

STALIN: What a barbarian you are, Andrei. There will always be miners, there will always be holes in the ground. But music sometimes drains away from an entire civilization. Do you know why? Because nobody cares about it. [*Pause. He goes over to SHOSTAKOVICH*] I think I'll give you a commission to write me a piece of music about this disaster in the Ukraine. It's a miserable, unhappy business and so it's right up your street. Why shouldn't you make a profit out of these miners?

SHOSTAKOVICH: [*Angrily*] Do you think I don't care about people?

STALIN: What are we short of in the Soviet Union? Miners or composers?

SHOSTAKOVICH: What is the matter with me? Come on! Let's have it.
Tell me!

PROKOFIEV: Dmitri, calm down.

STALIN: No, let him shout. I'm glad to see his eyes flashing behind his
bank clerk's spectacles. The blackbird is ruffled. This is what is the
matter with you. You have forgotten this.

[*STALIN goes over to the piano. He sits down and accompanies himself as
he sings a simple, melodic folk-song. It has a chorus which he encourages them
to join in. ZHDANOV does so with gusto. PROKOFIEV and
SHOSTAKOVICH make a half-hearted response*]

STALIN: That wasn't very good boys. Come over here and sing it again.
It's only a simple, peasant song. You keep quiet, Andrei. Let them do
it alone this time. One. Two. Three.

[*STALIN leaves the piano and conducts as choirmaster. PROKOFIEV and
SHOSTAKOVICH sing weakly and with reluctance*]

STALIN: Stop! What's the matter with you? You're sabotaging it, deliberately, you Russian snobs! Is a Georgian folk-song not good enough
for you? Now, listen, you two. Either you come down off your pedestals
or I'll have you shot. Do you understand? Shot. Andrei will take you
down to the Lubianka prison and have you done first thing in the
morning. So, stop wasting my time. Sing it again and put some feeling
into it.

[*PROKOFIEV and SHOSTAKOVICH sing the song with more
animation. Half-way through STALIN starts to smile and joins in, beckoning
ZHDANOV to do the same*]

STALIN: Not bad, not bad. Now, we'll take the parts. Andrei, you've got
an ear that is too easily influenced by what you hear around you. Stick
with the tune and start the verse with me. Prokofiev, try the baritone
line. [*Gives him a phrase*] Not difficult. Shostakovich, I think you could
manage the bass. [*Gives him a phrase*] It's not too low. If it is you can
switch to tenor. Improvise on it if you like. Let's see what we can make
of it. This first try is in the nature of an experiment, boys. Here's our
note, Andrei. Yours, Prokofiev; yours, Shostakovich. One. Two. Three.

[*They sing the song successfully in parts. STALIN is delighted*]

STALIN: Very good! You see how easy it is? I'm very pleased with that.
Hearing that old song took me right back. Can you hear the monks

running to stop us? We should have been singing hymns, not love songs. The piano may not be used for any purpose other than the practice of liturgical chants, anthems or, at the most, cantatas. Josef Vissarionvich Djugashvili is not to be permitted to use the piano again. He defiles it with secular filth! [*He takes the icon and carries it around the room held high above his head*] He will, for his punishment, carry the icon of our Lord in glory above his head around the refectory ten times before each meal and ten times after. No, not the one with the wooden frame. The one with the frame of lead. [*Pause. He stops and lowers the icon to cover his chest*] Now do you think that you have suffered more for music than I have? I was always in trouble. You see, we were forbidden to sing Georgian songs - simple, warm-hearted songs that we had learnt at home. Why? Because they tended to be about Georgian heroes, wild men, brigands, fighters for independence. The Orthodox Church didn't like that. Nor did the Imperial Russian Government. So, I ended up carrying Christ through the smell of boiled cabbage until my arm ached. But it was worth it, for music.

ZHDANOV: Those songs are worth suffering for. People can understand them. They belong to everyone. We don't even know who wrote most of them, they were composed so long ago. Or were they composed at all? Sometimes I think that word stinks. I think some music just comes out of people's souls.

STALIN: What do you know about Georgian songs, you ignorant lout?

ZHDANOV: I've heard them sung...

STALIN: Russian bastard! You can't speak a word of Georgian!

ZHDANOV: It's a difficult language.

STALIN: A dying language. I tell you Andrei, there is more music, more beauty, more great literature in Georgia than anywhere else. But no one knows about it because it was stifled. I wasn't allowed to be taught at school in my own language. How do you think that made me feel?

ZHDANOV: Yes, what I'm saying is...

STALIN: Shut up.

ZHDANOV: There's no need for that.

STALIN: You get drunk very quickly.

ZHDANOV: I'm not drunk.

STALIN: Whenever I get reports from you - decisions you've made, things you've done, excuses you're making - I have to ask myself, has he been drinking?

ZHDANOV: That's not fair!

STALIN: It's common knowledge that you were drunk from one end of the siege of Leningrad to the other. Ask Shostakovich. Isn't that common knowledge?

SHOSTAKOVICH: I don't know.

STALIN: Don't be afraid of him. I sent him to Finland on a delicate mission. It needed diplomacy, tact. There was a lot at stake. What did he do? Drunk for weeks, getting his hand up girls' skirts, falling over at receptions, sleeping at meetings, vomiting in hotel foyers...

ZHDANOV: This is a lie!

STALIN: And you were heard talking French! You fawning, snobbish, snivelling Francophone! You're like some bourgeois turd out of Chekhov. But you won't speak Georgian, will you? Why? Because it's the language of ordinary people who live natural, healthy lives - no affectations!

[*Pause. ZHDANOV is struggling to mind his tongue. He pours himself another drink and munches a biscuit*]

STALIN: I know I'll get more sympathy from my friends here than you, you arrogant Russian moron!

ZHDANOV: Whatever you say.

STALIN: These men are artists. They will know what I'm talking about. The agony of a nation made inarticulate. And don't you sulk, Andrei. You drive me mad when you sulk.

ZHDANOV: I'm not sulking. I was thinking about what you have said. Why don't we revive the language? Build up awareness of its existence. Start a campaign.

STALIN: Make it artificial? If that is what you want, go ahead. It's a natural thing. It's to do with pride, history. How do you stimulate nature? Eh? How do you wake people up to what is being taken away from them? [*Pause. He puts an arm round ZHDANOV*] He's all right. My oldest friend. One day he may succeed me, if he gets better. But I'll probably live to be well over a hundred, eh, Andrei? [*ZHDANOV roars with laughter*] Give Jesus a drink.

[*STALIN holds up the icon. ZHDANOV puts his glass to the mouth of the figure. He tips vodka over it*]

ZHDANOV: He doesn't want it. Not good enough for him. Perhaps he's developed a taste for vinegar.

[*ZHDANOV continues pouring vodka over the picture. PROKOFIEV watches with distaste but SHOSTAKOVICH is getting very agitated*]

STALIN: I know more about this man, Jesus Christ, than any other person. Don't drown him, Andrei.

SHOSTAKOVICH: You're spoiling that!

ZHDANOV: What?

SHOSTAKOVICH: You're ruining it!

ZHDANOV: So what? Who's short of icons? Stupid bits of painted wood. Never liked them, always staring at me.

SHOSTAKOVICH: Don't you put any value on it? I thought it was a gift. Why are you letting him destroy it?

STALIN: It's well varnished. No harm will be done. Don't venerate it, whatever you do.

SHOSTAKOVICH: Someone painted it. Even the artist needs respect. Excuse me.

[*SHOSTAKOVICH stalks across the room towards the washroom exit. ZHDANOV bars his way. He holds up the icon and spits in its face. SHOSTAKOVICH is horrified. PROKOFIEV turns away*]

ZHDANOV: Oh, what have I done? Sorry. Never spit into the wind. You never know who you'll hit.

[*ZHDANOV throws the icon on to the floor and bows SHOSTAKOVICH through. SHOSTAKOVICH goes into the washroom and closes the door. He leans on the wash-basin, head down, crying. ZHDANOV leans against the mantelpiece*]

PROKOFIEV: Why do you make yourself more ignorant and brutal than you are?

ZHDANOV: Don't talk to me, you lounge lizard.

PROKOFIEV: None of us can help our childhoods, where we came from.

ZHDANOV: Don't use that tone to me. We won a war, not a game of whist. It's about time that boy grew up. Sensitive about a bit of wood. What about him feeling for ordinary people instead of rubbish like that? And you as well, you intellectual. If I'd have pulled a poor man in off the street and spat in his face you'd have thought it was great fun. So much for your finer feelings. [*ZHDANOV sits down at the piano*] What do you think this is? [*Tinkles the keys*] It's just a big, black icon that sings. It's another of your holy objects. I saw you when you first came into this room. You didn't look at me. You looked at the piano. Well, you know what I say: people before pianos, people before Prokofiev.

PROKOFIEV: But not, and I may be guessing, people before politics.

ZHDANOV: What do you know about politics? You've spent most of your life throbbing in a greenhouse. You're a tomato, a green tomato, even an impudent tomato. Perhaps I'll string you up.

[*SHOSTAKOVICH washes his face and hands very thoroughly, almost obsessively. ZHDANOV starts to play the piano, which he does surprisingly well. He grins at PROKOFIEV and STALIN*]

SHOSTAKOVICH: I must not lose my temper.

ZHDANOV: Who wrote this? Keep quiet, Prokofiev, you're an expert. Let him guess.

SHOSTAKOVICH: I must stay cool and make as little comment as possible.

ZHDANOV: Come on. Who wrote it?

STALIN: Keep playing. I've heard it before.

SHOSTAKOVICH: Just survive, Dmitri, survive.

ZHDANOV: I'll give you a clue. [*Plays a flourish*]

STALIN: Glinka.

ZHDANOV: No! Glinka? Never!

[*SHOSTAKOVICH washes his hands again and again*]

STALIN: Skriabin.

ZHDANOV: Do me a favour!

STALIN: You're playing it badly. I can't tell.

PROKOFIEV: I disagree. He's making a fair attempt, I'd say.

ZHDANOV: You've no idea, have you?

SHOSTAKOVICH: I won't let them break me. I won't.

STALIN: Well, it's not Rimsky, it's not Tchaikovsky...

ZHDANOV: It's that mad Pole, that bloody mad, lecherous, lunatic Pole, Chopin! Failed, Josef Vissarionvich Djugashvili. Go to the bottom of the class. See, you assumed I'd only be able to play a Russian composer. But I'm a Renaissance man, a universal man.

[*SHOSTAKOVICH enters. He looks at ZHDANOV who is still seated at the piano. ZHDANOV winks at him*]

ZHDANOV: Hello, Comrade. Did you hear me playing? Go on, say that you thought it was a gramophone record of Arthur Rubinstein. Go on, flatter me.

SHOSTAKOVICH: The walls here are very thick. I didn't hear it.

ZHDANOV: I was quite good for a stupid soldier. I can play the piano, but can you fight?

SHOSTAKOVICH: I can fight.

ZHDANOV: Good. How about you, Prokofiev? Do you want a fight?

PROKOFIEV: Not in my best form at the moment but if someone will hold me up I'll have a go.

ZHDANOV: Good. That's what I like to hear.

STALIN: I reckon these two would tackle anything. They're good men. You'll have a go, won't you?

PROKOFIEV: Of course. We always have, as you might have noticed.

ZHDANOV: Steady, musician.

STALIN: The man is right. I have noted their efforts. [*Pause*] But they have not been good enough. So, why don't we get down to it and write the definitive new Soviet music together?

[*Pause*]

SHOSTAKOVICH: Sergei and I have different styles...

PROKOFIEV: Hold on, Dmitri. Do you mean that we should collaborate on something? Why not? We might be able to make it work. It will take time. Perhaps we could spend a couple of weeks together in the country? I'll look in my diary and see what time I've got free.

SHOSTAKOVICH: Yes, by all means.

STALIN: No! That is not what I meant! To ask you two to collaborate would be futile. You are so vain and envious of each other that it would be doomed to failure. I'm told that you don't even like each other all that much. [*He opens the piano lid and plays a couple of notes*] No, the four of us here tonight: me, Andrei, and you two, are going to compose something together.

ZHDANOV: A co-operative venture. Yes, it's a very good idea. We can make it work. I like the sound of that.

PROKOFIEV: Without wishing to be obstructive, Comrade Stalin...

STALIN: You refuse?

PROKOFIEV: No. I was just wondering if we might have some time to mull over the idea.

ZHDANOV: You've had plenty of time already. You've failed. If you'd done your job properly this wouldn't be necessary.

PROKOFIEV: I'm certainly not against experiments as such. Nor is Dmitri, I know. We both believe in a flexible approach. [*Pause. He looks at SHOSTAKOVICH*] If this is what you would like to do... we will help all we can.

STALIN: Good, Andrei and I are not unconscious of the privilege we are about to enjoy. Few people will have shared your extraordinary minds at such close quarters. Let us hope that we poor amateurs are not sucked in and lost without trace. [*Pause*] Do you know Rustaveli?

PROKOFIEV: I've read him in translation.

STALIN: The greatest of Georgian poets. We are going to set one of his stories to music; the kind of music that you two should have been writing. [*Pause. He looks at SHOSTAKOVICH*] Do you always have to look so unhappy?

SHOSTAKOVICH: I was thinking of the technical problems.

STALIN: What are they?

SHOSTAKOVICH: Music is a very personal language.

ZHDANOV: It doesn't have to be so private. You must learn to share. I'm a man, like you. You tell me what you're after and I'll tell you what I'm after.

SHOSTAKOVICH: But we're only dealing with sounds. That's very primitive. It can't be broken up, it's too basic...

PROKOFIEV: I think we'll have to judge the level of seriousness that the composition strikes very accurately. What it must do is suggest the... brotherliness of this venture... er, it will need an emotional balance that implies sharing, good nature... humour...

STALIN: Rustaveli is a very serious poet. I'm not having him trivialized.

PROKOFIEV: No, no, that isn't what I meant. Let me see... the mood of the piece should communicate this fusion of... different minds with a common goal...

STALIN: Yes, I see the sense in that.

PROKOFIEV: So, it must not be too individually tempered. After all, a group will always behave differently from a single person. Wouldn't you agree, Dmitri? For instance a crowd laughs more, because it is together. You must have noticed that in your audiences, Dmitri. [*Pause. SHOSTAKOVICH nods*]

STALIN: He still looks unhappy.

SHOSTAKOVICH: No, I'm adjusting my mind to the idea. Yes, I think we can make something of this! Why haven't we tried it before? What will they say at the conference when this gets out? They'll be amazed.

PROKOFIEV: We couldn't have it ready for the last day, could we? Imagine playing it to them, the looks on their faces. By the way, I haven't brought any score paper. Have we any?

STALIN: Everything we say is being recorded. We can go back over the tapes when we've finished and put the final score together. I've only got a few hours to spare so we will have to work quickly. [*Takes a paper from his inside pocket*] Here's the story that we have to set to music. We can start.

PROKOFIEV: May I ask a question?

STALIN: Certainly, go ahead.

PROKOFIEV: Have we decided whether this composition is to be a ballet, an opera, a song-cycle, concerto?

STALIN: What do you think?

SHOSTAKOVICH: Let's hear the story first, then choose the form that will suit it best.

ZHDANOV: Good idea. Let's see what we're dealing with first.

STALIN: From *The Knight in the Tiger's Skin* by Rustaveli. Are you ready? The speaker is Tariel, the knight himself: "As I came up the hill, the lion and tiger came walking together like a pair of lovers."

ZHDANOV: Bom-bom-bom-bom, oh-ho!

STALIN: Andrei, just hold back your creativeness for a moment. We need to get the story firmly in our minds. Keep quiet until I've finished.

ZHDANOV: Sorry. I got carried away.

STALIN: "As I came up the hill, the lion and tiger came walking together like a pair of lovers. Then they began to fight as lovers do. The tiger fled with the lion in hot pursuit. Then they sported gaily, then fought fiercely, neither seeming to have a fear of death. Then the tiger lost heart, even as women do, and ran away. The lion followed and tore at her unmercifully. This displeased me. 'Art thou out of thy wits? Why dost thou persecute thy beloved?' I shouted, rushing at the lion with my sword and spear. We fought and I killed him, freeing him from this world's woe. Then I threw away my bloody sword and embraced the tiger, wishing to kiss it on the mouth, my mind full of hot longings for my beloved whom I had left behind. The tiger roared at me and chewed my face so I killed it in rage and frustration, beating and dashing it to the ground, whirling it around my head, remembering my nights of passion with my beloved."

[*STALIN smiles and puts the paper on top of the piano. Pause*]

SHOSTAKOVICH: Well, plenty to be going on with there, eh, Sergei?

PROKOFIEV: A rich field indeed.

SHOSTAKOVICH: It has great musical potential.

STALIN: You're not just saying that, are you? You can hear what I can hear inside it. When I first read the piece it rang in my head for days. I couldn't get it out of my mind.

SHOSTAKOVICH: Can you remember the key it rang in?

STALIN: No. I should have tried to establish it but there was no piano available. I was in prison.

SHOSTAKOVICH: Oh... I see.

PROKOFIEV: Should the music be martial in character?

STALIN: Partly.

PROKOFIEV: With the greatest of respect to your intense, personal experience, we must have a key to work with - even if it is only a starting point...

STALIN: Let me be quiet for a moment. [*Pause*] Isn't it strange? I spent days humming the sounds that I heard in that piece. It nearly drove me mad. Couldn't sleep, couldn't think about anything else. Now I've forgotten. What a pity.

[*PROKOFIEV strikes a chord on the piano*]

PROKOFIEV: B flat major. How about that?

SHOSTAKOVICH: I don't think there's enough emotional resonance in B flat major, Sergei. This is no ordinary knight on a walking holiday. this is man... at a very fundamental level of feeling. Am I right, Comrade?

STALIN: You are. [*Blows his nose*] I don't fancy B flat major.

PROKOFIEV: Would you like me to play through all the major keys until we find the right one? I am presuming that it couldn't possibly be in a minor. [*Pause, then, with a touch of mischief*] Or atonal.

ZHDANOV: Under no circumstances. Would you like that, Josef? All the keys?

STALIN: Yes. Don't ever mention atonal to me again, you noisy child!

PROKOFIEV: The style of the melody must be governed by the mood of the words, and its shape by their sense and meaning. Are we agreed on that?

STALIN: I'm glad you mentioned a melody. And I don't want it ballsed up! D'you hear? I don't want you taking it to pieces and kicking it around until it's unrecognizable! Let's hear these keys.

[*Pause. PROKOFIEV starts to play through a series of major keys. He pauses at the end of each and looks questioningly at STALIN. STALIN waves him on each time. PROKOFIEV finishes and sits back*]

STALIN: Go on!

PROKOFIEV: That's the lot. We've run out of keys. There wasn't one that touched you?

STALIN: It was so long ago.

SHOSTAKOVICH: May I make a suggestion? To me there is a sadness in the violence of the story. It is Love and Death, the primitive and the civilized, conflicts that are acutely painful. Could we not consider the minor keys? They are very expressive of tragic conflict.

STALIN: No! You're dragging us down to misery again, you melancholy bastard! Make it... that third one you played... what was it? Near enough, near enough.

PROKOFIEV: An excellent choice. [*Plays the chord*] G major, as I live and breathe. G for Georgia, G for gorgeous. G *not* for avant-garde! This is wonderfully liberating, Dmitri. Right. I say we should have a French horn for the tiger and a trombone for the lion.

STALIN: No trombone. I don't like trombones.

ZHDANOV: Cut the trombone.

SHOSTAKOVICH: Could it be a brass trio? We could have a tuba for Tariel.

STALIN: I don't want a trio, or a tuba.

ZHDANOV: They're out for a start.

STALIN: This isn't going to be something a few street musicians can play. It's an important piece so it has to have majesty, power.

SHOSTAKOVICH: The knight, Tariel, is on a journey.

ZHDANOV: Without his tuba.

STALIN: A journey, a pilgrimage, a quest.

SHOSTAKOVICH: Ah. Questing music.

PROKOFIEV: In G major.

ZHDANOV: What is it you don't like about trombones?

PROKOFIEV: Let's find the melody. We can orchestrate later.

STALIN: Man's life is the theme. The journey. When the journey stops in the body but goes on in the mind. Do you know when that is? Prison or old age. This is what it's all about, Andrei. We're getting through to them at last!

PROKOFIEV: Of course, we'll need a striped theme for the tiger.

ZHDANOV: How the hell do we do that?

STALIN: Oh, it's possible, possible. Keep your ears open.

PROKOFIEV: [*Illustrating on piano*] There's black and yellow music. Music that eats one up. Man-eating music. How am I doing?

ZHDANOV: Got any tartan music while you're at it?

STALIN: Andrei! Stop being such an old sourpuss. This is great stuff.

PROKOFIEV: Rhythm, Dmitri.

SHOSTAKOVICH: Well, first part walking up the hill, wasn't it? That will have to andante, and I imagine that Tariel, being a knight, would be clanking up the hill in a suit of armour. so it seems that a clanking andante is what we're looking for. As he's probably quite fit he could keep up a simple quadruple rhythm of four minim beats in the bar. Or is that too fast.

STALIN: Georgian knights never clanked.

SHOSTAKOVICH: Oh. Wrong again.

ZHDANOV: We don't want any clanking in this. Or farting. Or train sounds or nasty factory whistles! Understand!

STALIN: Georgian knights never clanked. They were too brave to wear armour. Next to their skins they wore silk. And they were very fit.

PROKOFIEV: If they wore silk they'd rustle.

STALIN: I like the human voice.

SHOSTAKOVICH: An opera? Even Mozart couldn't write one in a single night.

PROKOFIEV: A song-cycle?

STALIN: Pooh.

SHOSTAKOVICH: Well, something for a large choir... a cantata.

STALIN: Thousands of voices. Thousands and thousands. In parts. That's what I want. You've hit it. Well done, what's your name.

ZHDANOV: Now we know where we are. That's a good choice. A huge cantata.

STALIN: A great work for the massed choir. Voices, melodies flowing in and out of each other. Just voices.

SHOSTAKOVICH: Then we will need the story to be adapted. We will have to have the words in a manageable rhythm. At the moment they are all over the place.

STALIN: I'll be in charge of the words. Have you forgotten I'm a poet? It takes a poet to understand a poet. I was publishing verses before I was twenty. This will pose me no problem at all. Thousands of people singing it. Millions perhaps. All together.

ZHDANOV: What am I going to do?

STALIN: Keep our glasses filled and hand round the nuts.

ZHDANOV: I thought we were all supposed to be composing this.

STALIN: You can be the continuity girl.

PROKOFIEV: Shall we get started? I suggest that everyone makes what contribution they are capable of. May I ask what kind of personality this knight, Tariel, has?

ZHDANOV: Sounds a mad bastard to me.

STALIN: Complex. Fiercely independent, yet basically a humble man who wishes to help others. He is virtuous but often appears to be evil because of the actions forced upon him by circumstances. Although a simple man who understands love he has a struggle to equate it with his duty to his people. He has great physical strength and moral courage. Tariel is a true hero.

[*Pause*]

ZHDANOV: How tall is he?

STALIN: What does that matter?

ZHDANOV: I need to see him in my mind's eye. If he was a dwarf...

STALIN: He's not a dwarf, idiot. Heroes aren't dwarfs!

PROKOFIEV: How about this? Walking up the hill, rustling along. Sun shining. A jolly nice day.

[*He plays a merry, mindless, fast tune*]

STALIN: I've changed my mind. I don't like this song-cycle idea.

SHOSTAKOVICH: This isn't a song-cycle. It's a cantata.

STALIN: You never hear of song-cycles in folk music. You never hear of cantatas in folk music.

SHOSTAKOVICH: We can't just sit down and write folk music.

ZHDANOV: Why not? We're folk, aren't we? Are you saying we're not folk? I'll punch your face in!

STALIN: I'm folk, for one.

ZHDANOV: So'm I.

STALIN: Are you? I'm more folk than you are. I'm more folk than any of you. To be honest with you, I'm the ultimate folk. [Pause] Prokofiev. Do you know what's left of you that is folk? The grave that is waiting for you. All your pretensions will drop away, my son. We'll dig you in like a spadeful of shit.

[*Pause. PROKOFIEV nods, smiles*]

PROKOFIEV: You would like us to imitate folk melodies? So, my pretensions must continue. If I'm not folk, as you assure me I'm not, I must adopt a pose. [*Pause*] It is a pity in music if we are not what we are, but... I can play the knight. I can play the peasant.

STALIN: All right, all right! Let's do this folk cantata. I'll adapt some of *The Knight in the Tiger's Skin.*

ZHDANOV: If you say so.

STALIN: You'll have to take it down as I recite it. It's a section that I learnt by heart. While passing it through my mind I'll improve it slightly. Just give me a moment to myself.

ZHDANOV: I hope you'll be able to read my writing.

STALIN: Shut up! [*Pause*] Silence, please!

ZHDANOV: Sorry.

[*STALIN closes his eyes, concentrating hard. ZHDANOV stands by him with paper and pencil. The composers wait at the piano*]

STALIN: I'm concentrating on the love theme, giving it an early development. What I thought might be a good idea is if the knight, Tariel, is thinking about his girl as he walks up the hill *before* he sees the lion and the tiger. So, he's striding along thinking the line: "My woeful heart is like a caravan."

PROKOFIEV: [*Pause. He frowns, shrugs, then improvises*] "My woeful heart is like a caravan."

SHOSTAKOVICH: [*Improvising with him*] "My woeful heart is like a caravan." I think it would be stronger as: "My woeful heart *is* a caravan."

ZHDANOV: Then, how about: "The wandering, trundling heart of Man?"

STALIN: Who d'you think you are? Rustaveli? The next phrase is -ah!

ZHDANOV: [*Writing it down*] "Ah!"

SHOSTAKOVICH: "Ah!"

PROKOFIEV: "Ah!"

STALIN: "To him who has been struck in the liver by a snake treacle is better suited than red candy."

[*PROKOFIEV and SHOSTAKOVICH falter on the piano. ZHDANOV looks startled. Pause*]

ZHDANOV: Would you mind giving us that again?

STALIN: "To him who has been struck in the liver by a snake treacle is better suited than red candy. To him who is dying of poison antidote is everything."

ZHDANOV: This is what is in the knight's head as he's climbing up the hill?

STALIN: Yes.

ZHDANOV: Mad bastard. Sounds as though he's suffering from a hangover.

STALIN: Just write it down, miss. Well, I think we've got a good beginning there. The mood should be reflective, like this. Move over.

[*STALIN pushes SHOSTAKOVICH off the stool and starts to improvise and sing. PROKOFIEV joins in on the piano*]

STALIN: "My woeful heart is a caravan."

PROKOFIEV: "My woeful heart is a caravan."

ZHDANOV: Everyone's heart is a caravan. How the hell do we get
  from his heart being a caravan into his liver being bitten by a
  snake?
STALIN: Sssh. Try that again. "My woeful heart is a caravan."
SHOSTAKOVICH: Wouldn't it be a more workable line if we lengthened
  if to: "My woeful heart is a caravanserai? Serai! Serai!"
STALIN: Show me.
  [*SHOSTAKOVICH builds the theme into what they have composed so far*]
PROKOFIEV: I quite like "serai". Do you like "serai?"
ZHDANOV: I love it. What d'you want? Plain "caravan" or "caravanserai?"
SHOSTAKOVICH: I think tagging the "serai" on to it would avoid any
  confusion. "Caravanserai" suggests camels, horses. "Caravan" could be
  motorized. That would make a different, non-medieval sound.
PROKOFIEV: No internal combustion engines in medieval Georgia.
  They hadn't invented it by then. Or had they? I'm quite happy to put
  one in.
  [*He plays an illustrative sequence*]
STALIN: I think it should be "caravanserai." That's another two syllables
  on that line. "Caravanserai." Do we all agree?
PROKOFIEV: I'm perfectly happy.
SHOSTAKOVICH: I think we've voted that one in.
STALIN: Let's try this. [*Goes to the keyboard and develops a phrase*] Good.
  Give me some of that walking music. [*He plays as PROKOFIEV
  accompanies him*] "To him who is dying of poison." Keep that serious.
  [*They play again*] Set that. We're doing well. It's working, Andrei. It's
  working. Let's try that, the four of us. Right. A few footsteps of the
  knight coming up the hill as a kind of prelude. [*They play*] Then his
  romantic longings make themselves felt.
ALL: [*Sing*] My woeful heart is a caravanserai. Ah! To him who has been
  struck in the liver by a snake treacle is better suited than red candy. To
  him who is dying of poison antidote is everything.
STALIN: Let's hear what that sounds like. It felt all right to me.
ZHDANOV: Sergeant! Play that back!
STALIN: What did you think, Prokofiev?
PROKOFIEV: I'd say we were breaking new ground, certainly.
  [*A babbling screech of backwinding tape over the amplifiers, then the replay
  starts. The four of them listen intently. STALIN is, at first, thoughtful, then
  incredulous, disappointed and dismayed in turn. PROKOFIEV and
  SHOSTAKOVICH watch STALIN wanly. ZHDANOV is visibly shaken*]

*but he keeps his eye on STALIN, watching his mood worsen. The replay goes through to STALIN's line:* Let's hear what it sounds like. It felt all right to me. *STALIN reacts angrily*]

ZHDANOV: That's enough, sergeant! Turn it off!

[*Pause. STALIN hangs his head*]

STALIN: [*Without looking up*] Andrei!

ZHDANOV: [*Going over to him and leaning down*] Yes, Josef?

[*STALIN beckons ZHDANOV to come closer so he can whisper in his ear. ZHDANOV listens, then straightens up*]

ZHDANOV: Face the wall, you two!

[*Pause. SHOSTAKOVICH and PROKOFIEV obey, bewildered and apprehensive. STALIN beckons ZHDANOV to lean down again. He whispers in ZHDANOV's ear*]

ZHDANOV: Certainly. Don't you go blaming yourself.

[*ZHDANOV goes round to where PROKOFIEV is facing the wall. He stands behind PROKOFIEV. Pause. Taking a metal-topped pen out of his pocket he touches the back of PROKOFIEV's neck with it. PROKOFIEV stiffens and almost cries out*]

PROKOFIEV: What are you doing?

ZHDANOV: Give me your handkerchief. You have made Comrade Stalin cry.

STALIN: That's right. I am crying.

ZHDANOV: He doesn't want you to see him like that. It makes him feel ashamed. Not that he need be. It takes a man to cry.

[*ZHDANOV goes back to STALIN with PROKOFIEV's handkerchief. STALIN takes it, wipes his eyes, blows his nose on it, then gives it back to ZHDANOV*]

PROKOFIEV: I'm sure we're all very sorry if we made you unhappy.

STALIN: Give him his handkerchief back. I'm all right now.

PROKOFIEV: It isn't that serious... [*Turns*] We can keep trying.

STALIN: [*Furiously*] Don't look at me. I'm very embarrassed.

[*ZHDANOV gives PROKOFIEV his handkerchief, deliberately opening it up and smearing PROKOFIEV's jacket as he sticks it back in his top pocket*]

ZHDANOV: I don't cry very often, so you see how crucial this has been to me. It means that the deepest part of the emotions has been disturbed. You have no idea how disappointed I am.

ZHDANOV: See what you've done? He reckons the whole things is his fault.

SHOSTAKOVICH: [*Still with his face to the wall*] We've only had one go at it. There's a lot of rewriting to be done. That's where most of the time and effort comes in. We'll just have to keep hammering away until we get it right.

STALIN: D'you think that I want to hear thousands of Russians singing that awful row? I never want to hear it again as long as I live. How black everything's got. Do you go through times like this?

SHOSTAKOVICH: Oh, often.

STALIN: You would. But I am not used to failure, boys. This has been a very strange experience for me. [*Pause*] They're not laughing at me, are they, Andrei?

ZHDANOV: If they are I'll kill them with my bare hands.

STALIN: I don't mind if they look at me now.

ZHDANOV: Turn round! If I see smiles on your faces you're dead!
[*SHOSTAKOVICH and PROKOFIEV turn round. STALIN looks up at them and smiles. Pauses*]

STALIN: I wish I didn't get this way, boys.

ZHDANOV: Don't make excuses to them, Josef. It was their fault. They misled you like they've misled everybody.

STALIN: And I was enjoying it so much. Did you enjoy it, Prokofiev?

PROKOFIEV: Yes. And I'm sorry that it failed but at least we all had the wit to realize it. After all, we can always try again.

STALIN: You'd do that with a good heart?

PROKOFIEV: Definitely.

STALIN: Shostakovich?

SHOSTAKOVICH: More time would help. You can't rush these things.

STALIN: I don't think you enjoyed it much. You don't enjoy anything, do you? Tell me, misery-guts, do you enjoy being alive?

SHOSTAKOVICH: Not always.

STALIN: Do you know, it's very odd, but whenever I make a mistake I do back in my mind to the days when I wanted to be a priest. I was always in trouble, always, but all I wanted in the whole world was to be the good shepherd in the valley of the shadow of death. Thy rod. Thy staff. Me comfort still. Fancy thinking that I was not cut out for it. [*He shakes his head and looks at his hands. He sings softly:*]He who clothes himself with light as with a garment, stood naked at the judgment...
[*He falls into a catatonic reverie, his eyes open. He hums a few more bars then falls silent. Pause. ZHDANOV has a good look at him*]

ZHDANOV: Josef!

[*Pause. ZHDANOV passes a hand in front of STALIN's face. He does not respond*]

ZHDANOV: Josef!

STALIN: Josef Vissarionvich Djugashvili is my name. I want to be a priest and save people. Have you any room for me?

ZHDANOV: Josef! Can you hear me? Do you want to go to bed?

STALIN: Josef Vissarionvich Djugashvili. The shoemaker's apprentice. God's apprentice. He's dead, you know.

[*ZHDANOV snaps his fingers in front of STALIN's eyes. STALIN laughs softly to himself, then suddenly grabs ZHDANOV's hand. He holds it and forces ZHDANOV down*]

STALIN: If you come in on me from the right side you get my good arm, Comrade.

ZHDANOV: [*Prising his fist loose*] Are you all right, Josef?

STALIN: Yes. I'm all right.

ZHDANOV: Good. [*Prises his hand out of STALIN's fist*] We still have these monkeys with us. Shall I get rid of them?

STALIN: They don't understand. But I want them. They're mine.

ZHDANOV: [*Standing up*] This man saved your country in its hour of peril. You are privileged to be near him. He won a great war.

STALIN: No one can take that away from me.

ZHDANOV: God help anyone that tries.

STALIN: God help anyone that tries.

[*STALIN suddenly gets to his feet and, very briskly, goes to the piano and pours himself a drink. He is full of energy again, back in command*]

STALIN: We'll have another go at it. But, I have to be frank with you, you made me suffer. I don't want to go through that again. All right, there're no guarantees, I know that, but we have to do a lot better this time. Well, say something! Come on! Andrei, I warn you, I'm starting to feel very hostile towards these two nincompoops. They're beginning to get on my nerves.

ZHDANOV: That's the brightest thing you've said all night.

[*STALIN throws his vodka full in ZHDANOV's face. ZHDANOV stands very still. STALIN pours another glass of vodka and walks towards SHOSTAKOVICH who sees what's coming and takes his glasses off. STALIN throws vodka in his face. He returns to the piano, fills another glass, goes to PROKOFIEV, dips his fingers in the vodka and sketches a cross on PROKOFIEV's forehead*]

ZHDANOV: In the name of Father, Son and Holy Ghost, amen. All is forgiven. We're back where we started from. But this time we've got to do better... or else!

SHOSTAKOVICH: Are we going to try and salvage anything from the first effort...

STALIN: That abortion is finished with. It never existed. We never did it. It never happened. Not that. Not us. A new sound has to come out of somewhere.

SHOSTAKOVICH: Then we must have a new story. It's essential!

STALIN: I could kick you for that. It wasn't the story that was wrong. See, you're trying to fix the blame on me. It was the music that didn't work. When I think of my poor father. A family of serfs we came from. Serfs. [*Weeps*] I'm off again. My mother was a saint. What she put up with. [*Takes a drink*] I was a great trial to her, you know. She knew about Tariel. She told me those tales in her own words. [*Pause*] I feel as though I've let her down. Something's gone wrong.

ZHDANOV: Josef, with respect, I think we'll have to rejig that old tale. It's marvellous, of course, but a bit antiquated. What's the relevance of Tariel and his queer battle with these animals - aren't lions and tigers extinct here now? - to the Soviet Union today, as it stands? Not only that but this is an elitist piece, drawn from one region, a region that is more fortunate than a place like, well, Siberia. At least let's move this knight to Siberia and let him run into a bear and a wolf.

STALIN: A wolf? Now you're talking!

ZHDANOV: Tariel comes face to face with real life, the truth, call it what you like. Don't you think that's a much better idea? And, while we're at it, do we actually need any reptiles around?

STALIN: I like wolves. Seven years of my life spent exiled in Siberia brought them very close. I used to watch the wolves running over the snow fields - dogs mating with bitches, cubs learning to hunt, scarred old loners hanging around on the edges of the pack, sick ones being picked off, old ones fading. Those animals kept me warm, reminded of life. Yes, I'd like to go back to Siberia on a sentimental journey. It was my second home.

ZHDANOV: Pack your kit! We're moving out!

SHOSTAKOVICH: I don't like the cold.

STALIN: Things are clearer in the cold. You see the world as it is: cruel, murderous, hostile. But the cold provokes life. All the energy has to

come from within. The cold is creative. The true, true sun is inside
oneself.

SHOSTAKOVICH: Inside one oneself. You.

STALIN: You can't take the cold, my son? How is it that Russia is your
home? What go ye into the desert to find? A man in soft raiment? Yes,
it's the sun inside me that keeps the land warm at all! Do you know
why Julius Caesar would not accept a crown? It was less than he had
already.

PROKOFIEV: Is that our insurance against the restoration of the Tsar?
[*ZHDANOV laughs*]

STALIN: I'm glad you're feeling easier with me. There is no insurance
any more. We nationalized it. [*Roars with laughter*] I am the past,
Prokofiev; I make the present; and I will supervise the future. No
wonder you feel more relaxed. [*Pause*] Why haven't you two set any
work by Jack London to music? He's the best writer the West has ever
produced. And a red-hot socialist into the bargain.

PROKOFIEV: Oh, you like him, do you? Doesn't he spend rather a lot
of time in the minds of animals?

STALIN: Yes. What's the matter with that? Look at yourself? You're
dying. Look at Andrei? He's on his way out. It's the animal part that
has the real power. Find the secret of that and you've solved everything.
Jack London. Wonderful writer. Probably a Slav in his family somewhere, eh? Beneath it all, all the talk, all the organization, we are
animals. *The Call of the Wild.* "The Indians tell of a Ghost Dog that
runs at the head of the pack. They are afraid of this Ghost Dog for it
has cunning greater than they, stealing from their camps in fierce
winters, robbing their traps, slaying their dogs, and defying their
hunters." Catch the mood, Prokofiev! Catch the mood!

PROKOFIEV: I'm not much of a one for the great outdoors.

STALIN: Hothouse plant! Orchid! How dare you write about wolves!
What d'you know about them? You've been misleading millions of
children with that *Peter and the Wolf* thing of yours. They'll think that
wolves are there to be played with.

PROKOFIEV: I don't know. My wolf is savage enough. [*Plays the Wolf
theme from Peter and the Wolf*] He eats people. I'd say he was a very
naughty wolf indeed.

STALIN: Where's his strength? Where's his power? The wolf is always
with us, waiting to burst out. "When the long winter nights come on
and the wolves follow their meat into the lower valleys, the Ghost Dog

may be seen running at the head of the pack through the pale moon-
light or glimmering borealis, leaping gigantic above his fellows, his
great throat a-bellow as he sings a song of the younger world, which is
the song of the pack."

[*Pause. PROKOFIEV lightly plays the Wolf theme again in a jocular way*]

STALIN: You're a thousand miles away with that. No wonder you can't
get through to ordinary people. They know what the power of Nature
is. They feel it.

[*STALIN goes to a huge wall mirror*]

PROKOFIEV: Do you worship Nature?

STALIN: I was taught to worship God. They were hard men who taught
me. They used force. We can all become God if we grind away at it.
That's Christian teaching.

[*STALIN stares into the mirror*]

PROKOFIEV: And the wolf? Can he become God?

STALIN: The animal is always holy. That was the first work of God, the
beasts. Grrr! Bahooo! White Fang! Red claw! Grrroah!

PROKOFIEV: Tariel, the oversexed Georgian outmoded militarist, a
man in the peak of condition, climbs a sharp gradient [Improvises]
encounters a lion and tiger in the act of bestial coition and Jack
London with an enormous wolf on a lead. Tariel is not confused. Being
an educated man his mind turns to thinking how to exploit this galaxy
of sexual opportunities. But what's this? The lion, the tiger and the
wolf have set up a ménage à trois and are tearing the seats out of
Tariel's and Jack London's trousers. "My God!" the humans cry and
run home to their respective mothers. Meanwhile, back in the Kremlin, Ivan the Terrible is growing hair all over his body... there's a full
moon... madness...

[*Pause. They look at STALIN who is grimly silent. Then ZHDANOV
suddenly roars with laughter. STALIN leaves the piano and goes over to
ZHDANOV. For a moment it looks as though he might hit him but he
merely slides his arm round ZHDANOV's shoulder then steals his drink.
They sport like a couple of boys*]

ZHDANOV: Get your own!

STALIN: Come on, meanie!

ZHDANOV: Get off me! I want my idea discussed seriously. I'm the one
who has to go back and chair that bloody conference tomorrow and I
must have something to tell them, be able to show we've made some
progress, taken a few decisions. Let's move the whole thing to Siberia.

STALIN: Too crowded!

ZHDANOV: Too crowded!

[*They roar with laughter, holding on to each other. PROKOFIEV nods and smiles, playing gentle music on the piano. SHOSTAKOVICH sings quietly. STALIN balances a glass of vodka on his forehead, gyrating slowly*]

SHOSTAKOVICH: My woeful heart is a caravanserai, serai, serai, serai.

ZHDANOV: All those who want this arsehole of a poncy, cock-eyed, idiot knight transferred to the bloody tundra say aye! [*Pause*] Aye!

PROKOFIEV: I'm easy.

SHOSTAKOVICH: Me too. You can send him to anywhere you like as far as I'm concerned. It's the story that matters. It's man against Nature. That's the theme. It's very sad.

STALIN: You always did write miserable music.

SHOSTAKOVICH: Did I?

STALIN: What have you got to be miserable about?

SHOSTAKOVICH: It just seems to turn out that way.

STALIN: Answer the question. Why do you write such miserable, whining, complaining dirges all the time?

[*Pause. ZHDANOV disentangles himself from STALIN*]

SHOSTAKOVICH: I write from what I feel. Maybe I'm a depressive.

STALIN: You abuse your status. People look up to you. And what do you do for them? You unload your own self-indulgent misery on them. You make them unhappy. That can't be justified.

PROKOFIEV: Perhaps it is melancholy rather than misery?

ZHDANOV: Don't split hairs, you fucking dilettante! Here he is, living in the most stirring times Russia has ever seen, and all he does is make people want to commit suicide. What right has he got to do that? Why don't you cheer the buggers up for a change?

STALIN: I know why he does it. He's disappointed with the way things have gone. He hates the Government. He feels out of place.

SHOSTAKOVICH: That's not so...

STALIN: Yes it is! You're undermining us! Sit down. Play us some of your miserable, horrible music so we can all have a good cry. Go on. I'm in the mood for it.

[*SHOSTAKOVICH sits down at the piano. PROKOFIEV gives him a pat on the shoulder and moves away*]

STALIN: Come on, make us miserable. We all want to die. Russia is a failure. The great experiment has been a disaster. All happiness has been destroyed.

SHOSTAKOVICH: I don't believe that.

ZHDANOV: Play or I'll smash your head in! My life's work being pissed on by a neurotic nancy-boy like you! Go on, tell me. Make me cry.

[*SHOSTAKOVICH starts to play a piano theme from the 14th prelude from Op. 34 - 24 Preludes for Piano. At first he falters but he becomes involved with the music and strengthens his playing*]

ZHDANOV: Boo hoo! Everything's a mess.

STALIN: Shut up, you ignorant pig! [*Pause*] Who is this music for, Shostakovich?

SHOSTAKOVICH: For the dead.

[*He plays on. STALIN drinks more. He leans against the mantelshelf*]

STALIN: Do you know how many died? I hardly dare think of the number. I could not bear to see it written down. Should I whisper it to you?

[*SHOSTAKOVICH plays on, shaking his head*]

STALIN: Twenty million. Don't tell anyone, will you? Twenty million. My heart is a caravanserai. To him who has been struck in the liver by a snake treacle is better suited than red candy. To him who is dying of poison antidote is everything. Twenty million. An entire generation.

[*SHOSTAKOVICH stops playing. STALIN goes over to him and takes his hand. He kisses it*]

STALIN: Do you know why your music isn't liked any more?

SHOSTAKOVICH: No, no.

STALIN: Remember before the war how they all loved you?

SHOSTAKOVICH: Yes, I do.

STALIN: You have lost that audience. Not your fault. They were the ones who died in the war, the twenty million.

SHOSTAKOVICH: I know, I know.

[*SHOSTAKOVICH lowers his head*]

STALIN: Now there are only old folk and children. All the life has to come from me. [*Pause*] You must stop mourning for the dead. Give the old folk and children what they need to cheer them up. They have to work hard these days.

[*SHOSTAKOVICH lowers his head until it touches the keyboard*]

STALIN: The old folk prefer old music. The children learn from the grandparents because their fathers and mothers are dead. So, it is old music we need - Tchaikovsky, I'm afraid, Rimsky, all the old favourites. Do it for me.

[*SHOSTAKOVICH weeps. STALIN sits next to him and plays the theme from the* Pathétique]

SHOSTAKOVICH: All I can hear is their silence. I don't know what they are saying. It's all been washed away.

ZHDANOV: They're saying get on with it!

STALIN: Prokofiev, you must face it as well. Your greatest fans are in the graveyard.

PROKOFIEV: I'll be joining them before long.

STALIN: Don't keep writing for them. You can compose like anyone you want. If I told you to imitate Beethoven, you could do it, and better the original.

PROKOFIEV: Could I? Beethoven was a German. If don't feel like writing like a German. Is that surprising?

STALIN: You know what I mean.

PROKOFIEV: We are already servants of one compulsion - our work. What you are asking would put us into a double servitude. Why not take what is Caesar's and leave us something to write with - a small freedom which is, after all, something of a secret.

STALIN: I don't like secrets. You'll do as you're told.

PROKOFIEV: You're expecting too much of us.

STALIN: Why? All I'm asking you to do is go back to being a student again. It's never too late to learn.

ZHDANOV: Do it for the cripples running the factories, the children in the fields twelve hours a day. Make sense of their drudgery. It will take fifty years for us to recover from the war. Extend our traditions of music to cover that period and Russia will be grateful.

STALIN: Exactly, Andrei, exactly. Well done. That's put it in a nutshell. They can do it. They're geniuses, these two. If you're a genius in the Soviet Union today you have terrible responsibilities - as I know, to my cost.

[*Pause*]

All those unfulfilled lives wasted in war are my destiny. I must live them out. I'll survive to be a thousand, a thousand thousand. In the stalks of young gooseberries is a substance that prolongs life. Georgian gooseberries, of course.

[*Pause*]

ZHDANOV: So you two know what you must do.

STALIN: They're good men. I trust them.

ZHDANOV: We'll go back to the conference and sort this out. I'm not going to stand up there and say - everyone has to write old music.

STALIN: Tsarist, bourgeois, capitalist music. Get it right. [*Picks up the icon*] Old friends are best. Old enemies are better.

ZHDANOV: I'm not going to say that. I'll find a way of putting it over. But I need your help with the decree. Am I going to get it?

[*Pause. STALIN sits down, holding the icon to his chest*]

PROKOFIEV: We will do what we can, within reason. Our kind of reason.

ZHDANOV: That's not enough...

STALIN: That is enough. They're going to write music like Tchaikovsky from now on. I know them. They're good Russians. They'll sacrifice their individuality like I have. Who am I now? I don't exist any more as a man. Stalin died in the war. Two lives I've lost. God lives in light, alone.

[*STALIN falls asleep. Pause. ZHDANOV looks at him, turns and looks at the composers, putting his fingers to his lips. He takes off his jacket and covers STALIN up with it. Pause. He holds out his hand for PROKOFIEV's and SHOSTAKOVICH's jackets. They take them and hand them over. ZHDANOV covers STALIN with them, then beckons the composers to leave. They wait for him by the door. ZHDANOV turns out the light*]

PROKOFIEV: Please pass our thanks to Comrade Stalin for a most instructive and helpful evening.

ZHDANOV: See you at the conference tomorrow. Good night.

PROKOFIEV: Good night.

SHOSTAKOVICH: Good night.

[*ZHDANOV ushers them out, then exits himself, closing the door behind him. STALIN sleeps on in the darkness. Bix Beiderbecke plays* Ol' Man River *on his cornet again as total blackout closes in*]


THE END

# MUSIC TO MURDER BY

*For Julian Leigh*

*Music to Murder By* was first performed by Paines Plough at the Gulben-kian Theatre at the University of Kent on 13 May, 1976, directed by Edward Adams, with the following cast:

PHILIP HESELTINE, *Stephen Boxer*
CARLO GESUALDO, *Eric Richards*
MARIA D'AVALOS, *Fiona Victory*
HELEN EUTERPE, *Mary Ellen Ray*
FEDERIGO, *Edward Adams*

# ACT ONE

[*A café in the gardens of the ruined palace of Gesualdo near Naples. Stage right an electric piano with a guitar on a stand. A blackboard sign reads* Rhythm n' Blues Napolitana Samedi 8.00 PM. *Stage left there is a table and four chairs in white metalwork, a furled parasol on a stand, and centre an orange tree in a pot. Right there is an upright piano*]

[*Strong sunlight.* FEDERIGO, *a waiter, is tidying the table as the audience enters. Then he sits at the piano and tinkles a few notes, swaps to the electric keyboard, experiments, then switches back to the piano and starts to play* St. Louis Blues, *gently*]

[*Enter* MRS EUTERPE, *a middle-aged American in summer clothes carrying a basket. She wears a headscarf and sunglasses. Sitting at the table she sighs with the heat, wipes her brow with a Kleenex, takes a tape recorder/cassette player out of her basket, puts the tape recorder on the table, lights a cigarette.* FEDERIGO *plays on, now with more animation and verve, oblivious*]

MRS EUTERPE: Hey!

[*FEDERIGO plays on*]

MRS EUTERPE: Hey! Can I have some service over here?

[*FEDERIGO plays on*]

MRS EUTERPE: [*Standing up and shouting*] Hey there! HEY!

[*FEDERIGO stops abruptly, stares at MRS EUTERPE, leaps to his feet, snaps in to his waiter's role and speeds across to the table*]

MRS EUTERPE: Would you spare a minute? A drink, eh? About time too. Do you have many tourists die of thirst around here? Who taught you to play the piano? The local blacksmith?

[*FEDERIGO is silent, napkin folded over his forearm, standing by her left side*]

MRS EUTERPE: No English? No English? Well, I got Italian. You want to talk Italian? Parla Italiano? No. Let's just keep it quiet then. And cool. Martini Seco, with ice, pronto.

[*FEDERIGO nods and crosses to exit.* MRS EUTERPE *presses the start button on the tape recorder and a Gesualdo madrigal is played.* FEDERIGO *halts in mid-stride. Enter* PHILIP HESELTINE *in a white suit and panama hat. Twenties style*]

HESELTINE: Buongiorno Federigo.

[*MRS EUTERPE is busy making notes on a pad. She stops the tape recorder. HESELTINE crosses to her, FEDERIGO exits. Pause. HESELTINE doffs his hat*]

HESELTINE: Good day to you.

MRS EUTERPE: [*Glancing up, then back to her pad*] Good day, good day.

HESELTINE: May I join you?

MRS EUTERPE: [*Pause*] Do you have to? I mean ... I'm trying to think right now. Don't be offended.

HESELTINE: Oh I'm never offended. [*Sits down*] And there are no other tables. You carry on.

[*MRS EUTERPE scribbles on her pad, head well down*]

HESELTINE: Doing the ruins?

MRS EUTERPE: Uh-huh.

HESELTINE: Pity they've let the old place go to seed like this don't you think?

MRS EUTERPE: Uh-huh.

HESELTINE: The Italian government should do something about it. You agree with that?

MRS EUTERPE: [*Looking up, now vexed*] Do you mind? I said I was trying to concentrate.

HESELTINE: [*Standing up abruptly, sticking out his hand*] Philip Heseltine. How do you do?

MRS EUTERPE: Do we have to? [*Pause, then takes his hand*]

HESELTINE: And your name?

MRS EUTERPE: Helen Euterpe, Mrs. Now, may I get on with what I'm doing? It is quite important.

HESELTINE: Recording your impressions of this shrine of musical history?

MRS EUTERPE: Yes, that's what I'm doing. Please!

HESELTINE: That looks an interesting machine. [*Looks at tape recorder*]

MRS EUTERPE: Please don't touch it. Cassette players come pretty expensive these days.

HESELTINE: What does it do?

MRS EUTERPE: Christ almighty ... will you stop bugging me? Are you saying you don't know what it's for?

HESELTINE: It looks most intriguing. Won't you show me?

MRS EUTERPE: [*Sighs*] Helen, what a sucker you are.

[*MRS EUTERPE presses the start button. Gesualdo's* Moro Lasso *is played for a few phrases then MRS EUTERPE turns it off*]

HESELTINE: Amazing! Quite delightful! What a useful box of tricks. What will they think of next? And so small and handy. [*Pause*] A good piece that.

MRS EUTERPE: Yes.

HESELTINE: One of his best.

MRS EUTERPE: You know Gesualdo's work?

HESELTINE: Intimately.

MRS EUTERPE: So do I.

HESELTINE: Do you indeed? Hm.

[*Enter FEDERIGO with drink on a tray, serves it, retires*]

HESELTINE: The old place is in a terrible state of disrepair. Chickens and goats all over the place. Very sad. I say, may I take off my jacket? It's dashed warm.

MRS EUTERPE: Do a striptease if you like.

HESELTINE: [*Taking off his jacket and hanging it over the back of a chair, then peering over MRS EUTERPE'S shoulder*] What have you said so far?

MRS EUTERPE: Pardon?

HESELTINE: What illuminating remarks have you put down for future reference?

MRS EUTERPE: Well, I got one down here that reminds me to avoid nosy Englishmen with bad manners.

HESELTINE: A lesson well learnt. Ah, I love the sun. Smell the breeze. Cypress. Sad cypress. [*Sings*] Sally is gone that was so kindly, Sally is gone from Ha'naker Hill...

MRS EUTERPE: [*Interrupting the song*] You're determined that I'm not going to get any work done, aren't you?

HESELTINE: Absolutely. When I saw you I said to myself, that charming and attractive woman in her early mature years seems to stand in need of entertainment. I will talk to her.

MRS EUTERPE: Thanks for the favour. What am I expected to do, throw myself at your feet?

HESELTINE: No, no. [*Sitting down close to her*] I'm not going to make advances. None of that. Ah, you're disappointed.

MRS EUTERPE: You've got a lot of gall Mr Heseltine.

HESELTINE: To raise the dead you must have gall. That is a quality which you and I share. Do you know how to raise the dead? I mean, the proper way. The professional way. The way that works. [*Pause*] Why, you're frightened.

MRS EUTERPE: No, but I think you might leave me alone.

HESELTINE: Abra-Melin the Mage gives precise directions on how to raise your Holy Guardian Angel. Mine is dead and therefore conjurable, so I suggest we start with him. [*Gets up, walks away R*]

MRS EUTERPE: [*Throwing down her notebook*] Okay, okay. I give up. You win. Let's raise the dead. Why not? I was getting bored anyway.

HESELTINE: This is a secluded spot. Here, I build my temple. Nothing too big, just a shelter. The temple must have a door opening northward on to a terrace of fine river sand. There, at the other end of the terrace, is a small hut for the evil spirits who will appear as a by-product of this summoning. They must go in to that hut, while I go here. In my temple there must be a window so I can keep an eye on them.

MRS EUTERPE: Wise. One thing you can't trust is evil spirits.

HESELTINE: Seven days and seven nights I wait, praying, concentrating. No food. A little water from the river. [*Kneels*]

MRS EUTERPE: Do I have to kneel with you?

HESELTINE: No, not while you are in a state of disbelief.

MRS EUTERPE: You're crazy.

HESELTINE: Seventh night, full moon. In the fine river sand I write his name and three signs known only to the Brethren. [*Writes with a finger on the ground*]

MRS EUTERPE: Who was it?

HESELTINE: [*Writing again*] Then three prayers. One in Egyptian. One in Greek. One in Gaelic. I should say that we are on an island off the west coast of Ireland.

MRS EUTERPE: Oh, are we? I like the air fares.

HESELTINE: [*Throwing his arms wide, declaiming*] From Hell, in the name of my life, my future, my hopes, I conjure you, your most illustrious and serene Highness, Don Carlo, third prince of Venosa, eighth count of Consa, marquese of Laino, Rotondo and Saint Stefano, lord of Gesualdo etcetera.

MRS EUTERPE: [*Surprised*] Gesualdo? He owned this place, I know him. [*Enter GESUALDO in sixteenth-century Italian court costume. He walks regally across the stage, turns, eyes MRS EUTERPE, gives a short bow*]

GESUALDO: Do you lady? Then you have the advantage of me.

MRS EUTERPE: [*Excited, humorous*] Sure I do. And you've managed to get a very good likeness. That's impressive. Yeh, that mean face, the beard. The costume's not bad either. Not sure about the boots though.

HESELTINE: Oh the boots are authentic, aren't they Gesualdo? True to life.

GESUALDO: As sincere as boots can be.

MRS EUTERPE: What is this? Some kind of carnival?

GESUALDO: It is indeed. Carni-val. *Carne-levare*.

HESELTINE: The Putting Away of Flesh.

GESUALDO: Enter the Flesh.

[*FEDERIGO plays a muted, tinkling pavan on the electric piano*]

[*Enter MARIA D'AVALOS, gorgeously gowned, hair up with long ornate curls falling, pale, very beautiful. She crosses to GESUALDO and takes his proffered fingertips*]

GESUALDO: Maria. Philip, my conjurer. An American lady whose name I did not catch.

MRS EUTERPE: Call me Helen. How do you do.

[*MARIA smiles and nods. GESUALDO turns her round, displaying her*]

GESUALDO: The most beautiful woman in the kingdom of the Two Sicilies, my bride, Donna Maria D'Avalos, twice married before I took her, twice seeded with children. Father considered both her enthusiasm and her fecundity to have been adequately proved. At twenty-six she was an experienced woman.

[*GESUALDO and MARIA dance a pavan to FEDERIGO's playing. At the points of change in the dance they pause and exchange the following section of dialogue*]

MARIA: Carlo.

GESUALDO: Maria.

MARIA: If you smiled more it might help your indisposition.

GESUALDO: None of my doctors have ever prescribed a show of teeth as a cure for constipation.

MARIA: Do I weigh you down? Is it me who makes you so miserable?

GESUALDO: No, it is purely a habit of mind.

MARIA: I have never known a man who enjoyed his misery so much. Even Christ laughed lord.

GESUALDO: Not on the cross lady.

MARIA: What crucifies you?

GESUALDO: Beyond the comical heaven promised to us by the Pope and his fellow-painters, I can see nothing to strive for. In confidence, I am a heretic. Heaven does not attract me, but death does.

MARIA: And my love?

GESUALDO: It takes away my power of thought.

MARIA: Then stop thinking.

GESUALDO: My first known ancestor had his head cut off by the Emperor of Byzantium and fired over the walls of Benvenuto by catapult. I guarantee he stopped thinking.

MARIA: But at least he was flying.

GESUALDO: Would you have me as your missile?

MARIA: If you would land over my walls, which are low enough.

[*The pavan ends. Music stops. A break of mood to informal conversation*]

MRS EUTERPE: [*Whispering*] Mr Heseltine, shouldn't we wait for more people to arrive? They're really great these two.

HESELTINE: Hush! Listen!

GESUALDO: Tell me about your first husband, the marquese of San Lucio.

MARIA: Only two years we enjoyed. Then, poor man, he died.

GESUALDO: How sad. The cause?

MARIA: An excess of connubial bliss.

GESUALDO: But Maria you were only fifteen years old at the time. Such enthusiasm for love from a child?

MARIA: He was admired by the whole nobility as an angel from heaven.

GESUALDO: You found a pleasant way to send him home. Your second husband?

MARIA: Ah, dear Alfonso, the Marquese of Giuliano.

GESUALDO: Now he would have lasted longer. These Sicilians are full of stamina, and at twenty you would have been more moderate in your demands.

MARIA: Three years of perfect happiness.

GESUALDO: He died as well?

MARIA: With a smile on his face.

[*MARIA and GESUALDO sit down at the table*]

MRS EUTERPE: Well, I've had three husbands and none of them committed suicide that way. They could have tried.

GESUALDO: Let us not forget the fruit of all this love-making. Three children by men other than myself.

MARIA: No Carlo, only two.

GESUALDO: Three.

MARIA: Carlo, I know how many children I have had. Two by my first husband and two babies by you, our sons. Don't you remember Emmanuel and ...

GESUALDO: The bastard?

HESELTINE: Now, now. Federigo!

[*FEDERIGO plays the introduction of* Lullaby. *HESELTINE sings the song, using his folded jacket as the child. When it is over GESUALDO and MARIA clap politely*]

GESUALDO: *Bravissima.*

HESELTINE: A carol of mine. You know I hated Christmas. England is a poor place when it comes to religious festivals.

GESUALDO: He hated Christmas so he wrote carols.

MRS EUTERPE: That proves he's got a sound commercial instinct.

HESELTINE: My lullaby was inspired by your treatment of your second son.

GESUALDO: [*Getting up abruptly, leaving the table*] Let us not go in to that.

MARIA: [*Savagely*] O yes, by all means let us go in to that!

GESUALDO: He was not my son!

MARIA: [*Pursuing GESUALDO*] He was. Every drop of his blood was yours, to his misfortune.

HESELTINE: [*To MRS EUTERPE*] Gesualdo finds this unpleasant. It affects his performance. I'll do it for him. Ho there... [*Strides about, giving instructions*] Bring the cradle and four silken ropes!

MARIA: My baby!

HESELTINE: Now, tie one rope to each corner of the ceiling and attach them to the cradle until it is suspended.

MARIA: [*Sinking to her knees*] Carlo! My son, my boy, my baby!

HESELTINE: Now, put the child in the cradle, get some long sticks, hurry along now...

MARIA: Innocent, a few months old, helpless ...

HESELTINE: Right. I want the four of you to keep prodding the cradle until we get a continuous, violent, undulatory motion. Non-stop. Three shifts. Twenty-four hours a day. Commence. [*Conducts*] One. Two. Three.

MARIA: No Gesualdo, cut him down!

GESUALDO: He is not my child. He is Carafa's.

MARIA: Have pity lord ...

GESUALDO: [*Demonstrating the action*] Together now. Do not lose the beat. In time. One. Two. Three. Four.

HESELTINE: [*In chorus with GESUALDO*] One. Two. Three. Four.

[*FEDERIGO plays* Lullaby *through the prodding, then in to the pause as they stop. Then silence*] Ah, the infant, unable to draw breath in this tempest, has rendered up its soul to God. Goodbye. Goodbye.

MARIA: Pig. [*Weeps*] My son. My son.

[*GESUALDO goes over to MARIA, offers his hand and raises her to her feet. She straightens up, frowns*]

MARIA: Why take out your bitterness on my baby, Carlo? What a thing to do. God will punish you for that.

GESUALDO: Not if I build him a monastery right here to atone for that fit of temper. Give the stonemasons their orders.

[*MRS EUTERPE laughs, sits back in her chair*]

MRS EUTERPE: You're good. You're all damn good. You're as good as I've seen anywhere. No wonder you Italians make such good movies. It this going to be a movie? Who is it? Fellini? It's his kind of subject. Of course, you've got the light here, like we have in California, pure...

GESUALDO: Federigo! Wine.

[*FEDERIGO exits. GESUALDO and MARIA sit down*]

HESELTINE: I was born out of my time. What I would have given to be a Renaissance man.

MARIA: Poor Philip. Always running away. Always the outsider. You would have been better off trying to love your own times.

HESELTINE: Would you like to try and live with the Great War Maria? Even you, with your appetite, you would have failed. It was a dismal time.

MARIA: I was born with one gift. Were you born for love signora? Were you trained that way?

MRS EUTERPE: No honey, I was intended for secretarial work but... well, I guess I was too bright, got too many scholarships, too many high grades. I was reviewing concerts for the San Francisco Examiner before I was twenty.

MARIA: You are nun to music like Carlo is a monk. Music is a substitute for love. At court we talked of nothing but love and dying for love.

MRS EUTERPE: That of course was a euphemism for orgasm. Did you realise that? Whenever Gesualdo here talks of dying, or even killing, take that phrase of his "d'amor empia homicida", what he's talking about is good old sex. Isn't that right? Come on now, your Highness, admit it.

GESUALDO: Even when I use it in reference to Christ? Many of my texts were religious.

MRS EUTERPE: Freud would have no trouble in tying those in with the others. What's a cross? Two phallic symbols. Two.

GESUALDO: Yes, we know Doctor Freud. Fortunately for us all he has stayed behind on this trip.

MRS EUTERPE: Now you're Gesualdo. Right? That's the idea?

GESUALDO: Correct.

MRS EUTERPE: [*Chuckling*] Since you're here, I've got a few things that I'd like to say to you. Do you mind straight talking?

GESUALDO: Admired it all my life.

MRS EUTERPE: Then I'll tell you something. You could be so pedantic. When you set words like *respiro, soletto, misero,* to the notes re, soh, mi, it really diminishes your stature in my eyes.

HESELTINE: Helen's absolutely right Gesualdo. Sheer academics.

GESUALDO: Am I not allowed to play games? Must one be serious all of the time.

MRS EUTERPE: [*Laughing*] You Italians are brilliant. You go the whole hog. I love it. You're all brilliant.

[*Enter FEDERIGO with a golden tray, jug and goblets held aloft. He serves it at the table*]

MRS EUTERPE: Christ, when's the chariot race? And I was starting to think what a dump this was. It's a festival. Did I come at the right time? Sure I did. What a terrific idea. You Italians do care about Gesualdo.

GESUALDO: This one does at least. How about you Maria?

MARIA: I did care. When I first married you. For four years I cared. I gave you everything I had.

MRS EUTERPE: You've had problems with him?

MARIA: [*Urgently*] Carlo, I am a woman. Do you understand that?

[*GESUALDO walks away from the table, MARIA following him*]

MARIA: Why have you stopped talking to me?

GESUALDO: You know my affliction Maria. It is not something which I care to juggle about in conversation.

MARIA: How can I share your sadness?

GESUALDO: I do not want you to.

MARIA: Then you exclude me.

GESUALDO: From sadness.

MARIA: And you.

GESUALDO: Do not torment me. Go away for a few days.

[*GESUALDO moves aside, standing by the orange tree. MARIA smiles, saunters to the table, smiling. HESELTINE picks up his guitar*]

MARIA: It is pleasant to be with friends in this beautiful garden. Such flowers, such pollen, such bees.

HESELTINE: [*Idling through a tune*] How is Gesualdo?

MARIA: As miserable as ever.

HESELTINE: He has gone back to the man he was before you married him.

MARIA: I have failed. Tried, but failed... ah! [*Holds her side*]

HESELTINE: What's the matter?

MRS EUTERPE: Are you okay?

MARIA: I think I'd better lie down.

MRS EUTERPE: You want me to come with you, see you're all right?

MARIA: No thank you. It will pass.

[*MARIA crosses to FEDERIGO, who is standing by the piano*]

MARIA: [*Holding out her arms*] Carafa, Carafa my love.

FEDERIGO: *L'amor che move il sole e l'altre stelle.*

[*MARIA and FEDERIGO kiss, then tumble down to the floor behind the piano sighing. They roll around, whisper, make love noisily*]

MRS EUTERPE: Well, she got better pretty damn quick.

HESELTINE: It was all a ruse. Carafa, the duke of Andria, has been waiting all morning in that pavilion. Maria was shamming. She is perfectly all right.

MRS EUTERPE: That's what it sounds like.

HESELTINE: She's a very hot-blooded woman, a natural giver.

MRS EUTERPE: Carafa isn't exactly stingy himself.

HESELTINE: Of course, this is Maria's third marriage.

MRS EUTERPE: Look at poor old Gesualdo. I feel really sorry for him.

HESELTINE: What the eye doesn't see... hm? You always behaved yourself?

MRS EUTERPE: No.

HESELTINE: And Gesualdo does have his best friend, music.

[*HESELTINE sings, accompanying himself on the guitar*]

HESELTINE:

A note is just a word,
[Don't be absurd],
A chord life's harmony,
[Don't talk to me],

A tune a conversation,
[Imagination]
Music a language lost,
[And what's the cost?]

[*MARIA has emerged from behind the piano. GESUALDO looks at her*]

GESUALDO: [*Bitterly*] Nothing. Music costs nothing.

[*Pause. MRS EUTERPE stands up, grins, holds out a hand*]

MRS EUTERPE: Gesualdo, come over here. Listen, I'll let you in to a secret.

GESUALDO: [*Not moving*] A secret? I am all ears.

MRS EUTERPE: You want to know why you were so miserable? I'll tell you. It was pathological.

GESUALDO: Signora, why wrap a secret in a secret? Pathological?

MRS EUTERPE: It's pretty straightforward. You were a manic-depressive.

MARIA: Should we congratulate him?

MRS EUTERPE: He was a man of extremes. One minute he was up, the next he was down.

GESUALDO: Signora, I am a composer, not a pump handle.

MRS EUTERPE: It all probably originated in Gesualdo's relationship with his father, Fabrizio. I think Gesualdo was suffering from an Oedipus complex.

HESELTINE: Federigo, I think you might as well bring a drink for Doctor Freud.

MRS EUTERPE: Didn't you hate your father?

GESUALDO: My father?

[*HESELTINE, MARIA and FEDERIGO form a triangular maypole dance with GESUALDO in the middle. they dance round him*]

GESUALDO: My father? In our circle that word had little meaning. You were lucky to know who your father was.

[*The dance stops. GESUALDO is opposite HESELTINE*]

GESUALDO: Signor, are you my father?

HESELTINE: No, only your mother's lover.

[*Dance resumes. Stops with GESUALDO facing FEDERIGO*]

GESUALDO: Signor, I am looking for my cousin.

[*FEDERIGO points at Maria*]

GESUALDO: Ah, my auntie's daughter, my wife. Who was your first husband again *carissima*?

MARIA: That was another cousin, the Carafa.

HESELTINE: But surely that was the name of your lover?

[*FEDERIGO looks shifty, moves the dance round*]

GESUALDO: Now who was it told me of Maria's affair?

HESELTINE: Why, your uncle, your father's brother, and Maria's mother's brother.

MARIA: He wanted me for himself, the lecher.

[*The dance breaks away from GESUALDO and proceeds round the orange tree. GESUALDO crosses to MRS EUTERPE*]

GESUALDO: There were three families in Neapolitan high society. We seldom married outside them and lived like gilded dollies under a glass dome. Incest, privilege and influence were the rats which gnawed at us, from the inside. I see it now. [*The dance passes in front of him*] D'Avalos, Carafas, Gesualdos.

[*The dance ends*]

MRS EUTERPE: But not then, eh?

HESELTINE: Helen, in your analysis of Gesualdo's music, have you yet detected a strain of the bagpipes?

MRS EUTERPE: The bagpipes?

MARIA: Philip, you're being wicked again.

HESELTINE: Not at all. It is my view that the purest expression of the melancholy spirit is produced by a sheepskin squeezed under a Scottish armpit.

GESUALDO: Enough Philip, I warn you, enough. Don't listen to him signora. Would you consider that any fraction of my work was stolen from the idiotic songs of King James of Scotland? That is what they said...

[*HESELTINE takes a bagpipe chanter from the branches of the orange tree and wails a few notes*]

GESUALDO: Such ignorance. Such pitiful ignorance. I found those chords. For the first time I used all twelve notes within the octave... [*Snaps his fingers. FEDERIGO illustrates at the piano*] While the English remained imprisoned in the seven notes of the diatonic scale.

[*FEDERIGO plays the opening of the National Anthem*]

GESUALDO: I increased the horizons of music by seventy per cent.

MRS EUTERPE: [*Very amused, going over to GESUALDO, friendly but patronizing*] Look Gesualdo, I don't want to hurt your feelings but you're considered to be a very... let me find the right word... isolated... eccentric...

GESUALDO: That's two words.

MRS EUTERPE: A blind alley.

GESUALDO: You know so much about me. No doubt you have studied my work closely, connected all the loose ends, made sense out of me. You can be trusted to do that after five minutes' conversation.

MRS EUTERPE: Gesualdo has to be viewed in the perspective of his time. There were other composers...

GESUALDO: Name them.

MRS EUTERPE: Nenna, Macque, Trabaci, Wert, Rore, Luzzaschi ...

GESUALDO: Pedants, stony ground, amateurs.

MRS EUTERPE: Would you care to give me an assessment of two madrigalists who are known to have been in your circle? Luigi Tansillo?

GESUALDO: Ape.

MRS EUTERPE: Giovanni Primavera?

GESUALDO: Vulture.

MRS EUTERPE: You certainly get involved with your role. Surely Gesualdo would have been more courteous?

GESUALDO: [*Sharply, with some iron*] Signora, you are the one who torments the dead. You asked us up. You want to know. To know you must suffer. Listen to this... One. Two. Three.

[*MARIA sings Gesualdo's* Moro lasso. *HESELTINE joining her and a third hidden voice filling three parts of the madrigal. Pause*]

MRS EUTERPE: That's really sad. you know, I think that is almost too sad.

HESELTINE: How dare you! How can you be so dogmatic? Is there a limit on how sad you can be? A ridiculous remark to make.

MRS EUTERPE: [*Slightly taken aback*] Okay, okay...

HESELTINE: I suppose you look upon music as a sedative like all the other sleepwalkers, damn fools.

MRS EUTERPE: I'm just saying what I think. There's no joy in that music. There should be some.

HESELTINE: There you go again, laying down the law. It's still going on. They never give up.

MRS EUTERPE: I've got a right to my own opinions.

HESELTINE: Of course you have. You are misinformed, prejudiced, poorly educated, inexperienced, insensitive, but honest. You know what you like and you're not afraid to say so.

MRS EUTERPE: I wish it were that simple.

GESUALDO: Signora, if you wish to investigate my music, you must have regard for me. I am my music. My music is me.

MRS EUTERPE: [*More confident. She gets up, takes the stage*] All right, you tell me. What is the energy that powers the creative process? What part of the personality does it flow from?

MARIA: She's talking about your soul Carlo.

HESELTINE: [*Cutting her out*] Helen, you are a critic?

MRS EUTERPE: Yes, I still do the occasional piece for the San Francisco Examiner.

HESELTINE: You hate me.

MRS EUTERPE: I do?

HESELTINE: Me, Philip Heseltine. You have your reasons. I might hold you in contempt, or have attacked your puerile efforts at composition. The whole thing is unreasonable and entirely subjective. You fear me, probably realising your own inferiority. Any composition of mine that I put in front of you will be rejected out of hand, smashed in to the ground, torn to pieces. You will delight in destroying it because you are destroying a part of me. Yes, you are vicious and vile.

MRS EUTERPE: I get it. I've got no objective standards. It's personal.

HESELTINE: Then, one evening, you go to a concert and hear a piece by a new composer. It enthralls you. No one has ever heard of the fellow before. He is yet to be discovered, and you're the one to do it. Oh, what songs, what music! Brilliant, moving, sincere. Back you scurry to your sewer in Chelsea and sit up all night writing a rave-review that will put Peter Warlock on the road to fame.

MRS EUTERPE: [*Thoughtfully*] Peter Warlock... Peter Warlock... [*Crosses to her books, looks in one*] Hm... now I have heard of you somewhere...

HESELTINE: She has heard of me Carlo, somewhere.

GESUALDO: Gratifying.

MRS EUTERPE: You see, my special period is pre-Baroque. I can't place you.

HESELTINE: Oh dear, that's me out. How sad. I cannot be placed. I am totally unmemorable.

MARIA: He means his music. Remember his music... please.

MRS EUTERPE: I have heard of you. I'm sure about that. Don't be hurt. Did you really change your name?

HESELTINE: Not only my name, myself.

MRS EUTERPE: And the critics didn't find out?

HESELTINE: Not until it was too late. Much as they would have loved to take back their garlands they could not without exposing their envious and vicious natures to public ridicule. You cannot compare me to Delius on Sunday and a corncrake on Monday.

MRS EUTERPE: Well, that serves them right. They must have been real slobs anyway. I don't know how people can get away with such dishonesty and get paid for it.

[*MARIA goes over to HESELTINE, takes his arm*]

MARIA: Peter Warlock. A striking pseudonym, eh signora?

[*MARIA rotates HESELTINE through a circle, one arm extended, finger pointed. Pause. Lights start to dim in to a green spot*]

MRS EUTERPE: Isn't a warlock a male witch?

[*GESUALDO stands behind HESELTINE, arms crossed over his breast*]

GESUALDO: A sorcerer to be exact. A seeker after change.

[*FEDERIGO lights three black candles*]

MRS EUTERPE: You say you changed yourself. How do you mean?

MARIA: [*Stroking HESELTINE's face*] He became someone else.

[*HESELTINE kneels in front of MARIA, his back to the audience*]

GESUALDO: Strange, strange. I will never understand it. Whatever did Philip ever find to admire in me?

MARIA: Come Carlo. Don't be so modest. He wants your power.

GESUALDO: My power? Power to what?

MARIA: Surely to create harmony.

GESUALDO: Does he care about music so much?

MARIA: Carlo, it is his life.

GESUALDO: Then he must live his own.

MARIA: It is not enough. He has asked for help, sought strength in strange places, like you Carlo.

GESUALDO: Me? What help did I ever get?

MARIA: [*Crouching with HESELTINE, holding his hidden face in her hands, pressing herself against him*] From another self within your self. Where else did that terrible strength come from? Not from the Carlo I married, but a new man. [*She stands up, leaves HESELTINE*] On the night of October the sixteenth fifteen-ninety, Carlo changed as Philip is changing now. Who was your model? Who made your music?

[*HESELTINE throws himself at GESUALDO's feet, face down, arms outstretched. FEDERIGO hits strong, dark chords on the piano*]

GESUALDO: The Devil! [*He raises HESELTINE, kisses him*]

[*MARIA and HESELTINE sing: They hold the three candles. GESUALDO sinks*]

Lucifer lux lucis light
cast in to eternal night
Lucifer lux lucis fell
had to light the fires of Hell
Lucifer lux lucis dark
could not generate a spark
Lucifer lux lucis bold

freezing in unlighted cold
Lucifer lux lucis see
here's the flame of harmony
Lucifer lux lucis found
chords which made a saving sound
Lucifer lux lucis then
composed himself for God again
But Lucifer lux lucis' crime
held him back for all of time.
[*Blackout. They snuff the candles as one*]

MRS EUTERPE: [*Crying out, alarmed*] Hey!

[*Lights up. GESUALDO is discovered sitting next to MRS EUTERPE, MARIA standing behind her chair, HESELTINE near the piano, bearded*]

HESELTINE: [*Coolly*] Are you all right?

MRS EUTERPE: The light...

GESUALDO: The lady is not well.

MARIA: She should go in out of the sun.

MRS EUTERPE: No, I'm fine...

GESUALDO: Come in to the shade. Federigo will take you indoors while we erect the parasol. Federigo!

[*They help MRS EUTERPE to her feet. She stares at the transformed features of HESELTINE, the new beard and moustache which are exact copies of those worn by GESUALDO*]

MRS EUTERPE: Why do you want to look like him?

HESELTINE: I am him. He has possessed me.

GESUALDO: We are brothers. We are one. It was his choice.

MRS EUTERPE: [*Groggy*] Maybe I should lie down for a while. That sun sure is hot. I should know better. You just carry on. Don't worry about me.

[*FEDERIGO helps MRS EUTERPE off. HESELTINE gives a hand*]

HESELTINE: We'll wait, Helen. We have all the time in the world.

[*Pause. They watch MRS EUTERPE go*]

HESELTINE: A stroll Gesualdo? Give her time to adjust. Federigo will take good care of her.

[*GESUALDO offers MARIA his hand. She gets up. They start to move off*]

MARIA: She is very difficult this one. Very defensive. What do you think she is looking for?

GESUALDO: Something to fill her empty days. [*On exit*] We have had them before.

[*They stroll off. Lights dim to blackout*]

# ACT TWO

[*Hurdy-gurdy fairground music in blackout. Lights up on the twirling parasol which has each panel decorated with a sign of the Tarot pack*]

[*HESELTINE, still bearded as Warlock, operates the spin. GESUALDO and MARIA enter hand in hand. FEDERIGO brings on MRS EUTERPE who has fully recovered*]

HESELTINE: Roll up! Roll up! Take your chance on the Wheel of Fortune. [*To GESUALDO*] You sir. From your eye I judge you to be a man in sympathy with the occult sciences. This system never fails. Call basta if you please. Any time, any time. Watch the Tarot.

GESUALDO: Basta.

[*HESELTINE stops the parasol, rests it on the ground supported on one panel*]

HESELTINE: What have we here? Ah, your friend and mine, the enigma, the Hanged Man. It could have been the Juggler, the Devil, Pope Joan or the Beggar in Rags, but no, it is the upside-downer, the Hanged Man, dangling by one foot.

GESUALDO: Interpret Signor Sorcerer.

HESELTINE: Warlock sees it thus: basing my analysis on the works of Eliphas Levi, I'd say this - the twelfth card is a symbol of Prometheus whose feet are in Heaven and whose head is in Hell.

[*HESELTINE stands on his hands, grinning up at GESUALDO*]

GESUALDO: Then only the feet are inaccurate. Congratulations.

HESELTINE: [*Standing again*] Helen?

MRS EUTERPE: No.

HESELTINE: Oh come on. It's only for fun.

MARIA: He's never right, are you Peter?

HESELTINE: Never.

MRS EUTERPE: Okay, but no bending the signs to suit your purpose.

GESUALDO: She doesn't trust you Peter. Wise woman.

HESELTINE: [*Twirling the parasol*] Shout basta if you please.

MRS EUTERPE: Basta.

HESELTINE: [*Putting the parasol down*] Ah, the Moon Card.

MARIA: [*Excited*] The Moon Card, you got the Moon Card!

MRS EUTERPE: Is that good?

GESUALDO: Wonderful, wonderful.

HESELTINE: It shows a dog and a wolf baying at a full moon while from the sea crawls a lobster. The moon has a woman's face and is shedding tears. In the background are two menacing towers.

MRS EUTERPE: Hm, well the towers are obviously my husband's, phallic towers. They menace the moon which is my career, my illuminated path through life...

HESELTINE: Hey, I'm supposed to be the sorcerer around here.

MARIA: And the lobster?

MRS EUTERPE: That could be Ernie.

MARIA: Ernie?

MRS EUTERPE: My third husband. He wasn't really phallic if you know what I mean.

MARIA: Oh I do, I do, don't I Carlo?

HESELTINE: The lobster is a crustacean. It has a thick shell. It is crawling out of the sea of life, going towards two towers. Could they be ivory towers? No, just high, isolated places overlooking the plain. No, that can't be correct. There are no windows in the towers. How strange. One could not look out. [*Pause*] Are you planning to do such a thing?

MRS EUTERPE: Such a thing as what?

HESELTINE: Become a recluse, look inwards only, shut out the world.

MRS EUTERPE: No.

HESELTINE: If you do then you will become the woman in the moon shedding tears. Don't run away Helen. If the lobster has any sense it will return to the sea and live.

MRS EUTERPE: After three marriages? And have you tried teaching? Think what it's like today. There's no discipline, no respect, the kids just lie around stoned out of their heads saying they're bored or its irrelevant.

HESELTINE: Oh dear, you have been badly treated.

MRS EUTERPE: Yes, perhaps I have.

HESELTINE: [*Pause*] Aren't you hoping to go somewhere away from it all and write a book about Gesualdo?

MRS EUTERPE: [*Hesitantly*] Could be.

HESELTINE: You won't admit it?

MRS EUTERPE: I'm on holiday. It was just a thought.

GESUALDO: It was just a thought? I'm not sure that is enough.

MRS EUTERPE: During the next two years I want to submit a thesis for my doctorate. I have to write about something. Gesualdo is just one of a short-list, you know, options, alternatives...

GESUALDO: [*Hemming MRS EUTERPE in with HESELTINE*]
Hmmm, options, alternatives, isolated, eccentric.

HESELTINE: Who else is on the short-list?

MRS EUTERPE: Er... I was considering Purcell actually.

HESELTINE: Purcell. She was considering Purcell, Carlo.

GESUALDO: An Englishman. Any other Englishmen whom you found worthy of your consideration signora?

MRS EUTERPE: My other possible was Monteverdi.

GESUALDO: I'm not at all flattered by the company you are keeping me with. Why not write your thesis about Peter? Very colourful career, hyper-sensitive, eccentric, went through agonies...

HESELTINE: Eton and Oxford.

MARIA: A broken marriage. Many lovers, many, many.

[*HESELTINE takes MRS EUTERPE's hand and leads her across the stage as FEDERIGO softly plays the theme of a song on the electric piano. MRS EUTERPE is nervous, but amused*]

HESELTINE: Helen, you are looking at a man who had a relationship with D. H. Lawrence, dark gods and all. I shared all the passions of Shakespeare, gold ladies and silver men. But I betrayed love, like Gesualdo did. Not even Carafa ever did that, did you maestro? What about you Helen?

MRS EUTERPE: What about me?

HESELTINE: Did you never betray love? Are those wrinkles round your eyes all from squinting at the sun?

MRS EUTERPE: I don't know what you're talking about.

[*She sits at the table*]

HESELTINE: Three husbands and you don't know what I'm talking about? Well, well.

[*HESELTINE slides away in a dance-step to the parasol, ducks under it and emerges with it over his shoulder, gay, debonair*]

HESELTINE: [*Sings*]
I knew only love when I first met you
All else that I called love was fantasy,
All that is good in me is you and you alone,
You have believed in me
Suffered and endured me,
Forgiven me
Even when I spurned forgiveness.

[*He dances with MRS EUTERPE, magically sticking flowers on her blouse*]

Yet I betrayed you
Ill-used you,and dismayed you
and finally made you
Go.
[*MRS EUTERPE joins in the spirit of HESELTINE's game with her, returns him one of the flowers and dances away back to the table, light-hearted. FEDERIGO crashes a discordant sound on the piano, throws a rapier at GESUALDO, attacks him, pursuing him across the stage with a rapier in hand*]
FEDERIGO: Bastardo!
GESUALDO: [*Refusing to fight*] No Carafa, I will not fight you now. It would merely be an exercise in swordsmanship at which you excelled and I had very little interest.
HESELTINE: It would be more honourable to fight him Gesualdo.
GESUALDO: [*Throwing away the sword*] No.
[*FEDERIGO gives a contemptuous sweep of his rapier, the salute to the coward, and returns to the piano*]
GESUALDO: [*Calling after him*] Shall a Gesualdo be a cuckold?
HESELTINE: Would you rather have a French horn or a cor anglais?
GESUALDO: I warned them. I saw to it that they knew of my displeasure.
HESELTINE: Carafa did get worried. He suggested to Maria that they stop the affair.
MARIA: [*To FEDERIGO*] If you are capable of sheltering fear in your heart, then chase me out of there and we will never meet again. If I die with you then at least it means that we will never be separated, which is all I want, to be always with you, my love. I have courage enough to endure cold steel, but not the bitter frost of your absence.
HESELTINE: Carafa, what are you saying? He speaks.
FEDERIGO: *Maria, ho una moglie che sara vedova, a quattri bambini che sarrano orfani per quest'azzione.*
HESELTINE: Maria, I have a wife who will be a widow and four children who will be fatherless by this act.
FEDERIGO: *Ma giacchè tu desideri morire, io moriro con te.*
HESELTINE: But since you wish to die, I will die with you.
FEDERIGO: *Tale e il tuo desiderio, tale e il mio amore per te.*
HESELTINE: Such is your wish, such is my love for you.
[*FEDERIGO takes MARIA in his arms*]
HESELTINE: So be it.

MARIA: Come tonight. Whistle from the garden. Carlo has told me that he is going hunting in the north, but it will not be for the pleasure of the chase, or in the north, but here and for us.

MRS EUTERPE: This is suicide.

HESELTINE: Not at all. They did not care to live without each other. It is an absolute love.

GESUALDO: You are testing me! Daring me!

MARIA: Enjoy your hunting Carlo. I am going to bed.

GESUALDO: I do love you Maria, but I cannot show it.

[*A whistle. FEDERIGO and MARIA face each other, embrace*]

HESELTINE: Gesualdo has assembled a chamber orchestra of arms, and musicians to play them: three arquebuses, three halberds, two rapiers, two stilettos. A well-balanced group that will create a new sound in music.

[*FEDERIGO raises his arms over his head. MARIA mimes dressing him in a garment*]

HESELTINE: Carafa puts on one of Maria's nightgowns. It is worked with lace and has a collar of black silk.

MRS EUTERPE: Why?

HESELTINE: He has decided to die like a woman. To die for love, not for honour.

MARIA: Make love to me for the last time.

[*FEDERIGO takes MARIA's hands, stretches them wide, holds himself against her, they slowly turn. HESELTINE plays soft music on the guitar, slowly building it to a climax as the lovers, through sighs and expressions only, revolve through mimed love-making. Pause. Silence*]

HESELTINE: It is quiet in the chamber. A miracle. They both fall asleep in each other's arms with Gesualdo waiting at the bottom of the stairs. [*Produces a conductor's baton*] Are we ready? [*Mounts a chair as a podium*]

GESUALDO: No, let them live. I cannot.

HESELTINE: Everyone is in place, tuning up, you cannot turn back.

GESUALDO: No, go home all of you.

HESELTINE: Begin! [*Conducts*] Rapid arpeggios! Up the stairs you go! You kick down the door. Hammer blows on the drum.

[*GESUALDO rushes across towards MARIA and FEDERIGO, mimes kicking down a door*]

GESUALDO: It is the worst sight that I have ever seen. Maria, in Carafa's arms, smiling.

HESELTINE: The shock retards the onward action. A pause of humming strings, then a deadly calm. A murmur from the woodwind.

GESUALDO: Kill Carafa!

HESELTINE: In a major key, sombre, majestic, just, powerful, the swelling chords of damaged pride.

GESUALDO: Drag him from the bed. Kill him here, at my feet.

[*FEDERIGO pitches forward. HESELTINE bends down, picks him up, dresses him in a nightgown with black and red streamers cascading down the front*]

HESELTINE: As in a dream Carafa allows himself to be placed on the altar.

GESUALDO: The head. The heart. The genitals. The genitals. The genitals. The genitals. The genitals.

HESELTINE: A wound for each note in the major scale. Timpani. Explosions. *Accelerando! Furioso!*

[*HESELTINE turns FEDERIGO towards the audience, holding him by the scruff of the neck, the ribbons sweeping the floor from his throat and chest*]

GESUALDO: Is he dead?

MARIA: He is dead.

GESUALDO: Make sure. Make sure.

HESELTINE: [*Holding the twitching body firm*] A spirited short attack, finishing on a dark smorzando, dying away to silence.

[*He drops FEDERIGO to the ground*]

[*Pause*]

GESUALDO: Maria?

MARIA: Carlo?

GESUALDO: Why?

MARIA: Love.

HESELTINE: A series of shuddering discords. The second movement. In those chords, the minor key, a mood of sadness, softness.

GESUALDO: You love that? That carrion?

MARIA: More than ever. Completely. Absolutely.

GESUALDO: Then join him! [*Slashes her across her eyes*]

[*GESUALDO hurls himself at MARIA in a frenzied attack, stabbing and hacking. MARIA screams*]

HESELTINE: *Presto!* The breast! *Apassionato!* The heart! *Tumultuouso!* The womb!

[*GESUALDO thrusts and skewers MARIA. The only sounds are MARIA's groans and cries. HESELTINE throws long red streamers over the locked pair as MARIA is battered and chopped to the ground*]

HESELTINE: A series of descending chords, still firm and buoyant in that major key, red in colour, now settled in adagio. She is still breathing.

GESUALDO: [*Kneeling by MARIA*] Die Maria, I beg you, die.

MARIA: I'm trying Carlo, I'm trying.

[*GESUALDO hurls himself at her again, hacking and stabbing*]

GESUALDO: Die, die, die, die!

[*Pause*]

HESELTINE: *Tremolo, tremolo*, the last breath quivering, leaving, the last sigh.

GESUALDO: [*Exhausted*] *Resta.*

[*Pause. HESELTINE sits down, crosses his legs*]

HESELTINE: The third movement. Waiting for the inspiration of grief, the uplift of remorse. Is it coming Carlc? Do I hear those strings stir?

GESUALDO: What is it? What is it? What is happening to me?

MARIA: Come Carlo, you are not finished yet. The coda, remember? You must strip me naked, drag me out to the palace steps.

GESUALDO: You were my wife.

MARIA: Come Carlo. Do not flinch. I am dead. I cannot argue.

GESUALDO: You humiliated me in front of the whole court.

MARIA: Naked, bloody, hacked about, ripped open, battered. Out in to the street. Come Carlo, drag me out like a carcase from the slaughter-house. Put me on the butcher's slab. Show these Neapolitans what you're made of. Expose me.

GESUALDO: Maria, I did love you. [*Seizes her, drags her round the stage, throws her down again*]

MARIA: Out in to the street!

[*GESUALDO turns MARIA over, grabs hold of her ankle and drags her round the stage, streamers trailing. He grunts, whimpers, cries, collapses by her feet*]

HESELTINE: The fourth and final movement. Slow, labouring devastation of all that is past, all other harmonies. Here, in this passage, a strange jubilation, underscored with pain unknown, unheard of, unalloyed. Then the mood expands, runs, pours, old obstacles are swept away on this mysterious tide and a fresh, invigorating freedom makes itself heard; positive, strong, new. The body works better. The blood freer. The ear is sharper. The eye clearer. The bowels become beautiful in themselves. In triumph this music enters daylight and the city of dreams.

MARIA: Leave me here in the street.

GESUALDO: My devil has left me. You have made him go. Bless you Maria.

MARIA: Here is a monk of Saint Domenic passing. He sees Donna Maria D'Avalos naked, dead, but still warm. Perhaps it is to be his great sin for which he will have to pray for the rest of his life, but he lifts his robe and thrusts himself upon me.

GESUALDO: I am reborn.

MARIA: [*Getting up*] And this is how I spent the morning; lying in blood and sperm upon the altar of your anger, and your devil, and your music, you pagan pig!

[*MARIA glares at GESUALDO then walks slowly towards MRS EUTERPE, the red streamers still clinging to her gown and trailing behind her. MRS EUTERPE retreats, gathers her belongings*]

MRS EUTERPE: Well er... I think I'll be getting along. I'm supposed to be in Naples tonight. I've got a room booked at a hotel.

HESELTINE: Don't go. Remember the lobster.

MRS EUTERPE: No, I'll find another subject for my thesis. I don't really dig his music anyway.

HESELTINE: What about mine?

MRS EUTERPE: Look, I get the picture. I see his motivation. Now I can't stand to be near the bastard. Let me pass.

[*MARIA threatens, blocking the exit, head down, glowering*]

HESELTINE: Why, what a coward you are Helen. And how ungrateful. Most people would be delighted to have a carnival centred around them. Doesn't it make you feel wanted?

MRS EUTERPE: Does it hell. All this for me? I know about it already. I know the story. I don't need to be told.

HESELTINE: But a book is no substitute for the real thing.

MRS EUTERPE: And neither are you.

HESELTINE: Correct. We are not a substitute for the real thing.

[*GESUALDO, MARIA, FEDERIGO and HESELTINE encircle MRS EUTERPE, menace her. Pause*]

MRS EUTERPE: Look, let's just call it a day. Leave me alone. I feel kinda upset. You're getting at me, you know that? It's damned impolite apart from anything else. I came here for a quiet look around and I get jumped on by a bunch of out-of-work actors.

HESELTINE: Helen, we are never out of work.

MARIA: We are regularly called upon, our services asked for.

GESUALDO: Our resurrections are continuous. We lead busy lives signora, more each year. You see, we *did*.

MRS EUTERPE: Yeh, yeh, so you're ghosts. Why not? Men of action.

MARIA: This is our garden. We have two homes, one for resting, one for working. Mostly we work in summer when people like you come looking.

MRS EUTERPE: Well this one has finished looking. [*Sits down at the table*] Find someone else to pester.

[*Pause*]

HESELTINE: Do the dead terrify you that much? Why anyone is afraid I don't know. We are timid, polite and quite powerless. The dead are stories, Helen, stories, ideas. We need your ears, we need your eyes. If you like you can keep your heart. Just study us, be professional.

MRS EUTERPE: I think I'm going to be sick.

HESELTINE: We'll turn our backs.

MRS EUTERPE: [*Flaring up*] Who needs your goddamned madrigals anyway?

GESUALDO: It would seem that you do. How else would you earn your living? I put the bread in your mouth.

MRS EUTERPE: No one needs a psychotic like you Gesualdo. Your music just isn't worth what you put into it. You disgust me.

HESELTINE: You disgust her Gesualdo.

GESUALDO: Then we agree on something, for I disgust myself. [*Bows*] Thank you signora.

HESELTINE: [*Breaking the mood, removing all traces of menace*] But be fair! See his side of it. He knew there was music in him. He had a court of poets and painters, all of lower caste than himself and they seemed happier, more talented. Even their kow-towing to him had a touch of insolence - great prince, at heart we are better off than you. We create. We bring fresh life. And you? Obsessed by our insincere obsecrations and your stinking bowels. Pity him Helen, pity him.

MRS EUTERPE: I wouldn't have minded if he'd taken the rap, but using his influence to keep it out of court... and that lousy painting? You've seen it? That's the end.

HESELTINE: I agree. That was going a bit far Gesualdo. It was almost ungentlemanly.

GESUALDO: The Church expected me to ask for forgiveness.

HESELTINE: That's not quite the same as giving yourself forgiveness, is it?

[*Twenties dance-band music. HESELTINE and MARIA dance by the orange tree. GESUALDO snaps his fingers*]

GESUALDO: Bring the artist to me.

[*FEDERIGO takes a menu to GESUALDO and stands by him like a waiter, pencil at the ready. As GESUALDO gives his order, FEDERIGO takes it down*]

GESUALDO: In the centre I want Christ in judgment, very regal, very stern. In the bottom left-hand corner myself, dressed in suitable black, with my uncle, Cardinal Borromeo, by my side, his arm around my shoulder, introducing me to the Redeemer. He should have an expression which says - this, dear Lord, is my erring nephew Carlo, pardon him. He is a good boy. He was wronged and he lashed out. Now he is sorry. He repents. On the left I think we will have the Blessed Virgin Mary, Saint Francis and the Magdalene interceding on my behalf. A useful combination. And on the right the Archangel Michael, Saint Domenic and Saint Catherine of Sienna. A powerful pressure-group speaking up for me. [*Pause*] The right hand of Christ should be raised in a gesture of absolution.

[*GESUALDO looks up at FEDERIGO who raises his hand in the correct gesture*]

GESUALDO: I have not quite finished. At the bottom of the painting there must be Hell, with flames. Hell should start a long way below the position occupied by myself and Uncle Borromeo. Yes, that will be adequate. And in Hell I want two adult figures, one male, one female, naked. They should be in the grasp of angels.

[*GESUALDO demonstrates that the angels must be pushing the man and woman down in to hell, not pulling them out*]

GESUALDO: That will be penance enough.

[*FEDERIGO bows, takes back the menu and returns to the piano. MARIA and HESELTINE finish their dance*]

[*The music stops*]

MARIA: Then you ran away Carlo. Go on, run. He's coming here to his castle, afraid of what my relatives might do to him!

GESUALDO: Cut down all of the trees! They could conceal an army. Lock the gates. Brother Giulio is coming!

MARIA: [*Sitting down at the table*] An extremely wild man. He would have killed Gesualdo given the chance, Carafa's nephew.

GESUALDO: I wish he had.

HESELTINE: Tosh. Don't talk such nonsense. But this friar did have a great unreasoning hatred of the creative artist. He thought they had little value, as witness his treatment of the poet Arcuccio who was passing along the street in Naples one day, reciting his own poems at the top of his voice. Our gentle friar begged him to desist and when the poet refused he raised his walking-stick and battered the poor fellow to death.

MRS EUTERPE: He didn't get through to you Gesualdo?

GESUALDO: No one got through to me.

HESELTINE: Except the Muse.

[*GESUALDO's madrigal* - Io sur respiro - *is played as background through this section*]

HESELTINE: Here in his castle, guarded on all sides, the devil appeased and gone, Gesualdo started to write his music. Can you imagine it? The strange new sounds coming from in there where the chickens are scratching. New music. Breakthrough music. Something original. Works of genius!

GESUALDO: The old forms could not communicate the pain. They were too stilted. I had to bend them.

MRS EUTERPE: You worked off your guilt on the keyboard. I'd call that masturbation.

GESUALDO: Madam, I can assure you that there was no pleasure in it.

HESELTINE: [*At GESUALDO's shoulder, in his shadow*] You are remembered Gesualdo.

GESUALDO: That is all that matters to you. I gained nothing. One devil having left me, the stopper from my music, there were a thousand to replace him. I could not move my bowels but twelve young men flogged me to force out the dirt. Three times a day I was beaten in order to perform the most humiliating of chores. My children died. My other wives drove me to concubines for what heat I had left from music.

MARIA: What a man you chose to imitate Peter. What a creature.

MRS EUTERPE: That I don't understand. How could you model yourself on him? He was a homicidal maniac.

HESELTINE: To me he was a success.

MRS EUTERPE: Then you're more of a damn fool than I took you for.

HESELTINE: It worked! When I became Warlock I found energy, confidence, power.

[*GESUALDO and HESELTINE suddenly thrust out their arms in perfect unison and give commands, HESELTINE in an echo*]

You will do as I say.

I will use you.

Your rents are increased.

Send me your daughter.

Love me at your peril.

Out of my way.

Drink deep.

Open your legs.

Do not argue.

Sit down and listen to this!

[*The madrigal rises, rises. GESUALDO's face is transformed. He is supremely happy. HESELTINE reflecting his joy. The music soars*]

GESUALDO: It is me. It is magnificent. I am working. I am creating!

[*HESELTINE jumps on GESUALDO's back and rides him round the stage*]

HESELTINE: We will hunt from dawn till dusk, driving our horses until they spew blood. Drink wine until our minds sail upon themselves. Whore in every village that we pass. Travel the length and breadth of Italy, Florence, Ferrara, Rome, Venice, battering at land and at people, punishing the earth. Me and this muse are boxers, knuckle to knuckle and nose to nose.

[*GESUALDO drops HESELTINE and they square up, fists raised, then break into laughter and hug each other as brothers*]

MRS EUTERPE: Did you imitate him completely?

HESELTINE: To the inch.

MRS EUTERPE: You murdered for inspiration?

HESELTINE: I did.

MRS EUTERPE: Your wife?

HESELTINE: No, myself. Poor old Philip Heseltine, that sensitive, shrinking violet. I killed him off.

MRS EUTERPE: You mean you completely changed your personality? That's impossible. We'd all be doing it twice a year if we had the chance.

HESELTINE: The will, Helen, the will. I had to change to survive. I left Heseltine behind on that Irish rock with the evil spirits in their hut. No doubt they tormented him. Then Peter Warlock entered London. [*Jumps up on a chair. Twenties dance-band music striking up behind him*] What fun I had.

MARIA: [*Kissing HESELTINE's feet*] Women flocked to him.

HESELTINE: Having ignored me till then. Ah the beard, the manner, the brute energy. They couldn't get enough of me. Helen, I dazzled them.

MARIA: His conquests were beyond counting.

HESELTINE: They came bright... [*Kicks MARIA away*] but went bruised.

[*Twenties dance-band music flows again. HESELTINE gets down off the chair, dances*]

MARIA: He became a celebrity. [*Claps*] Well done! You have made it. You have become someone.

GESUALDO: He was a truly amazing personality, a hyper-sensitive roister-doisterer, an alehouse Elgar. Tara! Enter Peter Warlock! He barges the door down, bangs on the counter for a quart of beer, jumps up on the table and serenades the astonished yokels.

[*HESELTINE strides across to the piano, vaults up and sits on the top. FEDERIGO plays and HESELTINE sings the drinking-song -* Mr Belloc's Fancy. *When the song is over he jumps down again, pleased with himself. GESUALDO and MARIA applaud. Pause*]

MRS EUTERPE: And did your music improve?

HESELTINE: It became more popular.

MRS EUTERPE: I didn't ask you that. I asked you, did your music improve?

[*Gets up from the table and meets HESELTINE eye to eye*]

HESELTINE: It appeared to.

MRS EUTERPE: Well, either it did or it didn't.

HESELTINE: At the time I would have said yes... but my earlier pieces, I still respected them.

MRS EUTERPE: So it didn't work?

HESELTINE: It was a deceit that the people who controlled and abused music in England forced upon me. My success was on their terms, not mine. To this day I hate them, and what they did to me.

MRS EUTERPE: I'd like to hear some more of your work. I could not give a proper evaluation until I had familiarised myself with it in depth. Forgive me for not knowing it as well as I should.

HESELTINE: Oh you should come back with us. Why don't you? My pieces are regularly performed with sympathy. You really should come back with us if you want to understand Gesualdo. He is usually the other half of the concert. [*Pause*] No? You won't go that far? Yours will be an incomplete work then. It cannot possibly be definitive unless you visit the country where the Prince of Venosa is held in his highest esteem. [*Takes a cassette out of his pocket*] However, I have this. A little toy. I believe it fits your machine. Would you like to play it? [*Takes

*MRS EUTERPE's tape machine out of her bag for her, gives it to her with the cassette*] Good, that is what I hoped you would say.

GESUALDO: You didn't bring along any of mine by any chance?

HESELTINE: Certainly not. You have Federigo here to play all your pieces. A satisfactory irony Gesualdo, the pieces playing your pieces.

GESUALDO: I understand that there are a number of records of my work on the market. They are receiving more attention each year. My reputation is growing. I am remembered, praised, studied.

HESELTINE: Thanks to me. I saved you from the archives Gesualdo, I brought you back from the grave. I wrote the first book which identified your genius. Don't forget that.

GESUALDO: There were other critics and commentators.

HESELTINE: I raised you from the dead. Me. I made your reputation for you.

GESUALDO: Nonsense. The music was there, it was there, waiting to be played.

HESELTINE: The gratitude of the artist is the blind man's thank you for a newspaper.

GESUALDO: You were a critic first, a worm in the liver of music.

HESELTINE: And where might you have got if you had not been a prince? Nowhere. You were indulged. Your worst pieces have to be heard to be believed. Trite. Absurd. Infantile.

GESUALDO: But they were mine. I did not prey on another's work, steal his forms and ideas.

HESELTINE: No? Gesualdo, your reputation rests on six madrigals pin-pointed by me, works like *Moro lasso* and *Resta di darmi noia*. And I detect influences. Perhaps Pomponio Nenna. You lifted some of his texts unchanged.

GESUALDO: [*Exploding with rage*] Pomponio Nenna? Take that back! Pomponio Nenna. I spit on Pomponio Nenna.

HESELTINE: [*Soothingly*] Remember Gesualdo, you're talking to the man who compared you to Debussy, Berlioz, Moussorgsky, Delius, even Wagner.

GESUALDO: Pomponio Nenna... I had instinct Peter, instinct. [*Sits down*]

MRS EUTERPE: [*Holding the tape recorder in her arms, cradled*] Okay if we play someone else's music now Gesualdo? You won't do yourself an injury?

GESUALDO: Signora, please continue.

[*MRS EUTERPE stands alone centre right. She has shifted into a classical pose, the muse, in her arms, music. She presses the start button. It is the pavan from the Capriole Suite. They listen. As the point where the solo violin emerges, HESELTINE darts across and jabs the stop button, then stalks away*]

MRS EUTERPE: Hey, I was enjoying that.

HESELTINE: I was not. I had not heard it before.

MRS EUTERPE: It doesn't give you any pleasure?

HESELTINE: It is imperfectly realised.

MRS EUTERPE: The conductor?

HESELTINE: No, one of the violins.

MRS EUTERPE: I couldn't hear anything wrong.

HESELTINE: That does not surprise me.

MRS EUTERPE: There was nothing to complain about. I thought the playing was excellent, in fact, superb.

HESELTINE: [*Angrily*] Madam, it was my piece! I should know!

MRS EUTERPE: That's where you're wrong.

HESELTINE: Wrong? How can I be wrong about the playing of my own work?

MRS EUTERPE: If you were a composer, and if you were dead, then you would know that whatever you had written belongs to us - if you were lucky enough to be any good. It is my ears that matter, not yours.

HESELTINE: You are the most impossible person I have ever met. What confounded arrogance! I appeal to you Gesualdo, what can one say?

GESUALDO: I think the violin that Peter is upset about was a sixteenth of a tone out, yes, a full sixteenth.

MRS EUTERPE: [*Sitting down*] Don't be ridiculous.

GESUALDO: Yes, a hemidemisemitone halved again. I heard it quite distinctly.

MARIA: Are you sure you did not hear it signora?

[*Pause. MRS EUTERPE glares at them defiantly. HESELTINE picks up his guitar and plays one high note*]

HESELTINE: Can you hear that?

MRS EUTERPE: Of course I can hear it!

HESELTINE: What note?

MRS EUTERPE: I'd have to be pitch perfect to be able to tell that.

HESELTINE: [*Plays the note again*] Come on, what note? [*Repeats it twice*] And how much difference between those two? A quarter? A half? How big must it be before you can tell? [*Dull twang*] Oh dear, an accident.

MARIA: Have you broken a string?

HESELTINE: How ham-fisted of me. I have a replacement. Will you be so kind as to get it for me Gesualdo? Carafa has one tucked away somewhere.

[*GESUALDO crosses to the piano and FEDERIGO hands him the packeted string*]

MARIA: Well, did you hear the difference then signora?

MRS EUTERPE: Look, I've got a perfectly good ear.

HESELTINE: You have the ear of a decomposing donkey.

MRS EUTERPE: You're very gallant.

GESUALDO: Why are you so unsympathetic towards us? Is it envy? Your unhappy love-life? Why?

MRS EUTERPE: Won't you two understand? I have nothing but contempt for what Gesualdo and Warlock did to themselves, and to others. It wasn't worth it. Anyway, they've been overtaken by greater talents, left behind...

GESUALDO: What you say may be true, though we do have our place which you obstinately deny us - and our reasons for acting as we did.

MRS EUTERPE: No. The pain and suffering you caused simply weren't worth it, they weren't. Not even that which you imposed upon yourselves. Look, if the Muse of music dropped dead tomorrow the world would carry on. Don't kid yourselves about that.

HESELTINE: Oh we don't, we don't.

MARIA: We know other people don't care so much, but that makes us care more to make up for it. Carlo and Peter work on, still composing, still striving for perfection.

HESELTINE: Wasting our time, according to you.

GESUALDO: We remain busy signora. We have great orchestras in Hell to play our work, brilliant musicians, the finest conductors who ever walked the earth look to us for new material. They expect new music.

HESELTINE: New music needs inspiration. Inspiration is hard to come by. We have to generate it in the only way we know how.

GESUALDO: Through the ultimate experience.

MARIA: Signora, join us in this thought. For once you are giving everything you have to music. The sacrifice is complete, absolute.

MRS EUTERPE: [*Coldly, picking up a book and opening it*] I'd like to be left alone now if you don't mind. Enough is enough.

MARIA: It would help us if you could offer yourself.

MRS EUTERPE: I said that's enough for Chrissake!

MARIA: Ah well, we tried. For us it would have been nicer if we could think that you saw the need and wanted to answer it.

HESELTINE: It makes the whole thing rather uncivilised, but necessary. [*GESUALDO opens the packet and takes out the guitar string*]

MRS EUTERPE: [*Concentrating on the book, refusing to look up*] I'm not listening. Go on, go away...

MARIA: After all, I died for music, Carafa died for music, Philip died for music, and eventually Peter Warlock died for music.

HESELTINE: By my own hand Helen. Picture it. A basement flat in Chelsea, early morning. A nameless woman has left my bed to go to another. On the piano a madrigal I cannot finish, in the manner of Gesualdo. I have dried up. There is no more music in me. I draw the curtains. Put out the cat. Then turn on the gas. It was easy, and inspiring. There is nothing to be afraid of...

MRS EUTERPE: Will you fuck off and leave me alone!

[*HESELTINE and MARIA retreat. GESUALDO stands up, the guitar string stretched between his hands*]

GESUALDO: Won't you believe in us? Believe in what we did? What we are doing?

[*MRS EUTERPE sticks to her book, stiff, intent*]

MARIA: Try for all our sakes.

GESUALDO: We would have killed you anyway but we always feel happier when the person sees things as we do. For the last time signora, give your all for something you profess to love, for music. [*Moves behind her chair*] You do love music, don't you?

MARIA: Of course she does.

HESELTINE: It will be worth it Helen.

GESUALDO: I, Carlo Gesualdo, assure you of that. And now, may we have some music to murder by?

[*GESUALDO slips the string over MRS EUTERPE's head and starts to garrotte her while HESELTINE and MARIA sing Gesualdo's madrigal* Or che in gioia. *They sing through her struggles until she is dead, then the three join hands and exit to the final bars. Lights dwindle down to MRS EUTERPE dead in the chair. Blackout*]

THE END

# NOTES ON THE MUSIC

In the Paines Plough production, the third voice was off-stage, also playing various instruments, e.g., glockenspiel and recorder. This was found to be an acceptable convention.

*PETER WARLOCK SONGS*
   *Ha'naker Hill* [Act One, page 73] can be found in *A Second Book of Songs - Peter Warlock*, published by Oxford University Press; *Lullaby* [Act One, page 77] can be found in *Warlock Songs*, published by Boosey and Hawkes; *Mr Belloc's Fancy* [Act Two, page 99] can be found in *Thirteen Songs by Peter Warlock*, published by Stainer and Bell. In the *Three-Families-Dance* [Act One, page 81], any simple 6/8 dance tune played on the recorder will be appropriate.

*OTHER SONGS AND ARRANGEMENTS*
   Permission to perform the following songs and arrangements can be obtained from John Johnson [Authors' Agent] Limited, Clerkenwell House, 45/47 Clerkenwell Green, London EC1R OHT. Tel: 071 251 0125

## A Note is Just a Word

*Words: David Pownall. Music: Stephen Boxer*
   The guitar accompaniment should play the tune throughout including the figures indicated in small notes. The first time through the words in brackets should be omitted and the tune played on the guitar, as if examples qualifying the previous phrase, i.e., A tune a conversation - and the next sequence of notes illustrates the musical conversation. A capo may be used on the third fret and the song played using an A min shape base.

## Moro Lasso

*Gesualdo, arr. Stephen Boxer*
   Like *Or, che in cioia*, this is considerably longer in its original form, and it would be inappropriate and impractical to sing the full five-part version. This shortened three-part version transmits the necessarily sad essence of the piece.

## Lucifer, Lux, Lucis Light

*Words: David Pownall. Music: Stephen Boxer*

## I Knew Love Only
*Words: David Pownall. Music: Stephen Boxer*

## Weep You No More
*Music: Stephen Boxer*

This was used for the Maria/Carafa love-making sequence in Act Two. It can be played on the guitar with a *capo* on the third fret, thus using a D min shape base.

## Or, che in gioia
*Gesualdo, arr. Stuart Morgan and Stephen Boxer*

The original madrigal is four times this length, and is written for five voices. This demanded more singing voices than were available, and was considered too long for the dramatic purposes of the play. This three-part arrangement successfully overcame those problems.

# ELGAR'S RONDO

*For Alex*

*Elgar's Rondo* was first performed by the Royal Shakespeare Company at the Swan Theatre, Stratford-upon-Avon, on 20 October, 1993, and transferred to the The Pit at the RSC Barbican, London on 27 April, 1994, with the following cast:

EDWARD ELGAR, *Alec McCowen*
ALICE ELGAR, his wife, *Sheila Ballantine*
AUGUSTUS JAEGER, of Novello's, *John Carlisle*
WINDFLOWER, Alice Stuart-Wortley, *Anne Lambton*
FRANK SCHUSTER, a patron, *Peter Bygott*
CARICE ELGAR, the composer's daughter, *Debra Gillett*
GEORGE BERNARD SHAW, *James Hayes*
MARK, a handyman, *Gary Taylor*
FATHER JOHN, a Jesuit, *Ian Hughes*
BANDMASTER, *Sean Hannaway*
KING GEORGE V, *David Weston*
ARCHIE, a gillie, *Alexi K Campbell*
PAUL HOOKER, a bassoonist, *David Delve*
CELLIST, *Tania Levey*
DOROTHY, a housekeeper, *Anita Wright*
BANDSMEN, *Jeremy Ballard, Leslie Cawdrey, Peter Fisher, Roger Hellyer, Andrew Hiles, Peter Morris, Clifford Pick, Robert Pritchard, Ian Reynolds, Michael Tubbs.*

Director, *Di Trevis*
Designer, *Pamela Howard*
Lighting design, *Rick Fisher*
Additional music, *Dominic Muldowney*
Musical director, *Michael Tubbs*
Movement director, *Jane Gibson*

# ACT ONE

*In blackout loud dance music. Lights up on guests in fancy dress, dancing in couples*
*[ELGAR, dressed as Satan, stands alone in the centre of them]*
ELGAR: Jesu Maria!
*[The music stops abruptly. The guests exit, leaving ELGAR alone]*
*[Lights change, discovering a high barn-like room full of curios and carpets in semi-darkness. Light from a roof window falls on the memorabilia of a rich man's world travels. From the ceiling hangs a giant stuffed lizard. Below the lizard is a table and chair with writing materials laid out, a metronome and a violin in a case. Beside the table are two old armchairs. Stage L is a hat stand. A door stage L leads to the main house across a garden.*
*This is Elgar's work-room, a detached studio in the grounds of the millionaire Frankie Schuster's Thameside house, 'The Hut', at Bray, near Maidenhead, May 1911, not long after the première of Elgar's Second Symphony]*
*[ELGAR goes to the table. He switches on a lamp which is a curio in itself, sits at the table, takes a tobacco pouch and pipe out of a drawer and starts to fill the pipe]*
*[A knock at the door. ELGAR sighs and carries on filling his pipe]*
*[Another knock]*
*[Pause]*
*[The door is opened sharply. The lizard swings in the draught. ALICE stands in the doorway, dressed as Nell Gwynn, with a basket of oranges, her eyes everywhere. Finally she looks up at the lizard]*
ALICE: Sorry. Forgot to come in carefully.
ELGAR: Why do you have to follow me all the time?
*[ALICE closes the door, her eyes on the lizard]*
ALICE: Horrible thing. I don't know how you can work with hanging over your head. Why don't you tell Frankie to have it removed?
ELGAR: I like it.
ALICE: *[Crossing the room to sit down in an armchair]* I wanted a quiet moment too.

*[ALICE starts to sit down. ELGAR warningly clears his throat. ALICE straightens up]*

ALICE: When you went off like that I thought: "Edu is finding this all too much". Frankie's invited far too many people, and the weather's so hot.

ELGAR: You misread the signs, as usual. Got it all wrong. Came for a smoke, that's all. Can't dance with a pipe in one's mouth.

ALICE: Did you have an idea?

ELGAR: About what?

ALICE: Don't be obtuse.

ELGAR: Am I being obtuse? Didn't mean to be.

ALICE: If the party wasn't in your honour I'd suggest we went home. I'm rather tired.

ELGAR: Home? Where's that? Oh, I remember. Where the furniture is.

ALICE: Do you promise to come back to the party once you've smoked your pipe?

ELGAR: No.

ALICE: I thought not, but I'm afraid you'll have to. There are so many people want to talk to the composer himself.

ELGAR: You talk to them.

ALICE: Me? Heavens, what would I say? They won't be satisfied with me. They want explanations. What's behind this? What does he mean? Is this to be Elgar's new style? You've caused an intellectual ferment over there.

ELGAR: That comes out of a champagne bottle. Look, Chicky, do me a favour, will you? Let me get over it in my own time.

ALICE: Get over what?

ELGAR: Don't soft soap me, Alice! You know what I mean. The audience sat there the other night like stuffed pigs, those that were there.

ALICE: They were thinking, that's all.

ELGAR: Thinking? Sleeping!

ALICE: It's the heat, darling. It makes people lethargic.

ELGAR: Come on, you've read the reviews.

ALICE: Yes, I have. They're very, very good.

ELGAR: Good? "A very sparse supply of melody?" "Elgar's charm and power diminished?" "Coldness and hardness?"

ALICE: Give people time to appreciate what you've done. They'll come round, I'm sure.

ELGAR: Pah! They hate it.

ALICE: These are awful times. Everything's so tense and unhappy. Nothing but war in people's minds. I think that deep down they want it to happen, don't you?

ELGAR: Well, they don't want my symphony, that's certain. And I'm not sure that I do. In fact, *I* hate the damn thing now.

ALICE: [*Shocked*] Edu! Don't say things like that.

ELGAR: I never want to hear it again. Now, leave me alone.

ALICE: Not when you're like this. Talk to me...

ELGAR: Oh, don't pry! After twenty years you still don't know what's going on inside, do you?

ALICE: I'll go, but I hope that you're not waiting for someone else's shoulder to cry on. That's my job.

[*ELGAR goes to the door and opens it sharply. The lizard swings*]

ELGAR: Damn!

[*ALICE moves unwillingly towards the door. From the curios JAEGER enters in the waistcoat and shirt sleeves of an office worker. He walks past ALICE, who cannot see or hear him, and stands stage L with the lizard directly over his head*]

JAEGER: I've come for your soul, Mephistopheles.

ELGAR: Have we got this the right way round?

JAEGER: Well. Alice would say: "Faust come, Faust served", I suppose. Deal with her, then we'll have a chat.

ALICE: Shall we go home tonight? I don't want to stay here.

ELGAR: I'll come back to the party when I'm in a better mood. [*He kisses ALICE on the cheek*] Must think things through.

ALICE: I don't like to imagine you sitting here all by yourself feeling so low. Let us cheer you up.

JAEGER: I'll cheer him up. Leave it to me.

[*ALICE exits*]

[*ELGAR slowly closes the door behind her*]

ELGAR: She never leaves me alone for five minutes.

JAEGER: Dear Alice. Your watch-dog.

ELGAR: What she doesn't realise is that I occasionally must have time to myself.

JAEGER: Under supervision. Was the Second Symphony for me?

ELGAR: Well, you know that everything I write is for you in one way or another.

JAEGER: [*Laughing*] I hope not!

[*ALICE opens the door cautiously and pokes her head round*]

ALICE: Did I leave my basket behind?

JAEGER: She's just checking. Someone might have slipped in without a pass.

[*ELGAR picks the basket of oranges up and takes it over to the door*]

JAEGER: She knows that in this room you wrote the B minor violin concerto for another woman, and that be major cause for anxiety. What she can't grasp is how such infidelity sounds so beautiful, even to her, whose failure as a source of romantic inspiration the B unfaithful concerto proclaims. But the Second Symphony was written here as well. That has some very strange sounds in it, she thinks, especially in the Rondo. They could be sounds of a man falling out of love.

[*ELGAR carefully opens the door to usher ALICE out*]

JAEGER: But she's got it wrong again, hasn't she? You're not falling out of love with your Windflower, your Alma, the dream-daughter, are you? You're falling out of love with the world.

[*ELGAR shuts the door*]

ELGAR: Why have you come to torment me tonight, of all nights? Haven't I had enough punishment?

JAEGER: You should never have turned your back on me. I warned you not to do it. I said that if you neglected those old friends who stuck by you in the hard times, you'd suffer for it.

ELGAR: [*Returning to the table*] I didn't neglect you. You were always in my mind.

JAEGER: Postcards!

ELGAR: I thought about you often...

JAEGER: Don't make excuses, Edward. You were up to your chin in affluent all of a sudden, drunk with it. Why think about me? What was changing for Nimrod? Same old office, same old advice, same old cough... I was on the slope down and no one could save me. You were right. What could you have done? We don't expect composers to find a miracle cure for TB... but for despair? Well, perhaps.

ELGAR: I did feel guilty.

JAEGER: Did?

ELGAR: Still do. You were my dearest friend. You helped me more than anyone ever did. I should have been with you at the end.

JAEGER: Really? [*He puts the metronome into motion*] Well, there was something about today that felt like an end so I thought I'd better come over to see you, before it was too late. It's a very good room for haunting. Everything in it was bought for you, offerings, inducements to release your essential self and make music. Dear Frankie. How hard he tries. This mansion of his is so near the river it must flood regularly. Could you handle Elgar's Water-Music?

[*ELGAR chuckles. JAEGER stops the metronome*]

JAEGER: Raised a smile? Any ideas for your Third Symphony now we've got the Second on it's way.

ELGAR: There isn't going to be a third.

JAEGER: I hoped not to hear you say that; but it is the fear that brought me hurrying over. How can a world-class composer stop at two? That's only one for each leg.

[*ELGAR sits at the table*]

ELGAR: Can't stand much more, I'm afraid.

JAEGER: Much more of what?

ELGAR: Everything! I'm giving up the music business entirely.

JAEGER: The great Elgar giving up?

ELGAR: Yes!

JAEGER: We must do something.

ELGAR: Nothing to be done.

JAEGER: No appeal I can make? If I remind you of those early days, the dreams we had - the man whose music would cross all frontiers. All that kind of thing. It meant a lot to me that a German and an Englishman could have that ambition together. We were brothers in it, Edward. I'm not sure that I understand.

ELGAR: It's my right to choose, isn't it?

JAEGER: Didn't you choose to become the only composer from these islands who's been able to hold his head up in Europe for two hundred years? Doesn't that mean anything to you any more?

ELGAR: No.

JAEGER: Then I'm dumbfounded. Where's your pride?

ELGAR: Gone.

JAEGER: What's done this to you?

ELGAR: I told you. I've given up. What kind of life is it? I run around the world buzzing like a blue-arsed fly. Don't like the places I have to go to. Can't stand the people. Haven't got a proper place to live. Can't earn a decent living...

JAEGER: You live like a lord! Do you know what I used to exist on at Novello's? The pittance that music publishers pay their staff! And living in the suburbs? [*Pause*] The importance people attach to place is strange. Even stranger once you've seen how small the world is. After all, life takes place, and that's about it, really. That could be quite a good theme for your Third Symphony if you were looking for one.

ELGAR: [*Jumping up*] Will you stop going on about my Third Symphony, for Christ's sake?

JAEGER: And the fourth will be inside the third. And the fifth...

ELGAR: Don't you dare!

JAEGER: Elgar's Fifth. That has a ring to it.

[*Pause. ELGAR grunts and sits down again*]

JAEGER: You've worked well in this room, horrible though it is.

ELGAR: It's a bloody madhouse.

JAEGER: You don't see all this, do you? Not when you're working. Not even your *deus ex machina*. I often used to wonder when you were doing *Gerontius*, *The Apostles* and *The Kingdom* - your religious phase - whether you had an idea what God actually looked like. [*He looks at the lizard*] And, if you did, if you used to forget about Him once you really got going. Do you ever think about all that now?

[*ELGAR does not respond*]

What about when you're sitting through yet another performance of one of your Catholic rhapsodies? Do you see God behind the conductor's arm? No. You sit there composing something new. Nothing gets in your way.

ELGAR: You're managing to. Could you haunt a little less heartily?

JAEGER: Do you want to work now? I'll just sit and be quiet.

ELGAR: I'd rather you went.

JAEGER: I have to keep an eye on you. You might start writing more quatsch. Alice is still nibbling away: 'A few little songs, a few doodles can't do any harm'.

ELGAR: Don't put it all on her. At least she knows what she wants. Give her a house in Hampstead, frequent trips to the Continent, the right dinner parties, she's happy. All I know is what I don't want. Music.

JAEGER:Why?

[*ELGAR shouts in rage, snapping his pipe*]

ELGAR: Broken a perfectly good pipe. One of my old favourites: That's all your fault, Jagpot, nagging at me again. You're worse than a woman.

JAEGER: Death is a very female thing, Edward. It enables one to see what has been wasted in a man.

[*The door is opened carefully and WINDFLOWER enters dressed diaphanously as a nymph. She closes the door softly*]

WINDFLOWER: I wonder if you can help me. Am I right for the sacred grove?

ELGAR: You took the wrong turning, Windflower. This is another place altogether.

WINDFLOWER: Well, it seems rather nice. Mind if I come in and look around?

ELGAR: I'd rather you didn't.

WINDFLOWER: Thank you. [*She walks in*] How marvellously distracting. Is the idea to take your mind completely off what you're composing?

ELGAR: Not my idea, but everyone else's, it seems.

WINDFLOWER: I never imagined it at all like this.

ELGAR: I'm mere bric-a-brac, darling. Not at all expensive. Whenever Frankie goes abroad he ends up in the souks and bazaars. When he gets back he chucks the stuff in here with me.

WINDFLOWER: I never understood why you didn't want me in this room. *Trés exotique!* But then, so are you, really. Come and dance with me.

ELGAR: No. I'd tread on your delightful toes.

WINDFLOWER: So, somewhere in all this was my music. Strange, It doesn't feel like me at all.

ELGAR: No, that was in me, not in the room.

WINDFLOWER: Have you run away from the party so everyone will wonder where you are? Aren't you getting enough attention?

ELGAR: Windflower, my darling, I'm angry. I'm miserable. I don't want you near me when I'm this way.

[*He ushers her towards the exit*]

WINDFLOWER: No! [*She shakes him off*] Otherwise, what use am I? I can't have you mooning over me one minute and throwing me out the next. Stop being so mysterious about your disappointments, Edward. It's silly. You're simply fed up because the première wasn't the howling success you expected it to be.

ELGAR: Hoped, is the word. All I ever wanted was for people to say that I'd made something that worked well. But even that they've denied me.

WINDFLOWER: No one saw me come over.

ELGAR: Then perhaps no one will see you return.

WINDFLOWER: What? Empty-handed? Defeated? My magic lost? Let me persuade you, Lucifer.

JAEGER: Perhaps it would do you some good? After all, you've had her a thousand times in your mind.

ELGAR: No! She'd shatter into a thousand pieces.

WINDFLOWER: What?

JAEGER: The fantasy produced the violin concerto. The fact might make a new symphony. Give it a chance.

ELGAR: Get out and leave me alone, you bastard!

WINDFLOWER: Bastard yourself... but, as you wish.

[*WINDFLOWER exits, slamming the door*]

JAEGER: She'll forgive you. Everyone has to. Do you trust her?

ELGAR: What d'you mean, trust? The woman's married!

JAEGER: To a very nice chap. Impossible, isn't it? Like writing another symphony. Oh, the joys of paralysis. The delights of the unattainable.

ELGAR: I'm taking this costume off. It seems to bring the worst out in you.

[*ELGAR starts to get changed out of the Satan costume. Underneath he is is wearing a pair of black trousers and a shirt. He rolls up his sleeves*]

JAEGER: I thought you'd given up.

ELGAR: Just a few loose ends.

JAEGER: Don't let me stop you.

ELGAR: [*Sitting at the table*] I won't.

[*JAEGER waits while ELGAR takes a pencil, sharpens it, draws a few bar lines on score-paper, then sits staring into space*]

JAEGER: Nothing happening?

ELGAR: Be quiet.

[*Pause. Suddenly ELGAR writes a note. Pause. He writes another. Then he writes swiftly*]

JAEGER: Coming fast!

ELGAR: Huh-huh.

JAEGER: What is it?

ELGAR: Wouldn't you like to know?

JAEGER: Is it big, abstract?

ELGAR: I can hardly keep up with it.

JAEGER: Keep going! Keep going!

[*ELGAR puts the pencil down. JAEGER tries to look but ELGAR covers the paper with his hand*]

JAEGER: Let me see.

ELGAR: For your own sake, don't look!

JAEGER: Show me.

ELGAR: Don't say I didn't warn you.

[*ELGAR takes his hand off the paper. JAEGER picks it up and looks at it. Music of the tritone is heard*]

JAEGER: The *diabolus in musica*. Over and over again.

ELGAR: A succession of little notes that threatened an entire civilisation, made the Pope turn pale and the Holy Roman Emperor's knees knock. Why? What power has music? Especially *ugly* music!

JAEGER: Hard on the ear. Pain has power.

ELGAR: It creates confusion. It throws a spanner in melodic counterpoints. It threatens the musical universe. It scoffs at the perfection of God. They had the sense to ban it, denied it access to their minds. If they hadn't it would have let the Devil in to do his work; and that is how I feel about the Second Symphony, especially the Rondo.

JAEGER: Edward, conservative you are, but not medieval.

ELGAR: The Rondo will take me places where I shouldn't go. If I could unwrite it, I would. I couldn't even find anyone to conduct the symphony. Richter refused. Beecham said no. Everyone sheered away from it. Why? Because they could see where I was going and they were damned if they were coming with me.

JAEGER: The Rondo's a long way from being atonal, Edward.

ELGAR: I've never had a moment's luck since I wrote it.

[*The tritone is heard again*]

JAEGER: For a new symphony to be imperfectly understood at its first performance is almost a compliment. It means that it has to be thought about...

ELGAR: I didn't hear you say that when my first was such an immediate success.

JAEGER: The second is better.

ELGAR: Aaaah! You terrible liar!

JAEGER: It is. The first is too English, too gentlemanly, to *nobilmente*, too *semplice*. The second is more complex, more dangerous, more dynamic, truly universal. And there are beginnings that I can hear in it for other great symphonies that will shake the world!

ELGAR: The Beethoven of Broadheath.

JAEGER: Brahms, beware. Look to your laurels.

ELGAR: Watch your back, Dvorak.

JAEGER: Don't get too grandiose, Berlioz.

ELGAR: More juicy than Debussy.

JAEGER: More art than Mozart.

ELGAR: Less luck than Gluck. Let's leave it at that.

JAEGER: [*Pause*] Oh, Edward. Why do we have to keep getting you off the ground?

ELGAR: Because that's what I always go back to. That's where, a country boy belongs, the ground. I've grown too far away from it. I want to go back. I want to sell potatoes for a living. I want to chase hares, fish the river, ride my bike.

JAEGER: Then do all those things. What's stopping you?

ELGAR: Music. It says I have to move on, but I don't want to.

JAEGER: [*Pause*] Yes. I see that. But you're too far in to pull out. Your first symphony has been played all over the world. The second will be when the times have become less toxic.

[*A thunderous knocking at the door that makes it shake*]

ELGAR: Good God, what's that?

[*The knocking is repeated with even greater force, then the door is opened carefully and SCHUSTER, dressed as a caveman, pokes his head round. Dance music can be heard off*]

SCHUSTER: Do you want to see what I'm knocking with? [*He holds out a large club, then enters*] You've taken your costume off, you old spoil-sport. And you looked so good in it.

ELGAR: You nearly had the roof down, Frankie.

SCHUSTER: Balsa wood. Amazing stuff. You can wallop yourself on the head with it and it doesn't hurt. Look.

[*He hammers himself on the head*]

Nothing.

[*He hits ELGAR on the head*]

See what I mean? You have a go. We've all been doing it to each other over there. Great fun.

[*ELGAR takes the club and hits SCHUSTER on the head with more force than he had expected*]

SCHUSTER: [*Blinking*] See, didn't feel a thing.

JAEGER: Sound but no pain. What a useful instrument.

SCHUSTER: It's from a tree that grows in the West Indies, *Ochrama Pyramidale...*

JAEGER: Frankie has been everywhere, looked at everything and collected many curiosities, including a composer, *Elgara Rhomboidale* that grows only in the English rain forest.

ELGAR: [*Handing back the club*] What do you want, Hercules, apart from to knock out my few brains?

SCHUSTER: I saw one of my nymphs running away from here. She said that someone had shouted at her in the most fearsome manner. Are you guilty of mood?

ELGAR: Definitely.

SCHUSTER: Then I've taken my life in my hands coming over here. No matter. How are you?

ELGAR: Much visited.

SCHUSTER: It is my house.

ELGAR: Look, bugger off will you? I'm busy.

SCHUSTER: No, I will not. If you're not over there in ten minutes, and on you're best behaviour, you're out.

ELGAR: Out?

SCHUSTER: Yes, out. You can pack up your things and go.

ELGAR: Well, that's easy enough!

SCHUSTER: Is it? You told me this is the only place you can work.

ELGAR: Well, it isn't.

SCHUSTER: You think I'll relent, don't you? Like all the other times. Well, I'm not going to. Before you stormed out of the party you managed to upset virtually everyone you spoke to. They're my friends, Edward...

ELGAR: Dregs and dimwits!

JAEGER: Careful. Don't completely alienate him. Well, not until you know there's somewhere else you can work.

ELGAR: [*Pause*] I don't know what's the matter with me these days, Frankie, old friend. Take no notice, please.

SCHUSTER: Don't apologise to me. The music must always come first. I was only trying to frighten you. Very hurt by your disappointment, you know. It always affects me when you're suffering. Can't understand because you're all joy to me. What a blunderer, eh? It was your women put me up to it. They challenged me to do something they couldn't by getting you over to the party.

[*ELGAR bursts out laughing*]

SCHUSTER: Are you mocking me?

ELGAR: God, no. It's just that you're in the same boat as I am. Everyone's telling you what to do.

[*ELGAR takes a bottle of whisky and two glasses from a cabinet amongst the curios*]

ELGAR: Two old chums haven't found time for a chat lately.

JAEGER: Don't keep him here too long.

[*ELGAR pours two tots and hands one to FRANKIE*]

JAEGER: I've got some ideas for you. What d'you make of this? Schoen-berg... has come up with it.

[*Phrases from the* Altenberg Lieder *are heard*]

ELGAR: Cheers.

[*ELGAR and SCHUSTER carefully sip their drinks. Only JAEGER and ELGAR can hear the music*]

SCHUSTER: Odd thing, you know... couldn't sleep the night after the concert.

[*JAEGER'S playing is now in studied experiments*]

SCHUSTER: Awful... like a *nuit blanche*... hovering... restless. What's this? I said. Whenever I've been to your concerts before I've floated home, slept like a baby...

ELGAR: Yes, I do have that effect upon people.

SCHUSTER: No, I didn't mean that. What I'm trying to say is that you resolve things for me. You put them into the most exquisite perspec-tives. But this symphony had a different effect. It disturbed me. You'd picked something up... I don't know...

ELGAR: Didn't want to, I assure you. Makes me feel like some old tramp going through people's dustbins.

ELGAR: How's business?

SCHUSTER: Buoyant. Good time to get in. A big boom is developing.

ELGAR: If only I had some spare cash.

SCHUSTER: Come on, Edward. You must have a few pounds. Every-where I go I hear nothing but your tunes in the street.

ELGAR: If you could see what I get out of it you'd cry, Frankie. Music isn't banking.

SCHUSTER: There's a very good copper share...

ELGAR: [*Putting an arm round him*] Dear Frankie.

SCHUSTER: I like to have you to myself now and then.

ELGAR: I hope so. [*Pause*] Frankie... I'd like to finish this little piece of work, then I'll come over. Is that all right? And I'll be charming to everyone, I promise.

[*SCHUSTER exits mollified. The lizard does not swing*]

JAEGER: Strange how you go from one German best friend to another. What is it you find in us? But he's been trained by Prussians.

ELGAR: That's not Frankie at all. He's soft.

JAEGER: Which must be why he's a millionaire. How has he become so successful in this country? By making pets out of artists? No, by investing in war. Treat Frankie like you did me. Once he's served his purpose, cast him aside. Be as hard as he is. If you weren't famous he wouldn't give you house-room.

ELGAR: Leave me something, Mosshead!

JAEGER: All I want to leave you is this: A boy listening to the wind in the reeds by the river. he has a few sheets of score-paper filched from his father's shop, some bread and cheese. This boy is teaching himself everything about music. he has never seen the inside of a conservatoire or a salon! Do you recognise him? Is he still inside you, or have you killed him off? [*Pause*] Everyone who rules your life now would have walked past and not given him a thought... well, everyone, that is, except me... Alice in her carriage... Windflower in her perambulator... Frankie in his Mercedes... but no... he'd have tossed you a penny! Oh, how you anger me, Edward! What better start for a true musician? You came out of the ground like a spring of pure water.

ELGAR: That's all very well but you try living by it!

JAEGER: Me try living by it? I lived *through* it for twenty years! Always remember that I wanted to compose, but I didn't have the spark. You took me as close as I could get. And we won through, didn't we? We brought you to greatness, to your proper recognition. Isn't that so?

ELGAR: Yes, you did.

JAEGER: Did I ever complain?

ELGAR: Well, you could be quite critical.

JAEGER: That was my job.

ELGAR: I sometimes wondered who was writing the music, you or me.

JAEGER: The tiniest suggestion and you'd go off in a huff!

ELGAR: You were wrong quite often... [*Pause*] There's no need to go on, Jagpot. I've let you down, I know. I've disappointed you.

JAEGER:Disappointed? Me! After that wonderful new symphony you've given us? Edward, I've been walking on air. Ecstatic, my dear friend. For me it's the fulfilment of a dream - the first time that you've broken out of your English chrysalis, and what a splendid butterfly you make. I'm proud of you - far more so than at any other time. Please believe me.

ELGAR: If only you were still with us.

JAEGER: But I am, Edward, always. I beg you - go down to the river again. Find that boy. Share his bread and cheese. He will sustain you through these dark times. All your strength is in him.

ELGAR: He's dead, can't you see? And you know what killed him. This cruel, bloody music business.

JAEGER: No, no, that's his life, his power. Relentless, perhaps, but who promised you mercy? That's only a sop to the faint-hearted. But indestructible glory, Edward, glory made in your mind? That must mean something.

ELGAR: If I could respond to anyone, it would be you. But I'm truly finished now. There's no hope at all. They're indifferent to my best work so that means they're indifferent to me.

JAEGER: Think of your brothers: Schubert, dead at thirty one - eight symphonies! Worked until he dropped. Mozart, dead at thirty six - fifty symphonies! Hounded by debt, persecuted! Mendelssohn, dead at thirty eight - eight symphonies! And you, at fifty four, honoured, famous, living off the fat of the land, defeated after two! It's monstrous!

ELGAR: You simply don't understand. You're a German and you don't understand how this country works. Why do you think English music was white and bloodless until I came along? No passion, no life! Because something was suffocating it. That's still there, and now all its attention is concentrated upon me!

JAEGER: No wonder when it *is* you. Your weakness. Your idleness. Your impatience. Your inane greed for things that don't matter.

ELGAR: How dare you insult my poverty!

JAEGER: No true artist is ever poor.

ELGAR: Dear old Mosshead. You were always such an innocent. Which was why I had to see less of you.

JAEGER: Don't give up, Edward, I implore you. Now now. Not when you've written such a superb symphony.

ELGAR: Tell them that.

JAEGER: I would if I could, but I can only talk to you. Be brave. Reject all this nonsense. Go forward. I'll be with you.

ELGAR: I daren't. It would take me into madness.

JAEGER: Choose the madness. Embrace it!

ELGAR: No!

JAEGER: Others risk it.

ELGAR: It's not as close to them. You know me, Mosshead, the way I am. It can't be helped.

JAEGER: I know you better now I've heard the Rondo. And I want to know more. Come on, make me tremble, make my knees knock! Rip the mask aside, Edward. Show us your demon at work.

ELGAR: Oh, leave off, will you! I say no! No! No!

JAEGER: [*Moving away*] Very well, Edward. Compose your English tea-time *quatsch*. I hope you drown in your royalties, O Gland of Mope and Borey. O Comp and Irkumstance! Forget the symphony. Become a dwarf. Shame your genius. From now on I shan't be listening. All that work, all those years coaxing you along, digging you out of your depressions. Now you've made it all pointless. Damn you for that! And damn you for making an absolute fool out of me!

[*JAEGER exits in a rage, slamming the door. The lizard does not swing*]

[*The door is flung open. The lizard swings wildly. Loud dance music is played by the band on the lawn outside. SCHUSTER, WINDFLOWER, ALICE, CARICE and the other guests in fancy dress tumble in, dancing and laughing*]

SCHUSTER: This is a deputation, Edward! We demand our rights! This is your party and you must come to it. If Mahomet won't come to the mountain then the mountain must come to Mahomet!

ELGAR: Please...

SCHUSTER: There's no please about it. All your friends are here but we can't have a good time without you. Now be a good boy, put your costume back on, join in. We're not leaving here until you promise.

ELGAR: If you insist.

SCHUSTER: We do, don't we?

[*The guests shout their agreement*]

CARICE: Come on, Daddy. You're missing all the fun!

ELGAR: If I can have your understanding...

SCHUSTER: You can have our understanding tomorrow.

ELGAR: Very well. I can see that I'm outnumbered. Give me five minutes.

CARICE: Hurray-hurrah! I knew he'd say yes! Well done, Daddy!

[*SCHUSTER leads the guests out. As ALICE is slipping out with the crowd ELGAR calls to her*]

ELGAR: Alice! That's the first time you've ever conspired to stop me working. Why?

[*ALICE closes the door*]

ALICE: They just swept me along.

ELGAR: You know the rules.

ALICE: I don't always know the rules between sulking and working, Edu. You make it difficult to distinguish between them sometimes.

ELGAR: I feel betrayed.

ALICE: Oh, don't be silly. You shouldn't work all the time. I think it's the work that makes you unhappy.

ELGAR: Ah! So it's work less, is it? Become more and more dependent on you.

ALICE: Hurry up and change, darling.

ELGAR: I can never write another symphony, you know.

ALICE: There are plenty of other things you can write.

ELGAR: Can't take the risk with myself... What have they been saying about me over there?

ALICE: Oh, you know them. Do put your fancy dress back on, darling. You can't be the only one in civvies.

ELGAR: [*Pushing her in a sudden outburst of berserk rage*] You destructive woman! You filthy philistine harpy!

[*ALICE falls to the ground. The oranges fall out of her basket and roll around*]

ELGAR: Alice... my dear... are you hurt?

ALICE: Edu... you don't really think that I'm destructive, do you? I couldn't bear that.

[*ELGAR helps her to her feet*]

ELGAR: Of course not.

ALICE: [*Gathering some of her oranges*] I only do what I think is best; but you must tell me what's important.

ELGAR: I'll get changed.

ALICE: We'll have a beautiful house in London... we'll be happy... lots of rooms... lots of quiet... you won't have to work in places like this, which upset you. Frankie's a good soul, but... well... he can be a bit of a nuisance. I know he's a good friend, but sometimes I wonder about his motives.

ELGAR: Did you hear me say that I'm abandoning the symphony?

[*ALICE hurriedly picks up the Satan costume and holds it up. ELGAR unwillingly starts to change back into fancy dress*]

ELGAR: Why don't you ever listen?

ALICE: You don't want me to understand really. This is damp.

ELGAR: Then I'll get the 'flu, won't I? I try to explain.

ALICE: You think you do. When you put things in your work you imagine you've said them, but you haven't.

ELGAR: What a little twister you are.

ALICE: I'm not, darling. We don't understand literally what you mean when we hear your beautiful pieces played.

ELGAR: What's the use of talking to myself?

ALICE: It's a lovely mystery. Who wants all their i's dotted and t's crossed?

ELGAR: Wherever it is my sounds come from... not from me, I never originate... Are you listening? Whoever, whatever that is, that's what's going mad, not me.

ALICE: You only feel that because you work so hard. Why don't we go away for a while. Rome would be nice.

ELGAR: Listen, will you? It is not *me* who is disintegrating! I can keep myself together. I know who I am. But the music comes from another source, somewhere outside me, and it's collapsing.

ALICE: How can it be when oo's music flows on so sweetly, darling?

ELGAR: And now I've started orchestrating the collapse!

ALICE: That's not twue. I always know whats twoubling my Edu. This time it's that ghastly, stupid audience who didn't listen pwoperly...

ELGAR: Stop talking like that!

[*Pause. ALICE busies herself buttoning up his costume*]

ALICE: You know I'm only trying to... [*She halts in mid-sentence, unable to follow her own thought through*] It's only the two of us.

ELGAR: Well, cut it out, will you? I don't want any more of it. We don't talk to each other so it means anything. If we can't do better than this absurd nursery chatter then perhaps we should shut up.

ALICE: It doesn't mean anything, darling...

ELGAR: Exactly! I'm trying to tell you something without using music... I'm at odds with everything I taught myself. I'm being driven to betray my own past.

ALICE: I'll help you, darling. For you and your heavenly music I would do anything in my power. Even take your insults.

[*Pause*]

ELGAR: Sorry. Not been a nice boy... humble myself... act of contwition... have mercy, Mummy. Don't know what's got into me.

[*He bows his head. ALICE gives him a cursory pat. She is still deeply indignant*]

ELGAR: Forgive poor old Mephistopheles for falling again.

ALICE: Well I do wish he wouldn't make such a habit of it.

ELGAR: Tell me I'm forgiven.

ALICE: Come on now, dear. Don't be silly. Straighten up now.

ELGAR: Forgive me.

ALICE: You are forgiven; But I do wish that you wouldn't make such a habit out of it. I've dedicated my life to you.

ELGAR: Every time you say that it makes me feel like a bloody cathedral!

ALICE: Don't blow up again, darling.

[*A sharp knock. The door opens sharply. The lizard swings. SHAW looks in. His fancy dress is Nero with his lyre*]

SHAW: Do I smell burning?

ALICE: Oh, Bernard, I wonder if you'd mind...

ELGAR: Why here's a man who can play the lyre.

SHAW: And here's a man who can explain the Rondo. Can't wait any longer. The only reason I came to this absurd party and submitted myself to this indignity was to hear from the horse's mouth why you wrote that Rondo.

ELGAR: You know me, Shaw. For money.

SHAW: Rubbish. You terrified that audience. Made them feel extremely uncomfortable. That's not like you.

ELGAR: Isn't it?

SHAW: What did you want to put into my head?

ELGAR: Only the dreadful beating that goes on in mine.

[*ALICE gives a cry and goes into a corner*]

SHAW: What's the matter? Were you in the middle of a domestic turmoil? You should have said. The Rondo is new Elgar. Suffering in psychic synthesis. Awful! The soul stretched on the rack. What I want to know is what you've seen. Where did that fearful sound come from?

ELGAR: I haven't the faintest idea what you're jabbering about.

SHAW: Magnificently horrible music. Bloodcurdling. Wouldn't have your imagination for anything.

ALICE: You really mustn't talk to Edward that way.

[*ALICE exits*]

SHAW: Take it as a compliment. I fear the power of your visions. I draw back where you plunge on. The symphony is superb, and the best part, the Rondo. You're changing, moving on. That's good news. We can expect great things. Now tell me, let an old socialist in on the secret: Was your inspiration something that you'd picked up in the Athenaeum.

ELGAR: I get less inspiration there than you do, I should think.

SHAW: I was sure that you'd heard something alarming. Whitehall gossip, you know.

ELGAR: It came to me in my sleep.

SHAW: Alice mentioned a street musician playing when you were in Florence. You copied down a phrase or two, she says.

ELGAR: Don't know anything about that.

SHAW: You'd just got news of Jaeger's death.

ELGAR: Never heard so much over-heated bosh in my life.

SHAW: I think you're hiding something. I'll get it out of you, never fear. [*Pause. He looks at the papers*] Working? I can see you are. I won't get in the way any more. [*Looks at the lizard*] Friend of yours?

ELGAR: He likes you to close the door very slowly when you go.

[*SHAW takes the hint and leaves, a finger to his lips. Pause. ELGAR sits very still, looking up at the lizard*]

ELGAR: What do you say? Why did I write the Rondo?

[*The Rondo begins. Blinded soldiers from the Great War enter being led by blood-spattered nurses in a slow dance that parodies the fancy dress party which opened the play. During the dance the scene is changed to a wooded garden in Sussex, and the time is shifted forward to 1918.*

*The first major part of the garden set to be brought on is a wooden sawing-horse. As the curios and carpets are removed and replaced by garden furniture, a handyman enters with a log and a timber saw. He takes off his shirt. This is MARK. He starts to saw the log.*

*This is the garden of Brinkwells, a cottage near Fittleworth. ELGAR enters R with a violin and a canvas chair. MARK glances up and sees him, then works on.*

*The composer is sixty, white-haired and moustached, very erect, and well dressed in a long-sleeved white shirt with collar and tie, a waistcoat, knee-length corduroy trousers, long socks and brown leather boots. He places the chair in the middle of the stage and stands by it, watching MARK who continues to saw energetically. ELGAR puts the violin and bow on the chair and exits R. As he goes, MARK glances up and grins, then takes a breather. As ELGAR re-enters with papers. MARK starts sawing again*]

ELGAR: Find something else to do now, Mark.

MARK: There isn't anything.

ELGAR: Find something.

MARK: You'll need some wood for the fire soon enough.

[*He starts to saw. ELGAR looks hard at him, then picks up the violin and bow and walks over. MARK keeps his head down sawing hard. ELGAR taps him on the shoulder with the bow. MARK yanks the saw out of the cut*]

MARK: Don't you go prodding me.

ELGAR: Take a rest.

[*MARK wipes the sweat out of his eyes and sits on the log which he has been sawing. ELGAR returns to the chair in his own time. He sits down, raises the violin to his chin*]

MARK: That silver birch has still got sap in it. I would have thought it might have dried up by now.

[*ELGAR ignores him, looking down at his papers. He lowers the violin from his chin resignedly*]

MARK: What kind of wood do they make violins out of, then?

[*ELGAR looks up*]

ELGAR: Shut up and go away.

MARK: I was only asking.

ELGAR: I was only telling.

MARK: What are you working on?

ELGAR: Music, strangely enough.

MARK: What kind of music?

ELGAR: I don't know yet. Be quiet, there's a good chap.

MARK: Suppose you'll be gearing yourself up to write a song for when we win the war?

ELGAR: Shut up.

MARK: It's a secret, is it? I was only saying in the pub last night: He won't want the peace, long-term. Bad for business.

[*ELGAR stares at MARK*]

MARK: It won't suit you, will it? People won't need your stuff.

ELGAR: God, how I wish I could give you the sack!

MARK: Well you can't! You're only a short lease and I'm here permanent. This is what I get for serving my country: Dogsbody to all and sundry. Now you, you've got a nice job. You can sort it out however you want. Take this victory thing you're working on. Doesn't matter when the war actually finishes you can whip it out of your drawer and say: "I've just done this, special!" [*Laughs*]

ELGAR: You're an insufferable idiot! For God's sake, go away!

FR. JOHN: [*Offstage*] Hello! Anybody there?

[*A bicycle bell is rung from the same direction*]

ELGAR: See who that is and tell them to go away too.

[*MARK exits R*]

[*ELGAR follows something in his notes with the end of his bow, then writes a few notes*]

[*MARK re-enters*]

MARK: It's a priest.

ELGAR: What does he want?

MARK: He says that your wife asked him to come over.

ELGAR: Tell him that my wife is out and I'm working.

MARK: You tell him.

[*FATHER JOHN enters R. He is a young Jesuit with a firm, brisk manner*]

FR. JOHN: Hope I'm not intruding.

ELGAR: You are.

FR. JOHN: Sir Edward Elgar? My name is John from Arundel. The bishop sends his compliments and begs you to be kind to me.

ELGAR: My wife isn't in. You'll have to come back another time.

FR. JOHN: It's you whom I have cycled over to see. A good ten miles, you know? And that last stretch up the escarpment is a killer.

MARK: Do you want him thrown out?

ELGAR: I can manage.

[*MARK turns to go*]

ELGAR: Excuse me, Father. Some unfinished business. [*He walks alongside MARK as he exits*] Violins are made of spruce or pine on the front, sycamore or maple on the back. Be kind-hearted and bring us some lemonade. We have an over-heated Jesuit.

FR. JOHN: You do indeed. May I sit down on your grass?

[*MARK exits. ELGAR returns to the chair*]

ELGAR: Are you saying that I'm the one my wife asked you over to see?

FR. JOHN: [*Sitting on the grass*] Yes.

ELGAR: For what purpose?

FR. JOHN: For two reasons: Firstly, that Lady Elgar suspects that you are losing your faith; and secondly that you have been talking about ending your life.

ELGAR: [*Sitting down*] Oh, I'm always doing that.

FR. JOHN: Lady Elgar has said so. But she added that this time she believed you to be in real danger.

ELGAR: That's always been the case, as she knows full well.

FR. JOHN: Then, on this occasion, she must be particularly concerned.

ELGAR: I'll sort this out with my wife when she gets back. I'm sorry that you've had a wasted journey.

FR. JOHN: Not at all. It was an excellent bike ride and I needed the exercise.

ELGAR: It's mostly downhill on your way back.

FR. JOHN: Do you cycle yourself?

ELGAR: Oh, yes. Love it. I've done up to sixty miles a day.

FR. JOHN: I couldn't help overhearing what you were saying to your man. How strange that a fiddle should be made of different types of wood.

[*Pause*]

ELGAR: Have you been in Arundel long?

FR. JOHN: Six months. I was a chaplain with the Army in Mesopotamia but I got sick and had to come home.

ELGAR: Aren't you rather young to be sent on this kind of mission? Haven't they told you how crabby I am?

FR. JOHN: I have plenty of experience. Soldiers, you know. They're not all good natured. One gets quite thick skinned.

[*MARK enters with a tray of glasses and a jug of lemonade*]

MARK: Where do you want it?

ELGAR: Over here.

[*MARK walks slowly over, trying not to spill the lemonade. He listens in*]

FR. JOHN: Are you losing your faith, Sir Edward?

ELGAR: [*To MARK*] Hurry up, nosey! [*To FR. JOHN*] Lost it years ago.

FR. JOHN: Oh.

ELGAR: Had to. It was getting in the way.

FR. JOHN: We could talk. Lady Elgar forsees a crisis.

ELGAR: Well, there isn't one.

[*MARK is now standing beside the chair with the lemonade*]

ELGAR: One day I'll get you to do as you're told. Give it here.

FR. JOHN: Let me.

[*FR. JOHN stands up and takes the tray off MARK, then puts it on the grass. MARK goes over to the sawing-horse*]

FR. JOHN: [*Pouring the lemonade*] Disillusionment with God in war-time is only to be expected. Have you ever read Kierkegaard?

ELGAR: Never heard of him.

[*MARK picks up the saw and starts on the log*]

ELGAR: Stop that!

MARK: You're not working now. You're just sitting there chatting. This is my job for the day. I want to finish it.

ELGAR: I'll call you when you can get back to it. Now leave us alone, please.

[*MARK picks up his shirt and puts it on, and exits*]

FR. JOHN: [*Handing ELGAR a glass of lemonade*] Kierkegaard was a Dane. A Protestant, actually. I've been reading him lately. Quite an eye-opener. Hard. Very uncompromising. I suppose what he insists upon is absolute submission to the divine will, but that can only be done with any credit from a position of complete individual freedom, otherwise it means nothing. Lady Elgar gave us to believe that your will is as solid as a rock.

ELGAR: Have you got a copy of this Kierky... I could read?

FR. JOHN: Strangely enough there's one in my saddlebag.

ELGAR: Did you offer him to the troops in Mesopotamia?

FR. JOHN: No. I didn't come into contact with his work until I came home on sick leave. I'm afraid that they would have used him as lavatory paper. Cheers. Here's to divinity.

[*FR. JOHN raises his glass*]

ELGAR: I've thought about killing myself all my life. In fact, it's almost a daily routine. Why Alice should have suddenly decided to take me seriously, I don't know.

FR. JOHN: The search for pure being.

ELGAR: Eh?

FR. JOHN: Extremely attractive. It's in your work, of course. Often. That sweetness, uplift, soaring. It's all going somewhere ruled by dreams. But the dream, as our Protestant friend implies, requires a dreamer with his feet on the ground, or at least in the bed.

ELGAR: You know my work?

FR. JOHN: Everything that I've been able to lay my hands on. Have you ever met anyone else who's played your *Five Intermezzos for Wind Quintet* under a sickle moon at the oasis of Sidi-Ben-Sik?

ELGAR: What's your instrument?

FR. JOHN: Oboe. Not too good really.

ELGAR: Is that in your saddlebag as well?

FR. JOHN: No, I had to sell it when I needed some money. D'you know, I have an inkling that your man has put something odd in this lemonade. In fact, I do believe he's urinated in it.

[*FR. JOHN takes ELGAR's glass from him*]

I got the impression when I arrived that he's not too enamoured of Catholics.

ELGAR: I'm so sorry. He goes with the place, I'm afraid. We're only renting. Sometimes I wonder if he's right in the head.

FR. JOHN: When your faith went, did it all go at once or did you dismantle it piecemeal?

ELGAR: Listen, bung yirds!

FR. JOHN: I beg your pardon?

ELGAR: Bung yirds. And in the distance a bog darking. Can't you fear them Hather? [*Cups his ear*] If you listen hard you can fear the gig buns in Flanders.

FR. JOHN: [*Laughing*] Very good, Sir Edward.

ELGAR: No, no. Gery vood, Er Sdward. Glay the pame, dammit!

FR. JOHN: I can't think quickly enough.

ELGAR: They're just noises. What does it matter which way round you hear them? In the name of the Sather, the Fun and Gholy Host, amen.

FR. JOHN: Can you really hear the guns from here?

ELGAR: I can. And I can't do anything with it. Out-of-date, you see. My name's not Stravinsky or Schoenberg. I just write heart-stirring slop for the masses, music to go over the top to. Death music. None of it makes sense any more.

FR. JOHN: You don't have to keep up with what other composers are doing. Your style is your own. I'd recognise it anywhere.

ELGAR: So there you are. I feel a failure. I fail Ophelia. My creative life is over. You should ask to be sent back to the Army and the real people.

FR. JOHN: Did you expect a pastoral visit?

ELGAR: [*Filling his pipe*] The penny dropped when I saw the sign-post in the village. Eight miles to Arundel - bastion of English Catholicism. It was no accident that my wife and daughter picked this spot for me to spend the summer. To be honest I expected the Cardinal and the Duke of Norfolk to make a two-pronged attack.

FR. JOHN: And all you got was me.

ELGAR: Yes, all I got was you. A retired front-line Army chaplain. The Last Rites are your speciality, I suppose.

FR. JOHN: I was chosen because I know your music... indeed, I talk about it a lot, fanatically, some might say.

ELGAR: Don't feel that you have to flatter.

FR. JOHN: I'm not flattering. For me, you say: "Life is unbearably sweet, and, life is sacred."

ELGAR: I'll go along with the unbearable but the rest is pure tosh. Life isn't sweet, it's bitter, and it certainly isn't sacred to anyone, and never has been. What people want to hear now is what they truly enjoy: Their brutality bumped up!

[*ALICE ELGAR enters with WINDFLOWER and CARICE. ELGAR gets excitedly to his feet*]

ELGAR: Windflower!

[*He hurries over and embraces her, kissing on both cheeks*]

WINDFLOWER: Hello, Edward. What a lovely place.

ELGAR: Was the train on time?

ALICE: Five minutes late. I told the station master what I thought of that.

[*MARK carries on a case and boxes*]

ELGAR: Did you piss in the lemonade?

ALICE: Oh, Edward!

CARICE: Daddy, don't be so silly. Mark wouldn't do that.

ELGAR: The rogue has to be watched.

[*MARK pushes past with the luggage and puts it down*]

MARK: When you know where you want it put, give me a shout. I'm coopering round the back.

[*MARK exits R*]

ELGAR: Come inside.

WINDFLOWER: I'd rather stay out, Edward. You're looking tremendously well. There are roses in your cheeks.

ELGAR: That's blood-pressure. This is my personal confessor, would you believe? We'll need more chairs.

FR. JOHN: I'll get them, Sir Edward. Lady Elgar. Lady Stuart Wortley. Miss Carice? John of the Society of Jesus.

WINDFLOWER: Hello. Have we met?

FR. JOHN: I don't think so. I would have remembered.

ELGAR: You have the chair, Alice, darling. I'm going to take my Windflower for a walk to show her my booful estate. Why don't you have a chat with this hard-pedalling saver of souls? He's a good egg, aren't you? By the way; what's the name of that book?

FR. JOHN: *Fear and Trembling.*

ELGAR: Don't want too much of that today, do we?

[*ELGAR exits L with WINDFLOWER talking*]

ELGAR: Over here is a tree... Another tree... Oh, what a delight to have you all to myself... Oh, look! Would you believe it? Another tree.

[*ELGAR and WINDFLOWER exit L*]

[*ALICE sits down tiredly. CARICE stays close to her. FR. JOHN brings over two straight-backed chairs and puts them down close to ALICE*]

FR. JOHN: Lady Elgar, the Bishop sent me over from Arundel.

ALICE: Oh. I thought that he would come himself, seeing it is who it is.

FR. JOHN: He didn't feel properly equipped to deal with Sir Edward. I hasten to say that he was not afraid, only humble. The Bishop is tone-deaf.

ALICE: That's got nothing to do with it. [*Pause*] Is there anything can be done?

FR. JOHN: Sir Edward seems to think that we're too late.

ALICE: Take no notice of that. Some steps have to be taken.

FR. JOHN: I have persuaded him, I hope, to read a book by a Dane.

CARICE: Well, he likes books, certainly. He's always reading.

FR. JOHN: The other thing I would say is that he must be encouraged to love the world once more.

[*FR. JOHN looks towards where ELGAR has gone*]

ALICE: Beauty he must have. There is no sin, be assured. [*Pause*] I did ask the Cardinal to speak to him, but he was reluctant. He passed it on to the Bishop whom he thought the braver man; in error, it seems.

FR. JOHN: All I can say, Lady Elgar, is that I was not chosen at random.

ALICE: I have never heard a Jesuit prescribe love of the world as a means of redemption before. The church is changing its tune, isn't it?

FR. JOHN: He no longer believes. If he doesn't have the world what does he have?

ALICE: Then make him believe! That's your job! Or aren't you up to it?

[*Pause. FR. JOHN picks up ELGAR's violin and bow*]

FR. JOHN: I'll put his fiddle in the shade. He wouldn't want it to get warped.

[*FR. JOHN puts the violin under a bush*]

ALICE: Come back here, young man. Don't be upset. I apologise for being sharp.

[*FR. JOHN returns to the chair*]

ALICE: I'm not very well. [*Pause*] Without me Edward is going to get rather lost. He has his ups and downs, some of them very extreme. I know the rhythm, when to be strong, when to be weak, when to give him his own way. There is no one who can take my place except the church. Do you understand?

FR. JOHN: How ill are you, Lady Elgar?

ALICE: Don't worry, I know what I'm talking about. The main thing is Edward's work. He has to be in a fit state to compose something of great importance.

FR. JOHN: Oh? What's this? Has someone commissioned a new work? That's the best thing to lift his spirits.

ALICE: Ssssh! Don't mention anything. It's a secret so far.

FR. JOHN: I see.

ALICE: We don't want to put too much pressure on him while he's like he is.

FR. JOHN: Yes, I can understand that. I'm so glad to hear that a new piece is in the offing. A major work? May we hope for that?

ALICE: Very major.

FR. JOHN: All the Elgar lovers have been waiting for something serious from him for so long.

[*A band offstage suddenly strikes up with* Land of Hope and Glory *and soldiers in full dress uniform enter from R in line playing, led by a bandmaster twirling a mace. ALICE gets to her feet thrilled. The band marches round the garden then comes to a halt in formation, the bandmaster saluting with his mace*]

BANDMASTER: Band of the Worcestershire Regiment reporting, ma'am. Is Sir Edward Elgar within earshot? We have orders to cheer him up.

[*Snap blackout*]

# ACT TWO

*Except for a few moments the scene runs on from act one.*

BANDMASTER: Stand at ease! Stand easy!

[*The band relaxes and lowers their instruments to the ground. Pause*]

ALICE: Have you come far?

BANDMASTER: We marched up from the station, ma'am. It's quite a steep hill.

ALICE: Oh, yes. And playing your instruments as well. Gracious me.

[*CARICE holds out her hand for the bandmaster's mace*]

CARICE: What beautiful thing. May I have a look?

BANDMASTER: [*Reluctantly handing it over*] Be careful with it, miss. That was carried right through the retreat to Corunna.

FR. JOHN: Who's idea was this?

BANDMASTER: Orders, sir.

FR. JOHN: Can you play anything of Sir Edward's other than *Land of Hope and Glory*?

BANDMASTER: Yes, sir. We can.

FR. JOHN: What?

BANDMASTER: *Imperial March. The Banner of Saint George.* A few polkas.

ALICE: You must have some refreshment. There's some cider that Sir Edward brought down. Will that do? Mark, see to it, will you?

[*MARK exits*]

BANDMASTER: Most grateful, ma'am. Do you think Sir Edward will be back before long? We're supposed to entrain at Fittleworth at seventeen hundred hours.

ALICE: Oh, he'll be back long before that. I'm so sorry that he wasn't here to receive you. I will thank Field Marshall Haigh personally. It was most kind of him to respond in this way. Oh, I do wish Sir Edward were here to listen.

BANDMASTER: That was the idea, ma'am.

[*MARK enters with a barrel of cider and sets it up on the sawing-horse*]

MARK: Come and get it!

BANDMASTER: Fall out!

ALICE: Carice, darling, run along and see if you can find Daddy, will you? [*Pause*] No, perhaps not. [*Looks at FR. JOHN*] Oh, dear. Mark?

FR. JOHN: I shouldn't send him. Did you ask the Commander-in-Chief for the band particularly?

ALICE: All I said to Douglas Haigh was that my husband's depression should be treated as a national emergency. You'd think Edward would have heard the noise and come back, wouldn't you? Well, I certainly won't go looking for him. We'll just have to wait until they see fit to return. It really is most annoying.

FR. JOHN: [*To the BANDMASTER*] Do you know any of the wind quintets?

BANDMASTER: We've had a look at them, sir.

ALICE: Oh, they're so lively. It's years since I've heard them played.

BANDMASTER: We've had a go at the music Sir Edward wrote when he was in Powick Asylum as well, but you can only play it at concerts and we don't do many of those it being war-time.

ALICE: My husband was never *in* Powick, as you put it. He was conductor of the staff orchestra.

BANDMASTER: Yes ma'am. There's a man in this band who was taught by Sir Edward when they were in there together. He can remember him sitting under an old weeping ash at the front door for hours and looking at the Malvern Hills. Then he'd come in and tell them, "I've got a tune."

ALICE: You've got it all mixed up. Sir Edward gave charity concerts for the inmates. He was never one of them.

BANDMASTER: Yes, ma'am. Memory plays such tricks.

[*A bearded man in waders, a tweed jacket and a fisherman's hat full of flies, enters R. Behind him is a gillie carrying rods and a fishing basket*]

ALICE: He's come! Thank God, thank God!

[*ALICE hurries across and curtsies. CARICE curtsies*]

ALICE: Your Majesty. How good of you.

GEORGE: Where is he, then? I've got something for him. Caught a couple of trout down there but my gillie says they're diseased. Some kind of fungus.

GILLIE: They've been coming up like that for a few years. Must be summat in the sea, sire.

[*Once the BANDMASTER and the bandsmen realise that it is the King who has arrived, they stand up, holding their glasses, not quite knowing what to do*]

BANDMASTER: Attention! [*He picks up his mace*]

[*The bandsmen stand to attention, still holding their glasses*]

BANDMASTER: Er... instruments! The National Anthem!

GEORGE: No, no. I'm Mr Windsor now. Must get used to the new monicker. Accept these trout for dinner, Alice. You can cut the white bits off.

[*The bandsmen remain at attention. The gillie produces the trout*]

BANDMASTER: Stand at ease!

GEORGE: Tell them to sit down and enjoy their drinks.

ALICE: [*Taking the trout which are gill-strung together*] Thank you, sir. Will you do us the honour of dining with us?

GEORGE: Can't do that, I'm afraid. I'm booked. but I'll have a glass of whatever they're drinking. It was hot work down on the river.

ALICE: Mark, bring some cider.

MARK: It's getting cloudy.

GEORGE: That don't matter. Cider always looks like the water of a sick horse anyhow.

[*GEORGE sits down in the chair. FR. JOHN edges himself forward and coughs lightly*]

ALICE: Sir, may I introduce Father... I do apologise... what is...

FR. JOHN: John, of the Society of Jesus.

[*FR. JOHN bows*]

GEORGE: Yes, the Cardinal told me you'd be here doing what you could. Did you know, Alice, that this young man would have the Victoria Cross if he were not in holy orders?

ALICE: He neglected to tell me that.

GEORGE: So you know the Cardinal sent a brave fellow on this mission. Now, John, have you spoken to Elgar yet?

FR. JOHN: Yes, I have.

GEORGE: And what kind of religious shape is he in?

FR. JOHN: Somewhat low, I'd say. But he claims that to be almost his normal condition.

ALICE: Oh, nonsense!

GEORGE: So, if anyone wanted something from him, now would be as good a time as any?

FR. JOHN: [*Pause*] I think that might depend what it was.

GEORGE: Only music, in this case, eh, Alice? Only music. There are other composers, of course...

ALICE: Do talk to him yourself, sir. That would do the trick.

GEORGE: Me? What would I say? Become a Roman Catholic again? Can't do that. I'm boss of the Church of England.

[*MARK gives the King a glass of cider*]

GEORGE: Elgar's way above my head.

ALICE: He will be greatly honoured that you have come.

GEORGE: Had to do my bit, but it's a minefield, isn't it, John? One has to tread very carefully. But if Germany heard that Elgar was on the slippery slope it would be a nice propaganda coup for them.

ALICE: He'd be very flattered to hear you say that, sir.

GEORGE: Well, they've got all the dead world class composers, Beethoven and all that lot, but our big gun is at least alive... well, half alive...

ALICE: Edward will do what's expected of him, sir. I'm sure of that.

GEORGE: Good. [*He turns to the men of the band*] Where have you come from lads?

BANDMASTER: From the Marne, sir!

GEORGE: Did you meet the Americans?

BANDMASTER: Yes, sir.

GEORGE: A million of them have been sent over. They've brought their own bands and their own music, I should think. You'll have to play harder to be heard above the Americans. They tend to play very loud.

BANDMASTER: Yes, sir! They told us they'd come to win the war for us.

GEORGE: Did they indeed? I hope you had a reply to that.

BANDMASTER: Yes sir! We gave as good as we got.

GEORGE: Alice, I think it would be best if Elgar believed that I'd dropped in because I was fishing down below and heard that he was hereabouts. The business I wished to talk about can wait until the... military situation gets clearer.

ALICE: Whatever you think best, sir, though I think it should be put in his mind as a possibility. That would have a very good effect.

GEORGE: You're sure that the notion of writing something triumphant would buck him up?

ALICE: Oh, yes! Yes! It's exactly what he needs. May I mention it to him?

GEORGE: No, that had better come from me when the time is right. Tell you what I'll do: Stay a little while in case he returns. After all, I lugged my bad back up that hill to see him.

[*GEORGE sips his cider and looks around. In the hiatus ALICE hands the trout to MARK*]

FR. JOHN: Sir, I am a little in the dark. Obviously my interest is specific but do I take it that you are going to commission Sir Edward to compose an occasional piece?

GEORGE: Oh, I don't know. Only if he can come up with the goods. It would have to be cheery. Hit exactly the right note.

FR. JOHN: In the mood he's in it might be best if it were delayed...

GEORGE: [*Snappily*] Well, events will take care of that, won't they?

[*GEORGE moves away*]

ALICE: [*To FR. JOHN*] How dare you interfere! It's not your concern!

FR. JOHN: Excuse me, but it is. The man has humiliated himself as an artist... he's heartbroken about what he's done...

ALICE: Absolutely not so! Edward can write these things standing on his head!

GEORGE: Bandmaster!

BANDMASTER: [*Scrambling to his feet*] Sir!

GEORGE: I'm going to sit under a tree and enjoy my cider. Play something... something light. Don't want a headache.

BANDMASTER: Sir!

[*GEORGE sits under a tree and pulls his hat over his face*]

BANDMASTER: [*Whispering*] Get your instruments. Stay seated. We'll do *La Brunette* by Sir Edward.

[*ALICE sits down. CARICE and FR. JOHN sit down on the grass*]

GEORGE: If I doze off, don't let me sleep too long.

[*The band plays the first of the five quadrilles which make up* La Brunette]

[*The King sips at his cider as he listens, beating time with a finger and smiling*]

ALICE: Oh, good, he likes it.

[*The band plays on. The King falls asleep. ALICE signals to the BANDMASTER that the music should be quieter. ALICE, CARICE and FR. JOHN sit still in the sun while the King sleeps*]

[*SHAW enters from the wood in hiking gear with a rucksack and a walking stick. FRANK SCHUSTER totters on behind him, similarly dressed, very fatigued. SHAW looks down at the King and lightly touches his foot with his walking-stick*]

SHAW: Frankie, look at this. A king guarded only by musicians. Well, well.

ALICE: Oh, no! Not you!

[*ALICE hurries across and pulls SHAW away from the King*]

SHAW: Hello, Alice. How's Edward? Any better?

ALICE: What are you doing here?

SHAW: We're trying to get Frankie fit. The man's a physical wreck.

SCHUSTER: If I wasn't before, I am now! I must sit down for a minute.

CARICE: Would you like some cider?

SCHUSTER: I'd love...

SHAW: No, thank you, Carice. I'm only drinking at holy wells on this trip. You shouldn't either, Frankie. Remember your vow.

CARICE: This is Father John of the Society of Jesus.

SHAW: [*Shaking hands*] Hello. I'm George Bernard Shaw of the Society of Authors.

ALICE: We can't talk now. Couldn't you continue your walk and see us later in London?

SHAW: Don't worry, Alice. If he wakes up we'll hide behind a bush. I wouldn't want that old gentleman to die of apoplexy.

ALICE: It really is most inconvenient today. Come on, get to your feet and carry on.

[*ALICE lifts SCHUSTER to his feet*]

SCHUSTER: Have mercy, Alice. Let me have a little rest.

SHAW: All right, don't molest him. How far is't called to Fittleworth?

ALICE: Barely more than a mile and it's all downhill.

[*ALICE herds SHAW and SCHUSTER towards the exit R from the garden. SHAW kisses CARICE's hand on the way. FR. JOHN follows*]

FR. JOHN: May I walk a little of the way with you?

ALICE: [*Disapprovingly*] Don't be too long.

[*SHAW and SCHUSTER exit with FR. JOHN. ALICE returns to her chair with CARICE. SHAW, SCHUSTER and FR. JOHN re-enter on the apron. SCHUSTER sits down*]

SHAW: We earned a big black mark there, I fear. Won't be forgiven for several months. It works on a sliding scale with Alice. For making a giant social error involving the monarchy I'll probably be banished till Christmas.

FR. JOHN: Lady Elgar was keen to get rid of you. That surprises me. What is she afraid of?

SHAW: I design my pilgrimages, young man. They all have a purpose. We're not on the inside, you see. Alice has created the inside, except for... well... the romantic heartland. There she is no longer queen. But she is overall empress, isn't she, Frankie?

SCHUSTER: Absolutely. I'm sure I've got another blister.

SHAW: Walk on it until it bursts. That's the best way.

FR. JOHN: If you had been able to see Sir Edward, what would you have said to him?

SHAW: To comfort him?

FR. JOHN: Yes.

SHAW: Not for your ears.

FR. JOHN: I'm only interested in giving the man the strength to write more music. That's his salvation as far as I'm concerned.

SHAW: Do you know the Rondo?

FR. JOHN: I do.

SHAW: I'd say to him - the Rondo is a terrible gift.

FR. JOHN: From whom?

SHAW: Here's where our swords cross. Are you sure you want this?

FR. JOHN: I want it.

SHAW: The Rondo was a vision granted him by a power greater than his God; a vastly evil, destructive power, so it might seem. But in its cruelty is regeneration, perhaps. Then I'd add - go on making the music, no matter what happens.

FR. JOHN: Now I can brag that I actually *agreed* with George Bernard Shaw.

SHAW: You'll be excommunicated. Frankie, I think you can trust this young man with what you want to tell Edward.

SCHUSTER: Oh, I don't know about that. It's a legal matter.

SHAW: A will isn't a legal matter. It's an affair of the heart. Tell him.

SCHUSTER: Oh, very well. I just wanted to inform him... no, this isn't how I imagined it.

SHAW: Tell him! You know how Elgar frets about money. It will quieten his mind. Give him a boost.

SCHUSTER: I've recently drawn up a will... keep this to yourself, won't you?

SHAW: This is a secret of the confessional, Frankie. he can't tell anyone but God and Edward.

SCHUSTER: Not Alice. But I expect Edward will tell her anyway. I wanted him to know that he'll be safe... it's quite a lot of money, this bequest. So he needn't worry. That's all.

SHAW: If you predecease him, which you won't once I've finished with you. On your feet.

SCHUSTER: Couldn't I just die here? Strikes me it would be better for everybody.

[*SHAW helps SCHUSTER to his feet*]

FR. JOHN: I'll find a time to tell Sir Edward. I have to assume that he will believe me.

SHAW: He will. Frankie's seen to that over many years. *Pax vobiscum.*
[*SHAW exits with SCHUSTER to L. FR. JOHN exits R and re-enters the garden*]
[*The band is still playing very softly so as not to wake the sleeping King*]

ALICE: [*To FR. JOHN*] Father, I forbid you to meddle. I asked for help from the Church with Edward's religious state, not his music. Do you understand? [*Pause. She looks at the King*] It's time to wake him. Could you do that for me?
[*FR. JOHN goes over to the King, looks down at him, pauses, then crosses to the BANDMASTER and whispers. The BANDMASTER silences the band*]

BANDMASTER: P.C. One.
[*The band play* Land of Hope and Glory. *FR. JOHN watches the King to see if it wakes him, but GEORGE slumbers on. FR. JOHN returns to the BANDMASTER and signals him to play louder. This still does not wake GEORGE. FR. JOHN signals that the band should play fortissimo and the BANDMASTER responds. The King still does not wake*]

ELGAR: [*Screaming off*] No! No!
[*WINDFLOWER runs on*]

WINDFLOWER: Stop! Please stop!
[*The band thunders on*]

ELGAR: [*Screaming off*] No! No!

WINDFLOWER: In the name of God stop playing that bloody tune!
[*The band look to the BANDMASTER for instructions. He quietens them to a fraction*]

WINDFLOWER: Shut them up!
[*The BANDMASTER points at the still sleeping King*]

BANDMASTER: Can't stop. Playing by royal command.

WINDFLOWER: You must! Sir Edward can't stand it!

BANDMASTER: Well, he wrote it! Anyway, can't stop. Orders.

ALICE: [*Whispering*] It's the King. He's come down specially to see Edward.

WINDFLOWER: I know! Stop them playing that music please! It's upsetting Edward dreadfully. He's in the wood howling his heart out.

ALICE: [*To the BANDMASTER*] Stop at once!
[*The band stops playing*]

GEORGE: [*Taking his hat off his eyes*] What's going on?

[*WINDFLOWER curtsies to the King.*]

ALICE: My husband isn't well, sir. I'm terribly sorry.

[*Pause. GEORGE gets to his feet*]

GEORGE: Needs some peace and quiet I should think. Hm, I was miles away. Must be off. Thank you for the cider.

ALICE: He will be desolé to have missed you, sir.

GEORGE: Tell him I'm staying at Petworth House. Do come over if you can. We can talk better there, I think. Afternoon to you all. Now you chaps, you can't cheer Elgar up, but you can me. Do you know *It's a Long Way to Tipperary*?

BANDMASTER: Yes, sir.

GEORGE: Good. You can play me down to me motor. Good afternoon.

[*Sets off to exit*]

[*The BANDMASTER brings the band to attention*]

BANDMASTER: Right turn! At the pace of the monarch, march!

[*The band strikes up and marches off, led by the BANDMASTER twirling his mace. As they go ELGAR emerges from the trees and raises his hand, trying to attract someone's attention in the band, but he is not seen*]

ELGAR: [*Shouting over the music*] Oi! Paul, don't rush off! Let's have a word!

[*ELGAR exits after the band*]

CARICE: What's the matter with Daddy?

ALICE: This is all my fault. I should have known better.

FR. JOHN: Can I help?

WINDFLOWER: No. You're part of the problem.

[*ELGAR re-enters*]

ELGAR: That was Paul Hooker. I used to teach him. Don't let him go. I must see him. I must see him. Please run after them and ask him to come back... please!

CARICE: Don't worry, Daddy. We'll get him to come back. Don't worry.

[*CARICE and ELGAR exit*]

WINDFLOWER: Alice, this is the worst I've ever seen him.

ALICE: Please don't let him realise how much he's upset you. That wouldn't help at all.

WINDFLOWER: Did you know that he has a rope tied to a tree back there, and a barrel to stand on?

ALICE: If you let me know where, I'll get Mark to go and remove them.

WINDFLOWER: Aren't you shocked?

ALICE: After thirty years with Edward? My dear, Death has been like one of the family.

WINDFLOWER: Hearing that tune does terrible things to him. He feels so guilty.

ALICE: No, no. That wasn't it. *Land of Hope and Glory* is one of his favourites.

WINDFLOWER: Then why did he break down?

ALICE: Just too much of everything. He'll be back on his feet very quickly, you'll see.

WINDFLOWER: Alice, the man's on a knife-edge. Can't you see that?

ALICE: You saw him just now. He's better already. As soon as there's something to occupy his mind, he recovers. That's his great strength. Here, let me help you with your hat.

WINDFLOWER: I'm amazed that you take it so coolly.

[*WINDFLOWER sits down. ALICE puts the veiled hat on for her*]

ALICE: You must adjust to his moods. Get out of the way. Don't try to do my part when he's blackest. You haven't got the experience to fall back on. Be his champagne, darling.

WINDFLOWER: And what are you?

ALICE: Oh, in the end I expect I'll be his hemlock.

[*ELGAR enters with an Aeolian harp. He puts it on a chair*]

ELGAR: Has Paul Hooker turned up yet?

ALICE: No. Do you want to work?

[*WINDFLOWER gets out of the chair and moves to get away from ELGAR*]

ELGAR: In a way, but there's no breeze for my Aeolian harp so I'll have a word with my Windflower. I think I might have frightened her.

ALICE: You did; and it was very silly of you.

ELGAR: I know. Is Edu's braut 'mmensely dispeased? Offaly contwite, he is. *Mea culpa,* mumsy.

ALICE: Very well. But you're not to think that you've got away with it.

[*ELGAR leans down for ALICE to kiss him on the cheek*]

ALICE: The King wants us to go over to Petworth. I'll make the arrangements. What about Saturday?

ELGAR: Saturday?

ALICE: Yes, I think so. I'll see if I can get us in to dine.

[*ALICE exits R towards the house. WINDFLOWER stands still under her veil. ELGAR walks around the garden picking up the glasses*]

ELGAR: That's all my Hereford cider gone. What a lot of guzzley-guts.

[*He puts the glasses down by the barrel, then returns to where he has spotted his violin under the bush. He picks it up. The light starts to go*]

ELGAR: I expect you're not talking to me. What a case.

[*WINDFLOWER makes no response*]

[*MARK enters from R with the gramophone*]

MARK: Where d'you want this putting?

ELGAR: Here.

[*MARK puts the gramophone on the table*]

ELGAR: Ask Lady Elgar to give you the record of my Sospiri.

MARK: What?

ELGAR: Sospiri. It means "a sigh."

MARK: I don't care what it means.

[*MARK exits R. ELGAR adjusts the gramophone and winds it up*]

ELGAR: *Sospiri* also means "a yearning." I've been lost without you, Windflower.

WINDFLOWER: Whatever I can do.

[*MARK enters with the record and hands it to ELGAR, then exits R. ELGAR wipes it with his handkerchief. He puts the record on, then sits down and stares at WINDFLOWER. Suddenly she crosses and takes the needle off the gramophone*]

ELGAR: Why did you do that?

WINDFLOWER: This is ludicrous!

ELGAR: Now you've broken the spell.

WINDFLOWER: Good. [*Sits down*] Leave me alone for a while.

ELGAR: Are you looking at me from under there?

[*Pause. ELGAR stalks round her*]

WINDFLOWER: Yes. I could be frowning.

ELGAR: What do you see? A man who's not much use to you? A man who's not much use to himself?

WINDFLOWER: Would I waste my time on such a fellow?

ELGAR: [*Taking her hands*] D'you know how many symphonies Haydn wrote? A hundred and four! He never resorted to hack-work. [*Pause*] Are you still under there?

WINDFLOWER: If it's money, Edward.

ELGAR: No, no... perish the thought. I want you to be my god.

[*He kneels by her*]

WINDFLOWER: I don't think I can manage that. I'm very earthbound.

ELGAR: I need someone. With Alice the music's all wonderful, gorgeous. I need someone to... I need...

[*PAUL HOOKER , the bandsman, enters R, breathless*]

WINDFLOWER: You have a visitor.

ELGAR: Paul!

[*WINDFLOWER stands up and walks to the back of the garden. FR. JOHN enters with PAUL HOOKER's bassoon and gives it to him, having carried it on his bicycle*]

FR. JOHN: I'll leave you. Would you mind if I went for a stroll and came back?

[*ELGAR takes no notice of what FR. JOHN has said. He is looking at PAUL HOOKER*]

ELGAR: When I heard the band play *Tipperary* I said to myself - I'd know that style of bassoon playing anywhere. Pure Powick!

PAUL: [*In a strong Worcestershire accent*] Hello, Ted.

[*ELGAR puts his violin down and crosses to PAUL HOOKER and offers his hand. FR. JOHN exits R. PAUL HOOKER awkwardly shakes ELGAR's hand*]

ELGAR: Come and sit down and tell me everything that's happened to you.

PAUL: Not a lot to tell.

ELGAR: It was a kind thought to have the Worcesters come and play for me. What a surprise. And you've kept well all these years?

PAUL: Well enough. And you?

ELGAR: Termenjously well, Paul. Termenjously.

PAUL: Aha! You remember!

ELGAR: Lummy days, I do.

PAUL: You didn't like the old *Brunette* we played? Was it done that bad?

ELGAR: Not at all. I wasn't ready for it. A bit overwhelmed, let's say. Voices from the past, and your sulphurous bassoon. Never mind all that. Tell me about yourself. Are you married?

PAUL: No, Ted. I always sheered away from having children. Wouldn't be fair. Couldn't take the risk they'd turn out like me.

ELGAR: Think of the places you must have seen. When you enlisted, what twenty...

PAUL: Twenty five!

ELGAR: ...years ago, you were off fighting and bassooning in South Africa, weren't you?

PAUL: Yes. I had five years out there.

ELGAR: All those exotic, faraway lands. Only place I've got to know is Germany.

[*Short cold pause from PAUL*]

PAUL: The Bandmaster asked if you could fix me up with lodgings for the night, if you know some place. The rest of them have got to go back on the train.

ELGAR: You'll stay here with me.

PAUL: We usually have our snap at this time, Ted, and I didn't remember to bring mine. Have you got anything to eat?

ELGAR: Lots. You'll have dinner with us, of course, but that's not till eight.

PAUL: I can't wait that long, Ted.

ELGAR: Bread and cheese?

PAUL: Capital, Ted.

ELGAR: An' a drop more of the old zuyder?

PAUL: That would do fine.

[*ELGAR exits R with his violin. PAUL looks at the Aeolian harp, smiles, touches the strings, blows through them, then carries it over to WINDFLOWER*]

PAUL: Things don't change, do they? At Powick in the old days, Ted always had his head in this contraption. He said he could hear music that was written on the skies.

WINDFLOWER: What is this place, Powick?

PAUL: Biggest madhouse in the Midlands, ma'am. And he always had an eye for the women, did Ted. He was in and out of love like a dog at a fair. Never a time when he didn't have someone in the sights of his French horn. Girls and his band is what Ted lived for in those days.

WINDFLOWER: What age was he?

PAUL: Oh, twenty-odd. Just a great boy.

WINDFLOWER: Was he writing music?

PAUL: I'll say he was. Yards of it! And trying it out on us at all hours. Gave us no peace. I expect you think a bit differently about him now. He won't have told you about Powick.

WINDFLOWER: Making music in a madhouse is very up-to-date these days. It seems Sir Edward was the first to do it and now everyone is copying him. So, he's gone up in my estimation. What's the matter? Didn't you want to come back and see him?

PAUL: No. Not when he couldn't be bothered to listen and told us to shut up. Got my goat, that did. He was ashamed of us.

WINDFLOWER: Ashamed? God, the poor man was overcome. Worcester is where his heart is.

PAUL: Then what's he doing here with you lot?

[*MARK enters with a plate of bread and cheese. PAUL puts the Aeolian harp down*]

MARK: Lady Elgar says you're to come round the back with me.

PAUL: [*To WINDFLOWER*] See what I mean? [*To MARK*] Right, mate. Just what I needed.

[*MARK leads PAUL off R. Lights dim. ELGAR enters from R with a notebook. He licks his finger and holds it up to the breeze. Picking up the Aeolian harp he sets it up on the chair to catch the breeze*]

WINDFLOWER: Edward.

ELGAR: Ssssh. [*Listens to the harp*] Very faint.

WINDFLOWER: Do be careful with that chap from the band.

ELGAR: Darling, would you mind taking yourself off?

WINDFLOWER: Can't it wait for a moment?

ELGAR: When did the wind wait for anyone?

[*WINDFLOWER exits. ELGAR listens to the harp*]

ELGAR: Come on. Speak to me.

[*A faint moan from the harp as a night breeze begins*]

ELGAR: Terribly faint.

[*The harp moans again*]

ELGAR: E flat? Again? The same key as the Second Symphony? That's cruel, even for you.

[*The harp moans again*]

[*ALICE enters dressed for bed, looking ill. She stands and watches ELGAR. The harp moans then fades*]

ELGAR: Don't go! I didn't catch that!

[*The harp moans strongly, flurrying*]

ELGAR: But what's the solo voice?

[*The harp falls silent*]

ELGAR: Oh, damn!

ALICE: I'm going to bed now.

ELGAR: Eh?

ALICE: Don't get cold out here.

ELGAR: Had the strangest advice.

ALICE: Lock the door when you come to bed.

ELGAR: Good night, Chicky. I'll be late, I think.

ALICE: Try not to wake me, there's a good boy.

[*ALICE exits R. ELGAR listens to the harp again*]

ELGAR: Come on, give me more to go on.

[*MARK and PAUL HOOKER enter, both drunk*]

PAUL: There y'are. I told you didn't I? He's at it again. Not changed a bit. A man in his position sitting in the dark talking to a box. What would you think?

MARK: I'd say he was fucking mad.

ELGAR: Ssssh!

MARK: Don't you shush me. I had just about enough of you today! You've been a right old sod.

PAUL: He was always like that. Fucking bossy. Got beyond himself now, though. Proper bloody mad, he is. Have you heard anything coming out of that box yet, Ted?

ELGAR: Do be quiet!

PAUL: What's in there? Your old Dad's piano tuning things?

MARK: He's not cottoning on to a word you say.

PAUL: Didn't mean to disturb you, Sir Ted. We're only taking a turn in the garden before retiring.

ELGAR: Can't you see I'm working?

PAUL: Call that working? [*To MARK*] What would you call it?

MARK: I'd call it fucking about.

ELGAR: Can't you keep your voice down? Come and listen to this.

PAUL: You'd think that in forty years he'd have improved a bit. Poor old Ted, you just never growed up, did you?

ELGAR: What instrument can you hear? Can't make up my mind.

PAUL: Don't ask me, Ted. I got all my marbles, a'nt I?

ELGAR: It's beautiful.

PAUL: Yes, I bet it is.

[*The harp moans louder*]

ELGAR: There! Did you hear it?

PAUL: Oh, isn't that lovely?

[*PAUL and MARK snigger*]

ELGAR: Go away, will you!

PAUL: Don't talk down to me, Ted. I'm not taking orders from you. I had enough of that in the old days, you bad tempered old bugger.

MARK: He's by far the worst tenant we've had here. never a word of thanks, no matter how much I put myself out.

PAUL: No one ever gets any thanks from him. He only talks to the wind. [*Farts*] Talk to that one then, Ted!

[*FR. JOHN steps out of the shadows*]

FR. JOHN: That's enough! Time you men went to bed.

PAUL: [*An automatic reaction*] Sir!

[*ELGAR is obliviously humming to himself, responding to what he hears on the Aeolian harp*]

FR. JOHN: Because you're stupid-drunk I'll say no more about this but you must learn to respect the sufferings of others. Dismiss!

[*PAUL and MARK exit R*]

[*FR. JOHN kneels a little way off. On the wind comes the* Nimrod Variation]

FR. JOHN: *Kyrie eleison, Christe eleison, Kyrie eleison*, Holy Mary pray for him, All Holy Angels pray for him...

[*A German soldier in mud-spattered uniform and carrying a rifle enters from the woods*]

FR. JOHN: Choirs of the righteous pray for him, All Apostles, all Evangelists, pray for him...

[*The German soldier walks over to ELGAR and stands beside him*]

FR. JOHN: All Holy Innocents pray for him, All Holy Martyrs, all Holy Confessors, All Holy Hermits, all Holy Virgins, All ye Saints of God, pray for him.

[*The German soldier rests on arms reversed. It is JAEGER's ghost*]

JAEGER: Hello, Edward.

ELGAR: [*Not looking up*] Where've you been all this time?

JAEGER: No-man's land.

ELGAR: [*Looking up at him*] Me too.

JAEGER: The King is going to offer you a commission to write a victory hymn.

ELGAR: Really?

JAEGER: Say no.

ELGAR: No.

JAEGER: Refuse.

ELGAR: I could do with the money.

JAEGER: You have squandered your genius!

ELGAR: It was that kind of genius.

JAEGER: Did it have to be wasted on such trivia?

ELGAR: Sssssh! Now you've made me miss something. Can't you see I'm working?

JAEGER: More *quatsch*? More bilge? More Elgar favourites?

ELGAR: Yes. No. Probably. What does it matter now?

JAEGER: The Battle of Somme cried out for a great symphony. Now the Marne does the same.

ELGAR: I'm not the one to write it.

JAEGER: They're both rivers. The wind blows through the reeds. Boys lie listening just as you did, hoping to hear the sounds of deliverance. When they die in such thousands don't you feel it in the air? Have you never been moved by their plight?

[*ELGAR turns his head away*]

JAEGER: Then you have failed!

ELGAR: Music has failed. This war is beyond it.

JAEGER: Nothing is beyond the competence of music.

ELGAR: Then where are your great German composers now? Show me the new Beethoven standing in the ruins. The Brahms of the trenches.

JAEGER: They will arise.

ELGAR: Never. Every heart is broken. Europe is mud. Jagpot... seven years ago you walked out... seven long, lean years. You shouldn't have deserted me. I might have fought my way back with a bit of help.

JAEGER: Tcha! You'd taken your decision. And what have you done since then? A bouquet for Poland, an encouragement for brave little Belgium. Why didn't you ask for a piano room in the War Office? How ashamed I've been. What do you think I've been fighting against? Who have I seen beyond the barbed wire? You!

ELGAR: Yes... but things are changing... I haven't given up entirely... I've written a string-quartet, would you believe?

JAEGER: A string quartet. One? Only one?

ELGAR: A piano quintet... a violin sonata... not at all bad.

JAEGER: My, this is corn in Egypt.

ELGAR: Well, it's a start. The war's almost over now.

JAEGER: Or for you, just begun?

[*Pause*]

JAEGER: So a hymn for victory would be quite out of place, wouldn't it?

ELGAR: I suppose it would. But I couldn't face a symphony.

JAEGER: Write for me. [*As he goes*] Write for me.

[*JAEGER's ghost returns to the woods. The* Nimrod Variation *fades, but not completely. FR. JOHN continues to pray. ELGAR crouches over the Aeolian harp*]

ELGAR: Nimrod, mighty hunter, forgive.

[*He weeps as the light fades to blackout. The* Nimrod Variation *continues, then fades to silence*]

[*Lights fade up on dawn in the garden and birdsong. A small tent has been pitched, using a cross-stage clothes-line. The barrel and the Aeolian harp and three chairs have gone*]

[*ELGAR enters from R with the canvas chair, his violin and a loosely tied pile of score paper. He is wearing pyjamas and a dressing gown. He sets up the chair, puts the papers and violin on it, then exits, returning immediately with a small table. He puts this by the chair, then moves the papers and violin onto it and unties the papers. He takes sheets of handwritten music from the pile and pegs them to the clothes-line, then pegs other sheets near the tent. The remainder he sets out in a semi-circle front stage. FR. JOHN pokes his head out of the tent as ELGAR walks away*]

FR. JOHN: What's this? An eviction order?

ELGAR: I've got someone coming down today to help me play a few ideas through. My old fiddle isn't enough. Did you sleep well?

FR. JOHN: [*Climbing out of the tent and buttoning up his trousers*] I never sleep in a tent quite as restfully as I sleep in a bed. I seem to hover, if you know what I mean.

ELGAR: Could you make yourself scarce for a while. There's some tea in the pot. I just want to get on with this thing I'm doing.

FR. JOHN: Certainly. May I wash in your sink?

ELGAR: By all means.

[*FR. JOHN goes back into the tent and brings out a wash-bag and his other clothes in a bundle, and exits R. ELGAR walks from one sheet of music to another, following his own notation in his head*]

ELGAR: Oh, rot... No, no, I didn't quite catch it...

[*PAUL HOOKER enters R, fully dressed, carrying his bassoon*]

PAUL: Pardon, sir.

ELGAR: Eh?

PAUL: Got to move off, sir.

ELGAR: Oh. Must you?

PAUL: Have to be agooin'.

ELGAR: Agooin'? Good luck to you. [*Shakes hands*]

PAUL: I should never touch cider, as you know.

ELGAR: Think nothing of it.

PAUL: It was my undoing in the old days. You were kind to me and I've repaid you with insults. I'm very ashamed and would like your forgiveness. You're a great man and I'm proud of you.

ELGAR: Good of you to say so. Cheerio.

[*PAUL HOOKER turns and exits*]

ELGAR: [*Watching him go*] Whiffley-whiffley-whiffley, zum-zum-zum.
[*ELGAR then works on, going from music sheet to music sheet. The birdsong gets louder. He stops, listens, makes an alteration on one of the sheets. ALICE enters R in a dressing gown carrying rubber boots*]

ALICE: Edu, what shoes have you got on?

ELGAR: Good morning, booful. Things are happening!

ALICE: You mustn't wear those slippers on the wet grass. Come over here and put these on. Whose tent is that?

ELGAR: The Jesuit's.
[*ELGAR comes over to ALICE and changes his slippers for the boots*]

ALICE: Did he ask if he could put it there?

ELGAR: Not that I remember.

ALICE: He should have got our permission first, don't you think?

ELGAR: Of course. Thanks for looking after that chap from Worcester. He seemed to enjoy himself. Good sort. Salt of the earth. I wuz jus' 'membering zumthing 'e a'told me once after a music lesson that made me ache wi' continuous an' strenuous risibility.

ALICE: I'll leave you to get on with your work, shall I?

ELGAR: See, you're off straightways! 'Twere a classic agrarian saga. My version were called *The Five Plum Trees*. 'Oo sure that 'oo wouldn't like to hear it? Though I might set it for the flute, or the clarinet, or both. Or brass, perhaps.

ALICE: Tell me your story if you will, Edu. I'm listening.

ELGAR: Have got time? It just arrived back in my 'ead when I said farewell to 'im. I'll have to do the old Wuster lingo. Sorry. I know it sets your teeth on edge. Wellity-well! Came a stranger. Meets a man on a country road. Most grandly pointed to five plum trees standing in a hedge. "Fellow", he says, "how came those to be there?" Sure you want me to go on?

ALICE: Yes, it sounds most entertaining.

ELGAR: The country man came back at him. "They plum trees wuz originerly planted in a fine meadow near Pershore weer the land be very kind to plums an' good bearings o' capital fruit they had on 'em. But misfortune for the farmer mon as owned 'm, theer wuz an owd rookery in some owd elms overanighst 'em an' soon as they plums wuz ripe they damned owd crows 'ud come an' settle on the branches of they plum trees an' peckety-peck-peck they 'ud go till they a yut a' the fruit there wuz. So the farmer mon sez to i'self, 'damn me if I don't set bird-lime for they owd crows', an' so 'e did, an' one fine day they owd crows a-settled on the bird-lime that 'ad been smeared on they plum trees by the farmer mon an' they got stuck fast an' could not move a foot. 'Lummy days', sez the farmer mon, 'I ha' got 'em this time! I'll git my owd gun an' shut the lot on 'em'. So off he guz to fetch 'un. They owd crows heerd what wuz said an' set up cawin' an' a-flappin' theer wings fit to bust an' soon as they see the farmer mon come back wi' 'iz muzzle-loader they made such a termenjous desperate flappin' that up come all five plum trees by the roots an' whiffley-whiffley-whiffley, zum-zum-zum, off they flies, plum trees an' all over toward Wuster. After they bin agooin' fur a while there comes a smartish shower 'o rain that washed most 'o the bird-lime away an' clunk-clunk-clunk down drops they five plum trees into this very 'edge where you see 'em now, an' they took root right here, but damme if I ever heerd what 'appened to those owd crows arterwards."

[*ELGAR laughs with enjoyment. ALICE smiles a little*]

ALICE: Very good. Wouldn't it have been a very bucolic piece if you'd set it?

ELGAR: [*Taking her in his arms*] Oh, Chicky, why can't I ever make you laugh?

ALICE: I'm a very serious person, Edu. And most serious fo all about you.

ELGAR: But it would help if you laughed with me... at me!... now and then.

ALICE: You are my life.

ELGAR: Oh, what a responsibility! [*Pause*] You deserve a better mon.

ALICE: Have you ever heard me complain?

ELGAR: Your poor old phiz is a bit careworn. [*Puts his arm round her and walks her a little*] Did you have a bad night? You were up and about.

ALICE: Edu, could we go to Rome?

ELGAR: Of course we could.

ALICE: Next week?

ELGAR: Well, we might be better advised to wait until the war is over.

ALICE: I'd like to take a closer look at the Sistine ceiling.

ELGAR: Wot, Michaelangelo an' such like? My darlin', that's just foreign rudeness on a gigantic scale. All it's good for is keeping the rain out.

ALICE: I'd love to go again. We had such a splendid time.

[*ELGAR bursts out laughing*]

ALICE: What's so amusing?

ELGAR: You're such an old fraud.

ALICE: Am I?

ELGAR: Am I subtle? Am I Machiavel? Off we go to see the Sistine Chapel. Here we are, craning our necks to look at God creating the

universe, surprise, surprise, here's old Pope Benedick playing my
setting of *Ave Maria* on his harmonica. You always want the top man,
don't you, Chicky? But leave it to the Jesuit here. He's cracked harder
cases than mine, no doubt.

ALICE: Did you have a good talk with him?

ELGAR: Yes, I think so. But he prefers people who've been shot.

ALICE: It was very late when you came to bed. I wondered where he was
going to stay but I was too tired to worry about it. I'll leave you to your
work but you mustn't let yourself get cold. Promise?

ELGAR: I promise. Kiss-kiss.

[*ALICE puts her face up to be kissed, then exits with the slippers. ELGAR
hurries back to his music*]

ELGAR: It's all in pieces! Nothing, nothing, nothing. No connections.
No theme!

[*He goes and sits in the chair*]

[*FR. JOHN enters with his wash-bag*]

FR. JOHN: Lady Elgar has just ticked me off for putting my tent up on
your lawn. Hardly croquet standard, is it?

[*He moves a sheet of music that is pinned near the entrance to his tent*]

ELGAR: [*With sudden sharpness*] You were glad enough to sleep on it!

FR. JOHN: Yes, I suppose I was.

ELGAR: I said, you were glad enough to sleep on it!

FR. JOHN: I heard you the first time.

ELGAR: Get out!

FR. JOHN: I beg your pardon?

ELGAR: Get out of here! Take your damned tent and go!

[*In a fit of fury ELGAR rushes over to the tent and tears it down, hurling the
tangle at FR. JOHN's feet*]

FR. JOHN: Calm down, Sir Edward!

ELGAR: What do you know? Nothing! Nothing at all!

[*FR. JOHN searches in the tangle for the sheet of ELGAR's music that was
pegged to the clothes-line near the tent and hands it to him*]

FR. JOHN: Here you are. Now, if you will give me a few moments I will
pack my things and get out of your way.

[*ELGAR snatches the sheet of music out of FR. JOHN's hand*]

ELGAR: How dare you impose yourself on us!

FR. JOHN: I was invited, if you remember. Could you possibly leave the
garden until I go? You've not only made yourself very angry but me as
well. I dislike that considerably.

[*ELGAR fumes, then turns abruptly to go*]

FR. JOHN: A moment. There is a duty I must discharge. A Mr. Schuster came by. In the absence of anyone better he asked me to tell you, in confidence, that he has made provision for you in his will. He implied that the sum concerned was large.

ELGAR: Hm. Good old Frankie. Who else has he got to leave it to?

[*ELGAR starts sticking the music up again, this time close to where the tent had been pitched. Then he starts to roll up the ground-sheet that had been left behind when the tent was pulled down*]

FR. JOHN: [*Angrily*] I'll do that. Please leave me be for a while.

ELGAR: [*Falling to his knees*] Help me, Father.

[*FR. JOHN goes quickly across to him and takes his hands. ELGAR is shaking. He kisses FR. JOHN's hands*]

ELGAR: Forgive me.

FR. JOHN: You are forgiven.

ELGAR: I know not what I do.

FR. JOHN: Stand up. You'll get rheumatism.

[*FR. JOHN helps ELGAR to his feet*]

ELGAR: I'm not fit for human society, you know. What can I do about myself?

FR. JOHN: Keep writing the music, then we can forgive you anything.

ELGAR: No! I don't want that.

[*FR. JOHN goes back to folding up his tent. ELGAR helps him*]

ELGAR: To be a nomad must be wonderful. Make a mess of this place, move on to that place. That would suit me. You know what's terrifying? No God, no wife, no woman, no friends, only me alone with the sounds.

FR. JOHN: Even though you have rejected him, God is with you.

ELGAR: That's not an official verdict, I'm sure.

FR. JOHN: You don't think that you will ever regain your faith?

ELGAR: Nein. I know it's mumbo-jumbo. Any sensible person does. Not that I'm a sensible person. And when you think of what's been going on over there for the last four years, how can the idea of a merciful God survive?

FR. JOHN: That is difficult. But Gerontius, The Apostles, The Kingdom - your great Catholic works - don't they mean anything to you now?

ELGAR: Can't stand 'em. And don't get me wrong. I don't give a damn about the yahoos getting slaughtered. We can afford to lose plenty of them. It's the poor horses. They've got no choice, have they? My beloved horses, standing there meekly, being shelled and machine-gunned in their thousands. That's what's finished me off.

FR. JOHN: I don't believe you mean that.

ELGAR: [*Passionately*] I do! We are a scourge on this earth, an affliction!

FR. JOHN: Yes... I can sympathise with that view...

ELGAR: Do you know the music of the enemy? Do you know the sounds that he has made? When I hear a Beethoven symphony I feel like a tinker looking at the Forth Bridge. And what must I believe? That these same Germans, the people of Bach, would spit babies on their bayonets and all the other vile propaganda?

FR. JOHN: In wartime truth does take a battering.

ELGAR: Truth? If you want truth where do you go? We have thrown truth on the rubbish-dump. I'm a musician! Germany is part of my very soul. The men who have helped me most have been Germans. My gods in music are German because there are no English ones. They speak for me. They prophesy for me.

FR. JOHN: Well, we have Purcell...

ELGAR: Pah! A boy! And he was two hundred years ago!

FR. JOHN: I won't mention Handel.

ELGAR: I should think not.

FR. JOHN: [*Pause*] I think that I'm beginning to understand.

ELGAR: No, don't. You'll be committing high treason in your mind. Wouldn't do for a hero.

FR. JOHN: When I was in the desert I took liberties with your setting of the *Beatitudes*. I made them into something I could sing myself; the words of Our Lord from the Sermon on the Mount. I cannot tell you how much it sustained me through some very dark times.

ELGAR: Awful stuff. Drivel. Poppycock. Slop. That makes you a fool. Time you went.

FR. JOHN: Very well. Give my thanks to Lady Elgar. There is a lot more to say but we'll leave it. Au revoir.

ELGAR: Don't forget that book you promised to lend me by Gurkykard, the Nane with the horrendous dame. I might dip into it.

[*Father John picks up his belongings and exits R. ELGAR returns to his music. FR. JOHN returns with the book and puts it on the table. By this time ELGAR is engrossed in his work and FR. JOHN now knows better than to disturb him. He exits R. A few moments later a bicycle bell rings. ELGAR turns, listens and grins*]

ELGAR: A good egg. How did it go? [*He talks/sings his way through his setting of the* Beatitudes. *Music is heard from* The Apostles] Blessed are the poor in spirit for theirs is the Kingdom of heaven... then in comes

Mary, John and Pete... then Judas, grr, grr. "He poureth contempt upon princes." Blessed are they that mourn: For they shall be comforted. John, Pete, Mary and John, Women, Men. Blessed are the meek: For they shall inherit the earth. People, Mary, John and Pete. People, Mary, John and Pete. Blessed are they which do hunger and thirst after righteousness: For they shall be filled. Mary, John, Pete and Judas, People. Blessed are the merciful for they shall obtain mercy. Blessed are the pure in heart: For they shall see God. Then People. Blessed are the peacemakers: For they shall be called the children of God. Blessed are they which are persecuted for righteousness' sake: For theirs is the Kingdom of Heaven. Pom pom. Rejoice. Tutti.

[*Pause*]

Then the Beatitude I added. Naughty. Blessed are they which have been sorrowful for all Thy scourges. What reward did we get? Can't remember?

[*FR. JOHN enters from L*]

FR. JOHN: I always meant to ask you, why did you leave the last Beatitude out?

ELGAR: No wonder the persistence of the Jesuits is legendary.

FR. JOHN: I remembered that I am a Jesuit and surrender is sin. Can you bring the last Beatitude to mind? I wonder what you'd have done with it? What we leave out is often more significant than what we leave in.

ELGAR: You should have kept going, Father. I'm a lost cause.

FR. JOHN: No, I'll camp close by, have an outdoor weekend.

ELGAR: Not on my property, you won't. [*Pause*] I'm sorry. Someone coming today. Musicians, you know. We have to get down to it. Yes, go on the common. You'll find a good site there.

FR. JOHN: The scansion of the last Beatitude is very difficult, I admit. Perhaps that is why you avoided it. Though I hesitate to confess this act of arrogance, I set it, for fun, when I was in Palestine, keeping to your style.

ELGAR: [*Immediately interested*] Did you really? Well, I'm blowed. What a cheek. Let's hear it then.

FR. JOHN: [*Singing well*] "Blessed are ye, when men shall revile you, and persecute you, and say all manner of evil against you falsely, for my sake."

[*Pause*]

ELGAR: It's not bad, though I'll sue you for plagiary, but I'd have to put the stress elsewhere.

FR. JOHN: Did you leave it out because it was the only one which might qualify for your blessing?

ELGAR: [*Impatiently*] What?

FR. JOHN: Whether you like it or not, you are blessed, and you cannot escape it.

[*ELGAR lowers his eyes. MARK enters R with a huge black coffin-like case on his back and carries it to centre stage. Behind him enters the cellist, a young woman of today in jeans and a T-shirt*]

CELLIST: Hello, Sir Edward. I came down on the early train.

[*The CELLIST looks at the music pegged around the garden*]

ELGAR: Thank you for travelling all this way to help me.

CELLIST: The journey simply flew past. It will be a privilege to work with you. May I ask the nature of the piece?

ELGAR: Oh... I suppose it's a kind of requiem... in the shape of a concerto... yes, a requiem for... [*He trails off*]

CELLIST: Oh great! I can't wait! I'll do everything I can to help.

ELGAR: Let's say... a requiem for a hundred or so unstarted, unfinished symphonies. I've got it all japed up around the garden. Will you follow me and I'll show you?

MARK: I'm not standing here any longer holding this.

[*FR. JOHN takes the cello from MARK*]

ELGAR: [*Going to the first sheet of music pegged stage R of the clothes-line*] Oh, your instrument. How are we going to move it around?

FR. JOHN: I'll bring it.

[*FR. JOHN opens the case and carefully, with great tenderness, lifts the cello out*]

ELGAR: [*Pointing at the opening bars*] This is the beginning. Four chords, *nobilmente*.

[*The opening of the* Cello Concerto *is heard. FR. JOHN picks the instrument up in his arms as if cradling a wounded man*]

[*Slow fade to blackout*]


THE END

# ELGAR'S THIRD

*A play for radio*

*For Martin Jenkins*

*Elgar's Third* was first broadcast on BBC Radio 3 on March 6th, 1994, with the following cast:

ELGAR, *Bernard Hepton*
SHAW, *Denys Hawthorne*
ALICE, *Anna Massey*
REITH, *Crawford Logan*
BALDWIN, *John Rowe*
LANDON RONALD, *James Taylor*
FATHER GIBB, *James Taylor*
MOUNTFORD, *Malcolm Ward*
DELIUS, *John Evitts*
DOCTOR, *John Evitts*
JELKA, *Margaret John*
MASE, *Gareth Armstrong*
CARICE, *Frances Jeater*
THOMPSON, *Colin Pinney*
GAISBERG, *Colin Pinney*
BILLY, *David Timpson*
AMERICAN GIRL, *Teresa Gallagher*
VERA, *Teresa Gallagher*
STENOGRAPHER, *Teresa Gallagher*
BBC ENGINEER, *Nicholas Boulton*
NURSE, *Nicola Jenkins*
REITH'S SECRETARY, *Nicola Jenkins*
PIANIST, *Tony Sellors*
VIOLA/VIOLIN PLAYER, *Michael Schofield*

Director, *Martin Jenkins*

Stage Manager, *Jondon*

# SCENE 1

[*Fade in room atmos*]

[Land of Hope and Glory *sung by a soprano on a scratchy record. The song finishes and the needle stays in the groove for a while, then it is lifted out. Someone else is in the room*]

ELGAR: I prefer the hiss of the aftermath. Never liked those words. If it had needed words, I would have written them myself, or got my wife to do it. I would never have come up with Land of Hope and Glory and she would never have come up with Mother of the Free. If it had to have a lyric then something noble and simple is what I'd have looked for. [*Sings to himself*] "Let's go down to Alfonso's, he'll accept rubber cheques", that kind of thing. You disapprove? Then you do better. Now, listen to this...

[*A record of the opening of Elgar's First Symphony. Once the main theme is established, the needle is taken off*]

ELGAR: Why hasn't some pushy poet set that to words. Same kind of stuff, surely. *Nobilmente e semplice*. And when I did my version of *God save the King* did you know that I submitted seditious words? [*Sings*] "God save old Kaiser Bill. No other bugger will". Got me nowhere, of course. Wasn't the right time for it. Now, no talk from thee about patriotism. It's something beyond you. All you can do is sneer. One can't sneer in music. One has to be wholehearted or nothing. Yes, I have been wholehearted since the war, whatever you say. Wholeheartedly casual. Why not? Nowt to do with the war. Nowt to do with Alice's death. Of course I've been tinkering. Tinkers tinker, don't they? Mend old pots and pans. No-one wants anything new from me. I only wish they did... Would I? I'd jump at it! But I can't beg, Bernard.

# SCENE 2

[*Cut into telephone bell ringing on distort. Enter line connection as the telephone is picked up*]

SHAW: Victoria 3160. [*On distort*]

ELGAR: Morning, Shaw. The BBC has come up with a commission for a symphony. I've just been told this is your doing. Do you confess?

SHAW: Are they offering you decent money?

ELGAR: A thousand on completion and a thousand for the year I've been given to work on it.

SHAW: Are you happy with that?

ELGAR: Damn dictatorial but the wolf's at the door.

SHAW: Is a year long enough for a symphony?

ELGAR: Has to be. Though I do have this opera to think about, and other things. Also I have to go to Paris on business.

SHAW: I thought you were short of work.

ELGAR: Have you any idea what's involved? The sheer slog!

SHAW: Hold on. I was only going by what you told me.

[*Pause on the line. ELGAR can be heard breathing*]

SHAW: You're a strange old fox. Sometimes I wonder if it hadn't been better if you'd been kept hungry. [*Pause*] Well, Reynard?

ELGAR: Can a fox feel shame?

SHAW: Shame? What are you talking about?

ELGAR: These are my orders: It has to be a symphony on a *grand scale*, and dedicated to the Corporation. Talk about pompous!

[*SHAW laughs*]

ELGAR: Glad you find it funny.

SHAW: Working on a grand scale comes naturally to you.

ELGAR: But my dedications should be my own. Can you imagine what it feels like to be told that one has to dedicate the final... [*Agitated breathing*] ...to a *corporation*?

SHAW: Ignore it. Have two dedications. Be devious. Be yourself. Weave something into the score. Enigmatise them.

ELGAR: Got to have the money. So I've signed up.

SHAW: D'you want me to complain about the dedication?

ELGAR: No. There's been enough backing and forthing. Landon Ronald's handling all the business side for me. I'm hopeless with all that. And I still resent the fact that the bloody BBC didn't think of the idea themselves.

SHAW: They're probably frightened of your reputation as a human gorse-bush. Come on, Edward, be glad. A new symphony will be born.

ELGAR: That's easier said that done. You just churn things out. With me it's a painful labour, you know, not like shelling peas. I sometimes wonder if you've got any notion at all of what we musicians go through!

SHAW: You must learn to be more robust with yourself, Edward.

[*Click as ELGAR puts the phone down*]

ELGAR: [*In his head*] Insulting, insufferable... taking a hell of a lot on himself without me actually asking him to... Grrrr! Makes me feel like a bloody schoolboy who's has the prize-giving rigged in his favour.

# SCENE 3

[*Guildhall banquet*]

RONALD: [*Fade in*] ...and I can hardly express my delight and appreciation of this festival given by the BBC for my dear friend's music - great favourites! Great works!...

ELGAR: [*In his head*] Oh do get on with it, Landon!

RONALD: ...a festival that the BBC has organised, it has to be said, in response to public demand for the return of this great composer to his proper pre-eminence after years of undeserved neglect...

ELGAR: [*In his head*] Do we have to go over all this?

RONALD: ...one has to ask, why? What is it in our national character that makes us turn away from what is best in ourselves at crucial moments? In the last decade what terrible times we have been through... The General Strike... Now the Depression... and yet we saw fit to keep this great healer in the shadows.

ELGAR: [*In his head*] Get to the point, or it will mean my meringue chantilly right in your face!

RONALD: ...a new symphony for a new time, a time of hope, a time of redemption.

[*Cross on applause and cheers into:*]

# SCENE 4

[*LANDON RONALD's apartment, London*]

RONALD: [*Fade in*] Well - what did you think of my speech?

ELGAR: Seemed to hit the nail on the head.

RONALD: I thought about showing you the draft but then I thought, no, I'll surprise him. Did I succeed?

ELGAR: Went down very well, Landon.

RONALD: You used to make speeches. Your professorial lectures at Birmingham were excellent. Now you seem to avoid it. Such a pity. You're much better than I am.

ELGAR: Daren't open my mouth in public.

RONALD: Oh why?

ELGAR: Might blurt something out.

RONALD: Whisky?

ELGAR: A small one. With lots of water.

[*RONALD moves to pour whisky*]

RONALD: That means you've already started work on the new symphony. I know you. As the whisky gets weaker the music gets stronger.

ELGAR: No. It's because it keeps me awake.

RONALD: Alice would have liked being here tonight. She'd be so proud you're still creative.

ELGAR: Yes.

RONALD: Did I say something wrong? Oh, I'm sorry. Sometimes one's oldest friends are the clumsiest.

ELGAR: No... I'm just a bit glum. All the sound and fury gets on my nerves. Yes, Alice would have loved it! [*Laughs*] She really did enjoy the big occasions. I used to say to her - you should have been the composer, if composing is what it's about.

RONALD: Odd that no great music has come from the female.

ELGAR: I don't find it odd. They don't know much about forces outside themselves.

RONALD: One has to remark: Your audiences are full of women.

ELGAR: I didn't say they don't care to listen. Do you think Virginia Woolf might work on an opera with me?

RONALD: What a wonderful combination! What gave you that idea?

ELGAR: Everything she writes comes from within, and everything I write comes from without.

RONALD: D'you want me to ask her?

ELGAR: No. She'd run me ragged. [*Pause*] Landon, what have I taken on with this symphony?

RONALD: Don't you want to do it? There's still time to get out of the contract. They'll understand if I talk to them.

ELGAR: It's all right. Just a moment of panic.

[*Dance music heard from the adjoining apartment*]

ELGAR: Who's next door?

RONALD: Oh, they're always having parties. Couple of American girls. They're very wild.

ELGAR: Could we go round?

RONALD: That would be difficult. You see I've complained about the noise several times.

ELGAR: That was silly of you. I like this tune. Do you know Nat Gonella? Lovely stuff. Monah, Monah... Dance with me, Landon.

RONALD: Don't be absurd.

ELGAR: Then I'll dance with myself. [*Sings*] Monah, Monah... Sheer delight. If I come back to earth I want to be either a stag or a saxophonist. What would you like to be?

RONALD: Myself.

ELGAR: Oh, Jesus Maria! How tiresome. You've lived all this time without dreaming of a better deal for yourself? I'd like to be next door right now, breaking glasses.

RONALD: Look, Edward, I'm off to bed. I've got a lecture at nine in the morning. Help yourself to whisky. Goodnight.

[*Door shuts*]

ELGAR: [*Humming*] Oh, Monah, Monah, say you'll be mine.

[*ELGAR opens LANDON's flat door - goes along corridor, still humming*]

[*A knock*]


# SCENE 5

[*Door opens*]

AMERICAN GIRL: Hi!

ELGAR: I'm from next door.

AMERICAN GIRL: Have you come to complain? Feel free!

ELGAR: Well, my choice is this: Either I complain because I'll never get to sleep, or I come to the party.

AMERICAN GIRL: Then come to the party. They'll love you.

[*Door closes*]

AMERICAN GIRL: What's your name?

ELGAR: Horace.

AMERICAN GIRL: This is Horace, everyone! Well, Horace, I'm Sally. Say, haven't I seen you somewhere?

ELGAR: Oh, I'm all over the place. Look round any corner and you'll find me. Now will you teach me this dance they're doing?

AMERICAN GIRL: Sure.

[*They dance. Pause*]

AMERICAN GIRL: I've got a feeling you can do it already.

ELGAR: Very good on rhythm.

AMERICAN GIRL: What do you do?

ELGAR: I'm a playboy.

AMERICAN GIRL: Are you married?

ELGAR: Me? Ha! Would I be? [*Pause*] Was. Long dead. Left me to bat out my innings.

AMERICAN GIRL: Was she very beautiful?

ELGAR: Never. You're much better. My arm's aching. D'you mind if we get closer together? It would ease my arthritis.

AMERICAN GIRL: You don't say.

ELGAR: You're without doubt the best all-round good-looking girl I've ever had the pleasure of smooching with. I'm so glad I didn't go to bed with a good book.

[*ALICE on slight echo. Dance music is still audible*]

ALICE: Edward, she's not actually all that pretty.

ELGAR: I know.

ALICE: Why are you trying to turn her head?

ELGAR: One gets desperate for proof one is still alive.

ALICE: Don't hold her so close. Everyone is laughing at you.

ELGAR: I don't care, Chicky. Perfume, a few dance-steps, a drink, where's the harm?

ALICE: You should be preparing yourself.

[*Cut into*]

# SCENE 6

[*Aircraft interior. Sound of De Havilland Rapide in flight*]

ELGAR: Are you frightened of flying, Richard?

MOUNTFORD: No, Sir Edward.

ELGAR: Well, I am. I don't expect to come back from this experience alive. As your employer I feel responsible for the fact that you will share my demise. A manservant shouldn't have to go that far.

MOUNTFORD: We'll be all right, Sir Edward. The pilot told me there are no strong winds over the Channel today.

ELGAR: I don't care about the wind. It's the engine. If it's anything like the other machines I've to deal with, it'll break down and then we've had it.

MOUNTFORD: It won't, sir. They service it after every flight.

ELGAR: The vacuum-cleaner broke down at home yesterday, didn't it?

MOUNTFORD: We're not flying in a vacuum-cleaner, Sir Edward.

ELGAR: Wish we were. There's less to go wrong. We should have taken the boat. No matter. How long will we be up here at the mercy of some sprocket?

MOUNTFORD: The pilot says the average time between Croydon and Le Bourget is two and a quarter hours.

ELGAR: Let's hope to God we don't fly into the Eiffel Tower.

[*MOUNTFORD laughs*]

ELGAR: [*In his head*] Alice, my dear little Chicky, I'm closer to you now than I've ever been - if your cock-eyed ideas about heaven are to be believed. I expect you to fly alongside on your angel's wings and look through the window any minute. But you would never have come on this aeroplane with me if you were alive. How it would have offended you! What a fuss you'd have made about the noise.

MOUNTFORD: The coast of France, Sir Edward.

ELGAR: [*In his head*] You would have loved to come to Paris with me. This boy, the Menuhin lad, what is he? Seventeen? Seventeen and playing the violin concerto! Can you imagine it? He's hardly started shaving yet!

[*The cadenza of the* Violin Concerto *on echo*]

ELGAR: [*In his head*] And such a courteous and good-natured youngster that I can't help being nice to him.

MOUNTFORD: Bethune... Neufchâtel... Forge-les-Eaux...

ELGAR: [*In his head*] And I've arranged to visit poor old Delius. Blind and paralysed now, poor sod. Lives near Fontainbleau. Hasn't got long, they say. Like to chat to him about it all. Swap a few horror stories.

MOUNTFORD: The Somme, Sir Edward.

ELGAR: [*In his head*] When I think of that little lad standing up in front of the whole of Paris with his fiddle playing my concerto I can hardly breathe.

MOUNTFORD: Are you all right, Sir Edward? Is this altitude affecting you?

ELGAR: [*Mumbling*] No... no...

MOUNTFORD: It hasn't brought on your sciatica again, has it?

ELGAR: No... no... I was day-dreaming.

MOUNTFORD: I can ask the pilot to fly lower, if you wish. We might get a better view of the war-damage at Beauvais.

ELGAR: I can do without that, thank you, Richard. Actually what I'd like is a drink.

[*Fades*]

# SCENE 7

[*Cross on aircraft noise into Salle Concert Hall. Many German voices importunate and urgent*]

VOICES: Herr Elgar! Herr Elgar! Remember me? I sang the Angel of Agony in *Gerontius*, Dusseldorf, 1902! What a night - like this!

ELGAR: Ja... Sehr freundlich... er... danke... danke... [*In his head*] German Jews! Nothing but German Jews! Don't you find that a mite strange, Chicky? I come to Paris and it's full of musicians from Berlin. Where do I fit in? Who have they come to listen to? This boy Menuhin or me? Selah!
[*The very end of the* Violin Concerto *and passionate applause*]
[*Cross into*]

# SCENE 8

[*Birdsong. Delius's garden at Grez-sur-Loing. The sound of a car drawing up, a door slamming, the car driving off*]

DELIUS: Is it him?

JELKA: I think so. He has come the forty miles from Paris by taxi to meet the great Delius. Must have cost him a fortune.

DELIUS: Describe him for me.

JELKA: Shouldn't I go out and greet him?

DELIUS: You won't be able to describe him while he's here. You wouldn't be able to tell the truth.

JELKA: How's he going to get back? Did you invite him to stay?

DELIUS: If he likes. Now get on with it!

JELKA: Very erect, soldierly... almost Prussian... large tapering moustache... very ill at ease, not at all sure that this is the place he's looking for. He has a fierce eye. Carries a furled umbrella. Flares his nostrils a lot like a horse. Pouts!

DELIUS: Is he coming in?

JELKA: Ah he's spotted us. Should I wave?

DELIUS: Yes, but tell me how he walks before you go to meet him. I want to know if he marches.

JELKA: [*Calling*] Hello! [*To DELIUS*] Very stately... with his umbrella held at his hip like a sword. head held high. Not too fast. He's waiting for me to open the gate! How *seigneurial*!

DELIUS: Excellent! Go! Go! Don't let him fumble with that rusty old latch! But note very carefully how he smiles - if he does - and what he says. You can tell me all that after he's gone.

JELKA: Don't you find it odd, Frederick, that people say that you remind them of an ascetic archbishop, and that Elgar should be so like a silvery, sad general? What self-important people write English music!? [*She laughs as she goes*]

# SCENE 9

[*Chime of glasses, a cork being pulled, wine poured*]

ELGAR: Is hounding talented people out of Germany because they're Jews purification? Sounds like lunacy to me.

DELIUS: Strauss has offered his services to Hitler. And Furtwangler has done the same. They must know what they're doing.

ELGAR: Well, it's a mystery to me. And all this rot about Schumann and Mendelssohn being corrupting influences. How can he say that?

DELIUS: In Germany he can. Music has been put in its place, you see. And it's spreading, this practice. Ask Prokofiev where he stands in Russia. He knows very well. The state will decide what is good and what is bad. Why should it be left to individuals? What do they know? What do we know, if it comes to that? Leave it to Hitler and Stalin. There'll be destruction, then truth.

ELGAR: I can't believe you mean that.

DELIUS: Then let's leave it to Wagner. [*Pause*] I'm well past being concerned. I know that music is like the curse of the Egyptian mummy. It will outlast the opening of the tomb, and the fall of the final pyramid. So why worry?

ELGAR: I didn't say I was worried. I said I didn't understand.

[*Wine sipped*]

ELGAR: You've been happy here?

DELIUS: Yes. the French are very tolerant of artists in their midst. They make allowances, and they enjoy making those allowances. You've never thought of living abroad?

ELGAR: No.

DELIUS: Good for the health. If I'd stayed in England I'd have been dead twenty years ago. And not with bronchitis.

ELGAR: Well, I'm still here.

DELIUS: I wish that I'd been able to hear this *wunderkind* playing your cello concerto...

ELGAR: Violin, actually.

DELIUS: Of course. But Paris is too far these days. I'd like to hear something of my own as well! I've been living in France for thirty-five years and they've never done any of my work.

JELKA: Not even his *Paris Nocturne*. Isn't that ridiculous?

ELGAR: Very short-sighted of them. [*Pause*] French can be very provincial when they like.

DELIUS: It's never bothered me particularly. What does it matter where one lives? While I've been here much of the time I've been composing pieces up on the Yorkshire Moors.

ELGAR: But if you'd stayed it might have strengthened the music?

DELIUS: No. I needed to miss it. These days I often think about a piece dedicated to sight. But I never start it because I can still see in my mind and that is the more intense experience.

ELGAR: Why not give it a try?

DELIUS: Would be worse than whimsical. I can see. I can see everything. The more incapable I become, the more I can do to help myself.

ELGAR: Should be useful. [*Pause*] Setting out on a new symphony when I get back.

JELKA: There you are, Frederick. I told you that's what I'd heard.

ELGAR: Been sculling around in my mind for years. BBC heard of it and offered a commission. So, my bluff's been called, as it were. Got to come up with the goods.

JELKA: How very brave of you.

ELGAR: Brave? I had to accept. I was spending all my time at the races, getting nothing done.

JELKA: Can you tell us what it will be about?

ELGAR: Probably quite abstract, if you know what I mean. No real programme for it. [*Hesitant*] I am somewhat on a mountain top looking over again, that's the way I feel, anyhow. There're rivers, the hills, people are specks... Difficult to explain, perspective.

DELIUS: I don't think you should do it.

JELKA: Frederick!

DELIUS: Music has no perspective. It destroys perspective! Why do you think being blind troubles me so little? I've been blinded by music all my life. You must abandon that plan, Elgar. Think of something else.

JELKA: Don't be so dogmatic.

DELIUS: Why should I encourage him to waste his time? He hasn't much left. Do you still feel with the same power you used to?

JELKA: How can he possibly answer that?

DELIUS: Because he's talking to me. Neither of us have been too good at explaining ourselves except in what we hear inwardly. The composer's ears aren't stuck on either side of his head at all. They're elsewhere.

JELKA: There you are, Sir Edward. Tiresias has spoken. Is that what you came for?

ELGAR: I came to pay my respects to a fellow artist. What I did not expect was such perfect understanding.

DELIUS: I never liked the symphonic form. Enormous abstracts don't bring out the best in me. How can anyone hear what an abstract is saying? Now poetry is another matter. I can hear what a poet is doing to me. Have you read Nietzche? He sings to me.

ELGAR: I do get a bit lost with him...

DELIUS: Keep trying. Read *Thus Spake Zarathustra*.

ELGAR: I have.

DELIUS: Then read it again! Know the superman, the will to power, the magic of sublimation, master-morality, slave-morality and the great cycle which governs human time! *Wunderbar!*

ELGAR: Maybe I'm not up to it. Shelley and Longfellow are more in my line.

DELIUS: Shelley would have loved Nietzche. They'd have been the closest of friends. Not an ounce of mediocrity between them. It's been so good having you here. Now I'm a little tired, if you'll excuse me. There's so much more to talk about. [*Dozes off*]

JELKA: [*Whispering*] Come and walk down to the river with me.

[*They move away from the sleeping DELIUS*]

JELKA: You will, of course, ignore all Frederick's advice.

ELGAR: I'm not sure that I shall. Except the bit about reading Nietzche again. That wouldn't do me any good at all.

JELKA: I knew you were a wise man the moment I saw you.

[*Cross on JELKA's laughter into:*]


# SCENE 10


[*BBC office*]

MASE: Broadcasting House, the BBC, 21 April, 1933. Dear Sir Edward, I wonder if you could yet tell me whether the new symphony will be finished in time for our big series of concerts next year...

# SCENE 11

ELGAR: [*In his head*] There are fragments, Alice. You know me. Bits and pieces everywhere. I know you disapprove that I've been shooting my mouth off about how far I've got and that it's the strongest thing I've ever done, but I have to keep the BBC quiet while I work on it. They do harry one!

# SCENE 12

[*Marl Bank. ELGAR plays fragments of the* Third Symphony]

ELGAR: What d'you think, Shaw?

SHAW: I get the feeling I've heard some of it before.

ELGAR: That's an illusion.

SHAW: I don't have illusions.

ELGAR: And what do you think, Vera?

VERA: I can't wait to hear it.

ELGAR: But you did hear it.

VERA: When it's finished, I mean. I find it very difficult to judge from... well, little bits.

SHAW: Have you started to string them together?

ELGAR: They're not onions, Shaw! You're very hard to please, the pair of you. Will you play some of the "little bits", as you call them, for me on your lovely viola? That would be a great help.

VERA: Is anything scored for viola? Might I be able to play in the orchestra when the symphony is first performed?

ELGAR: Of course, darling. That looks like being at the BBC Festival in nineteen thirty four. Here we are. have a go. Nice and steady.

SHAW: So you've got a deadline?

ELGAR: Oh, that don't worry me. I'm well ahead. You know my style. I bring it all together at the last moment.

[*VERA plays a fragment*]

ELGAR: [*In his head*] You would like Vera, Chicky. She's been such a friend over the last couple of years. I don't know why but she seems to prefer my company to that of men of her own age.

ALICE: [*On echo*] I thank God that this girl does not play the cello. The way that the instrument is held between the knees has always appalled me.

ELGAR: [*In his head*] Oh, Alice...

ALICE: [*On echo*] I was glad when your cello concerto fell into disregard. All those young women queueing up to play it. Don't they understand what you're doing to them?

ELGAR: [*In his head*] As time goes by even the memory of you seems to give me less and less understanding.

ALICE: [*On echo*] Return to your faith, Edu, my darling. Go to the priest. Let him help you find self control.

ELGAR: [*In his head*] I haven't got time to think about that mumbo-jumbo. The opera... the symphony... so much to do.

[*The viola playing has stopped on the word* symphony]

VERA: Are you all right, Sir Edward?

ELGAR: [*Coming out of a daze*] Eh?

SHAW: I'll call his man. You should be in bed, old boy.

[*SHAW opens the door*]

ELGAR: No, no... thoughts, only thoughts. You played so well, Vera, that I was mesmerised. Bless you. [*Whispers*] I do love you so.

[*Door closing*]

ELGAR: Who was that?

VERA: Mr. Shaw going out.

ELGAR: And is Mr. Elgar coming in?

VERA: I'm sorry... I don't follow.

ELGAR: Oh, leave it, you dunce!

[*Out*]


# SCENE 13


[*Fade in BBC office and radio broadcast. Typing can be heard from outer offices*]

BROADCASTER: ... there were extraordinary scenes in the Reichstag. Chancellor Hitler attacked the Social Democrat deputies in the most threatening manner. "From now on," he said, "we National Socialists will make life impossible for you. You think that your star will rise again. That the bourgeois world will re-assume its stranglehold on the workers' throat. No! It won't! In the life of nations what is rotten, old and feeble passes and does not come again."

[*Click as the radio is turned off in Sir John Reith's office*]

REITH: I can't imagine Ramsay MacDonald talking to MP's like that.

MASE: Might do them some good, Sir John. Shake their ideas up a bit.

REITH: Mm - you wanted to talk about Elgar.

MASE: I wondered if you'd heard anything.

REITH: He wrote to me a few days ago and said that he'd played parts of what he'd written so far for his friends and they'd loved it.

MASE: Well, his music publisher hasn't had anything from him at all. Usually he sends it in piece by piece as he completes it.

REITH: Oh. That's bad news.

MASE: If he's still at the stage of tinkling a few phrases over tea for his friends then I think we should put some pressure on him.

REITH: Do you indeed, Mase?

MASE: Should I go to Worcester and get him to play what he's got so far?

REITH: I don't think so.

MASE: When Mr Shaw suggested the commission to you, what was at the back of his mind?

REITH: You're asking me what's at the back of George Bernard Shaw's mind? Who do you think I am?

MASE: But hadn't Elgar been fishing for this commission? I remember something in the papers. He was complaining no one was interested in him any more. And I hear he's short of cash.

REITH: Stop beating about the bush, man. What are you trying to infer?

MASE: Well - I don't know if we should actually expect a 75 year old to deliver a symphony. If the commission was just a hand-out I'd rather know so I can forget about it and get on with other work. It does happen, Sir John.

REITH: Of course we expect a new symphony! What's the matter with you? D'you think I'd throw away two thousand pounds...

MASE: If I'd been consulted about this - which I wasn't - I'd have said that at 75 he's far too old and there are plenty of younger composers who would have benefitted more from a commission like this. Since the war all Elgar's composed is trivia, and not much of that either.

REITH: And that's your considered opinion, is it?

MASE: Yes, Sir John, it is. And many people think his work is essentially vulgar and insular.

REITH: They do?

MASE: If someone doesn't take himself seriously as a composer any more I don't see it as our business to wave a cheque in his face.

REITH: So Elgar's to be written off? Our greatest composer!

MASE: I didn't say that, Sir John. It's a case of not casting seed onto stony ground.

[*Out*]

# SCENE 14

[*REITH's office*]

REITH: [*Fade in over intercom*] Bring me in that George Bernard Shaw letter about Elgar, will you? And my notes.

SECRETARY: [*Over intercom*] You didn't leave any notes for filing, Sir John. I'll bring the letter in.

REITH: [*In his head*] I made notes. I know I made notes. Notes on why I supported the venture.

[*Door opening*]

REITH: Thank you. No sign of my jottings?

SECRETARY: You often take things home with you, Sir John, and we don't see them again.

REITH: Do I? Must watch that.

[*Door closing. Rustle of letter in REITH's hand*]

REITH: [*Reading the letter*] Dear Sir John, may I make a suggestion? In 1823 the London Philharmonic Society offered Beethoven fifty pounds for the manuscript of a symphony. He sent them the Ninth. In 1827, when Beethoven was dying, the Society sent a further one hundred pounds as a gift. Beethoven said "God bless the London Philharmonic Society and the whole English nation." This is by far the most creditable event in English history. Now the only composer today who is comparable to Beethoven is Elgar... [*To himself*] Is he? What about vulgar? Insular? Trivia? I must find those notes!

[*Out*]

# SCENE 15

[*Fade in ELGAR's workroom and ELGAR playing fragments for the first movement fretfully and impatiently on the piano*]

ELGAR: [*In his head*] Oboi.. Corno Inglese... Clarinetto Basso... Contra Fagotto! Oh, Contra Fagotto! God damn you to hell! What am I doing this for? Tromboni tromboni arpa arpa!

[*ELGAR crashes his hands on the keyboard*]

ELGAR: Nothing. [*In his head*] Why should I give them any more? They enjoyed my silence often enough. Why do they want me to make a noise now?

[*Door opens*]

MOUNTFORD: Did you call, Sir Edward?

ELGAR: No. I did not call.

MOUNTFORD: I'm sorry. I must have been mistaken. As I'm here perhaps you'd like to know Marco has been sick.

ELGAR: Oh dear! Where?

MOUNTFORD: On your bed, I'm afraid.

ELGAR: Tut, poor little fellow. Where is he?

MOUNTFORD: In the garden.

ELGAR: That's right. Punish him, and make him feel guilty! It's not his fault, is it? He couldn't help it. Is Mina all right?

MOUNTFORD: Yes, Sir.

ELGAR: You've given them bad meat. Well, I can't carry on with this. Really, Richard, you must take better care of those dogs. They're the only friends I've got.

ALICE: [*On echo*] Edu, the dogs... I can't tell you how it disgusts me... in the bed, in the bath, sitting up at table... I prefer the viola player, to be honest. Move her in! Marry her, if you wish. But the dogs... ugh! Why do you have to treat them as if they were more than scruffy, dirty little animals?

# SCENE 16

[*Fade into ELGAR whistling his dogs repeatedly in the garden*]

ELGAR: Where are you? Marco! Mina! Come to Daddy. Good dogs!

[*Spaniels barking and running towards ELGAR*]

ELGAR: There, there, my little babies. Have you been poisoned, my Marco? Is your tummy hurting? Daddy'll soon get you better. [*In his head*] What I love about you is how completely you ignore music. You will not even come to my whistle, bless you.

[*Cut into*]

# SCENE 17

[*ELGAR's workroom. ELGAR plays a fragment of the first movement on the piano*]

ELGAR: This is your theme, Vera.

VERA: Oh.

ELGAR: It will be re-stated, of course, my darling. Often.

[*He plays it again*]

ELGAR: Do you like it?

VERA: Oh, yes.

ELGAR: Does it mean anything to you?

VERA: In terms of being about me?

ELGAR: The theme is in your possession, as I am. This will be *your* symphony.

VERA: [*Upset*] No... don't do that... I don't deserve it.

ELGAR: Can't be helped. You have my heart. That's what the theme is saying.

VERA: Is that what people will expect from a man your age?

ELGAR: I don't care. [*Angrily*] What other life is there? Eh? Don't you want your theme? We can tear it up if you like!

VERA: No, no... I'm a little frightened, you understand.

ELGAR: Of me? I'm the one who should be frightened. It shakes me, this love. It scatters my thoughts but then re-gathers them into one meaning, Vera... Veritas... So late in my life you choose to come along... Truth, mistress, wife, lover, angel...

VERA: Sir Edward please... Don't make too much of me.

ELGAR: Can I help it, damn you? You're so hard! [*Pause*] Nothing to offer, I suppose. What's a symphony if you compare it to a lusty lout with his shirt off? Eh? Wasting your time on an old fool! What's the matter with you? [*Pause*] Accept my gift, at least. The symphony is yours.

VERA: I'm not worthy of it.

ELGAR: Nonsense. To be young and beautiful is worth a thousand bloody symphonies.

[*ELGAR plays the theme again*]

ELGAR: Now you hear it. Now you don't. Gone. Disappeared.

VERA: Don't keep playing it. Not now. Give me some time to get used to the idea. You're taking me very far, you know.

[*ELGAR plays the theme again*]

ELGAR: I don't have to have your permission, darling. It exists. Elgar's written it out. [*Sharp intake of breath*] Damn! What a pain! Get Richard for me.

VERA: Shall I help you to the sofa?

ELGAR: [*Yelling at the top of his voice*] Richard! It's another of God's little jokes!

[*Bring in running footsteps which go into echo*]

ELGAR: [*On echo*] Marl Bank, Rainbow Hill, Worcester, 7th October, 1933. Dear Sir John, I have to go into a nursing home today for a sudden operation - gastric. This upsets all plans. I am extremely sorry to tell you that everything is held up for the present. I am not at all sure how things will turn out...

[*VERA's theme played in disintegrated form on the piano*]

REITH: The BBC, Broadcasting House, West One... 9th October, 1933. Dear Sir Edward, I am greatly distressed at the news which you send in your letter just received. Of course the postponement of the work is a great disappointment to us but it is not of this I am thinking, but of the inconvenience and discomfort caused to yourself... The man's starting to disintegrate, obviously. 75! He's already got one foot in the grave. What was I thinking of? Two thousand pounds!

[*cross into*]

# SCENE 18

[*Private hospital ward*]

DOCTOR: You can get dressed now, Sir Edward. I'm afraid the sciatica was wrongly diagnosed, it was a tumour at an early stage pressing on the nerve.

ELGAR: [*Testily*] All right, all right, you don't have to go into detail!

DOCTOR: You said that you wanted to know exactly what was the matter. I'm trying to tell you.

ELGAR: But do it in an overall way. [*Dressing*] I don't want to know about the finicky things.

DOCTOR: You have cancer.

ELGAR: Ah.

DOCTOR: And it is malignant.

ELGAR: Oh.

DOCTOR: If you had not asked to know then it would have been kept from you.

ELGAR: Why?

DOCTOR: So you could live in hope for as long as possible.

ELGAR: I've lived without hope for twenty years. Why should I need it now? Pass my shoes, will you? How long have I got?

DOCTOR: Six months.

ELGAR: You say that as if you ought to have added: "If you're lucky."

DOCTOR: It's a rule of thumb, that's all.

ELGAR: Hmph! [*Pause*] I'd always hoped to be taken suddenly. I don't like long, drawn-out endings.

DOCTOR: We will do all we can with palliative treatment.

ELGAR: Why the hell did I want to know?

DOCTOR: [*In difficulty*] Because... some people feel that they have the inner strength to face everything... hiding from the truth shames them.

ELGAR: Not me. I like to keep the puzzle going. Too bad. It's out of the bag now. Thank you, doctor. Sorry to have put you through the hoop. Now I'd like to see my dogs.

DOCTOR: Your dogs?

ELGAR: Are you deaf, man?

DOCTOR: We can't have dogs in the nursing home, Sir Edward.

ELGAR: Why not? They're clean, cleaner than a lot of people. [*Pause*] How do I deal with this? [*Pause*] Imagine it was you.

DOCTOR: Remain within your life.

ELGAR: What does that mean?

DOCTOR: Don't let go... I wish I was better at this...

ELGAR: So do I. Go on, get out.

DOCTOR: I am very sorry.

ELGAR: [*In his head*] Hear that, Chicky? Very odd. I knew I should never have started talking about a new symphony. This tumour started its life the very same day. That's what I heard! I've been scoring my own death, darling. *Arpa, arpa, arpa! Tuba! Timpani! Elgare funerale!* Much pomp coming up. Filthy fanfares! But at least I have the consolation of knowing that the thing will certainly get finished one way or the other.

[*Out*]

# SCENE 19

[*BBC office*]

REITH: [*On the telephone*] Yes, we'll put you in touch. I'll give him your extension number, if I may... No, I don't think Elgar would go along with homeopathy somehow... Thanks for your help. Goodbye.

[*Telephone receiver being replaced*]

REITH: Not much hope there, I'm afraid. The best the Ministry of Health can advise is something called the Brompton Cocktail, a mixture of morphine for the pain and cocaine to keep him happy. He said that psycho-surgeons in the United States claim to have located part of the brain that controls artistic activity but they don't know yet how to stimulate it.

MASE: Give them time.

REITH: What rotten luck for this to happen now.

MASE: If Elgar had tried to take out a life insurance policy on the day we gave him the commission they'd have turned him down.

REITH: [*Going*] The BBC is not a life insurance company, Mase.

MASE: Not even a cultural life insurance company?

  [*Out*]


# SCENE 20

[*London embankment, 1933. Sounds of barges passing, people at work*]

SHAW: My letter was clear enough. The man was in need. I said - give him some money - encourage him to come to life again as a composer. Was that such a bad idea?

REITH: Not at all. It was a very noble idea.

SHAW: And you wish that you'd had it yourself.

REITH: With his illness, should we abandon the whole thing?

SHAW: So you can have your money back?

REITH: The money is secondary.

SHAW: Second is right behind first.

REITH: Please accept my assurance that this is not about penny-pinching.

SHAW: Then what is it about?

REITH: We feel...

SHAW: Is this the royal pronoun we are using now?

REITH: Everyone who has been involved...

SHAW: D'you mean the BBC Board of Governors? Who are we talking about? You know how edgy I am about power structures. Especially if I'm being blamed for something.

REITH: No one is blaming you, Shaw. But it was through your influence that the commission came into being, and we thought it might be appropriate if you could use your influence on Elgar to complete it.

SHAW: My friendship, you mean.

REITH: He's all we've got.

SHAW: Nonsense. Vaughan Williams. Arnold Bax. Delius.

REITH: Delius had Teutonic parents. Bax only seems to write about Ireland. Vaughan Williams has a very Welsh sounding name.

SHAW: [*Laughing*] Oh, now you've got me interested! We have to have the last gasp of the quintessential English sound! Is that it? But why keep it alive artificially? If it hasn't reproduced itself then let it be consigned to history. I wonder what kind of sound this place *Britain* might make, given a chance.

REITH: It is too soon for that, perhaps.

SHAW: Said like a true Scotsman!

[*Cross on SHAW's laughter and striking of Big Ben*]


# SCENE 21


[*Nursing home. Night*]

ALICE: [*On echo*] It's very sad news, Edward, but we must be brave. I knew, of course. I could have put my finger right there.

ELGAR: Of course.

ALICE: There is no part of you where I am not present. Your pain is my pain. If only you had started this new symphony earlier!

ELGAR: Without the commission it wouldn't have been worth it.

ALICE: While I was with you a thought like that would never have come into your head. I wouldn't have let it near you.

ELGAR: Chicky.

ALICE: Yes, darling?

ELGAR: You know how I've always admired your simple faith. Can you assure me you got one thing absolutely wrong.

ALICE: Whatever can you mean?

ELGAR: This medieval notion of music in the afterlife. You know, harps and trumpets, angel choirs, all that. Can't be true, can it?

[*Out*]

# SCENE 22

[*Party and hum of conversation. Ministry building, large room*]

REITH: Have you time for a word, Mr Baldwin?

BALDWIN: When the BBC speaks who dares not listen?

REITH: The Prime Minister suggested I should raise this with you. I can only describe it as an issue affecting, in the most subtle sense, our perception of national unity.

BALDWIN: Good Lord. Sounds very serious.

REITH: As a man of Worcestershire you may think so. Elgar, that famous son of the shire, is ill.

BALDWIN: Very ill, so I've heard.

REITH: You are well informed.

BALDWIN: It is my parish.

REITH: You know that we have commissioned a new symphony from him? Something tells me that he has not got very far.

BALDWIN: Not surprised, are you?

REITH: I wondered if there was an encouragement... that could be given.

BALDWIN: What have you in mind?

REITH: We really would like the symphony to be completed. He's already a baronet, and an OM, he has the GCVO. All these are very important to him. He responds well to recognition.

BALDWIN: Artists and earldoms don't quite fit somehow. And we do like to sell them if we can. How much was the commission worth?

REITH: Two thousand.

BALDWIN: If a sum as big as that can't do the trick then I think it's not our kind of intervention he needs. But leave it with me.

[*Out*]

# SCENE 23

[*Nursing home*]

MOUNTFORD: Good morning, Sir Edward. How are you feeling?

[*Door shuts*]

ELGAR: First class. Never felt better. Ragingly well.

MOUNTFORD: That's good to hear. I've brought your post. There's quite a lot of it.

[*Letters put down*]

ELGAR: Nothing like reading get well cards when you know it's impossible. Bucks one up no end.

MOUNTFORD: I'll leave them with you. There's a few words I want to have in the kitchen of this establishment, having cast an eye over what has been offered you as an excuse for luncheon.

ELGAR: Yes - you go and roar at them, Richard. Tell them it has to be caviare or nothing.

[*Door opens and shuts. Sound of letters being opened*]

ELGAR: How thoughtful... up and about! Yes, I'll be up and about, my friend. [*Pause*] Her handwriting... can't find it... Vera, where art thou?

[*Sound of letters being searched through anxiously*]

ELGAR: [*In his head*] Nothing. It will come tomorrow. No, it won't... She'll come instead...

[*Sound of letters being opened*]

ELGAR: [*In his head*] Poems... that's a change... get well poems... Oh, no... "Dear Sir Edward Elgar, I send the enclosed unworthy verses to you with much self doubt"... I know what's coming, you sly oily rascal... "Wondering if you might consider setting one or two of them to music... Much separates us in terms of time and experience. I am at the beginning yet I keep hearing your music... haunting." Wystan Hugh Auden, Esquire! Hmm, *quel nom*! You perisher!

[*Reads*]

Oh what is that sound which so thrills the ear
Down in the valley drumming, drumming?

[*Drums in his head*]
Only the scarlet soldiers, dear,
The soldiers coming.

[*Marching in his head*]

O what is that light I see flashing clear
Over the distance brightly, brightly?
Only the sun of their weapons, dear,
As they step lightly.
O what are they doing with all that gear;
What are they doing this morning, this morning?
Only the usual manoeuvres, dear,
Or perhaps a warning.

[*Drums and marching build up to crescendo then stop abruptly*]

DOCTOR: Sir Edward.

ELGAR: Don't touch me!

DOCTOR: It's time for your injection. Will you turn on your side please?

[*Out*]

# SCENE 24

[*Nursing home*]

CARICE: Daddy. Daddy. It's me.

ELGAR: [*Hazily*] Eh?

CARICE: I'm sorry if I woke you but I've only a short time before I have to go... I didn't want to leave you without saying hello...

ELGAR: Darling, I'm so glad you came. I've been waiting for you. How was the concert? Did you play well?

CARICE: What concert?

ELGAR: Who's that?

CARICE: It's me, Daddy. Carice.

ELGAR: Oh.

CARICE: [*Upset*] Your daughter! Who did you think it was?

ELGAR: What do you want?

CARICE: I came to see you... Oh, Daddy I don't know... I brought you some books.

ELGAR: Good.

CARICE: Your Shakespeare.

ELGAR: Good.

CARICE: Your Bible and your Missal...

ELGAR: What did you bring that for?

CARICE: Father Gibb thought you might need it.

ELGAR: Take the Missal and the bloody bible back with you. I've had enough of all that. And you tell yon sly priest to stay away from me, d'you hear?

CARICE: Yes, Daddy.

ELGAR: I only want to see... fellow sufferers.

CARICE: What do you mean, Daddy? Fellow sufferers?

ELGAR: Musicians. Ask Billy Reed to come and see me, and tell him not to forget to bring his fiddle with him.

CARICE: Will the doctor allow it?

ELGAR: The doctor will do as he's told! I'm paying for this, aren't I? Besides, this dump needs cheering up! [*Pause*] Sorry Fishface. I shouldn't shout at you.

CARICE: That's all right, Daddy.

ELGAR: But you must watch out. People will use you to get at me. You know how it works. They all want to get in on the act. Keep the priests away. Keep the hangers-on away. Get hold of Vera for me... Please ask her to come... I need her, you understand...

CARICE: Oh, Daddy, must I?

ELGAR: Yes, Fishface, you must! Now... Be on your way... Bye... Lovely to see you...

CARICE: [*Upset*] Bye, Daddy. I'll be back soon.

ELGAR: Don't forget Vera.

CARICE: Oh, God forgive you!

   [*Out*]


# SCENE 25

[*Nursing home. Solo violin fades in playing a fragment. Door opens*]

THOMPSON: I'm afraid that will have to do, Sir Edward, lovely though it is.

ELGAR: Don't stop me working, for heaven's sake! We've only just got going.

THOMPSON: I'm sorry but I have to insist.

ELGAR: You're a hard man. Billy, this is my medical consultant, Arthur Thompson. He thinks music is bad for you.

BILLY: Are we disturbing people? I kept it as quiet as I could.

THOMPSON: Perhaps it's not the volume that worries, but the intensity.

ELGAR: All that matters to me now is this symphony. I must finish it, come hell or high water. [*Flares up*] I've given my word as a gentleman!

THOMPSON: Calm down. Don't put yourself under such a strain.

ELGAR: It's the frustration that's the strain, not the work. My self-respect as a musician is at stake. Isn't that so, Billy?

BILLY: Well, Sir Edward, I wouldn't dare argue with a doctor.

ELGAR: I must use what time I've got left to the full! I can do it, I know... It's all there, it's just a matter of getting the damn stuff down on paper.

THOMPSON: No more for the present. I can't allow you to overtax your reserves of strength at this stage.

ELGAR: Huh! Might as well be dead already.

THOMPSON: That's an option you could be forcing on yourself.

ELGAR: D'you expect me to just lie here and wait to die like some stupid peasant? Go on, leave us alone. I'll be all right.

THOMPSON: Sir Edward, either you obey my instructions or I will take no further interest. Is that what you want?

ELGAR: No. Oh, have your way. We'll stop. Put your fiddle away, Billy. We'll chat now... You can get on with your rounds.

THOMPSON: But can I trust you? No more work today. I'll be listening. [*He exits. Door closes*]

ELGAR: Will you come again tomorrow, Billy?

BILLY: Yes, Sir Edward.

ELGAR: Good. We've got lots of things to think about. What did you think of that last section we did? Good isn't it?

BILLY: Can't wait to see how it develops.

ELGAR: Oh, it's leading somewhere. Come on. Let's do a bit more.

BILLY: Got things to do, Sir Edward.

ELGAR: *Et tu Brute?* Off you go. But tomorrow - forward! [*Broken, fitful playing of fragments*]

ELGAR: [*In his head*] Yes, I had overdone it, I'm afraid, Chicky. Not long after Billy went I blacked out when I tried to get up for a pee. Never happened to me before. Very odd. Like somebody turning the light out.

ALICE: A little warning, Edward, that's all - from someone with your ultimate interest at heart.

ELGAR: The whole nursing home went into a spin, apparently. They were convinced that I was on my way out - and here's me with five months to go!

ALICE: Darling, that's not guaranteed, you know.

ELGAR: While I was unconscious the idiots panicked and called in a priest. I woke up to find the oil of final unction smeared on my forehead. Oh, Chicky, by hell I was angry! I'm not dead yet, I told them. Not by a long chalk!

ALICE: Edward, you must not fight the inevitable.

ELGAR: More than twenty years ago, before the war, I gave up writing symphonies, remember? I was scared, and I couldn't stand the pain of it. Now pain is everywhere, every day, and I must atone for my cowardice. I could have fought on, taken the risk of losing an easy life.

Been brave. I had enough examples in Flanders. Looking back on it, everyone was being brave but me.

ALICE: I refuse to listen. You've no idea what you're saying. It's all those narcotics in your bloodstream talking. Can't you do without them?

ELGAR: [*Shouting*] No! No!

THOMSPON: Sir Edward.

ELGAR: [*Waking*] Uh... what's up?

THOMPSON: A bad dream.

ELGAR: Horrible.

THOMPSON: Are you afraid?

ELGAR: No. [*Pause*] Well, not of what you think.

THOMPSON: What then?

ELGAR: Unwritten music. Music I could have written but didn't. Music from a part of myself that I need now, but I put it to sleep in 1911 in a fit of *pique*, would you believe! [*Pause*] Why am I telling you all this? You'll laugh.

THOMPSON: Don't I deserve a laugh now and again?

ELGAR: No more symphonies, I said. They're too much like hard work. They don't pay. And they take me places I don't want to go. Rather be at my club, frankly. But actually I'm terribly good at symphonies. Better at them than anything else, if the truth were known. So here you have a patient who deserves no sympathy at all because he cut off his nose to spite his face. [*Pause*] That's where you're supposed to laugh.

THOMPSON: And you expect to make up for all that wasted time *now*?

ELGAR: When else?

[*Fades. A strong unified section played on violin. Cut into:*]


# SCENE 26


[*Nursing home, private ward*]

ELGAR: [*Fade in*] You must never let the priest loose on me again when I'm helpless.

CARICE: No, Daddy.

ELGAR: I'll look after my own eternal soul, if you don't mind.

CARICE: They meant no harm.

ELGAR: I think you should have said *we* meant no harm, don't you?

CARICE: It's very difficult. I'm not a great one for religion.

ELGAR: It's got nothing to do with you. It's what *I* want. How you could let them do that while I was helpless.

CARICE: They told me it was for your own good..

ELGAR: My own good? [*Laughs*] Thank you, Fishface. I needed a laugh. Anyway, next time you'll have no excuse. You know my wishes. No church. No fuss. Put me down where the Severn and the Teme meet, as I asked.

CARICE: Yes, Daddy.

ELGAR You must stop letting people shove you around, or me.

CARICE: But they all say - "He's the man who wrote *The Dream of Gerontius, The Apostles, The Kingdom!*" What do I say to that?

ELGAR: That was someone else, another man. A man with a faith.. Well... half a faith if the truth were known... That's all over now. It'll be oblivion, a drink at the waters of Lethe.

CARICE: Oh, Daddy, please...

ELGAR: Stop whimpering! [*Pause*] I still have a lot to do. The only important thing left is the symphony. Must clear the decks, you see. Get everything else out of the way and forge on! [*Out*]


# SCENE 27


[*Edge in BBC REITH's office*]

REITH: Now is a time for visions, Mase. Why shouldn't Elgar have one? Dying men frequently do.

MASE: Yes, Sir John.

REITH: Vision created this corporation, Mase. Let us never forget that.

MASE: No, Sir John.

REITH: I've never been afraid of visions; having them or encouraging other people to have them.

MASE: Absolutely, Sir John.

REITH: It was a stroke of genius to commission this symphony. John of Gaunt on his death-bed. "I am a prophet new inspired and thus expiring," etcetera. D'you see what I mean?

MASE: Should I come back a little later, Sir John?

REITH: No, no, stay, stay! It's all becoming clear. It's odd the way one does something and then has to wait for the reason one did it to emerge. I tell you, Mase, I think this symphony could be the final nail in the coffin of the *ancien regime*.

MASE: Pardon, Sir John?

REITH: Think about it, man! The British Empire at its final high point. Mussolini resurrecting the Roman Empire. The Germans flexing their muscles again. And what do you have?

MASE: And what do you have, Sir John?

REITH: Elgar up there with Beethoven and Verdi! A new imperialism that will create democracy afresh by non-democratic means!

MASE: I never thought of that, Sir John.

REITH: That's where the vision comes in, Mase.

MASE: Yes, Sir John.

REITH: That's what Elgar's Third will be all about. A new sense of nationhood.

MASE: This will take some time to sink in.

REITH: Don't be so dull, man. This will be a great British symphony. Not insular but global! Not vulgar but strong, dynamic and refined. Do you know that Great Britain has been a political reality for over two hundred years but it has never been a cultural reality? But suddenly it is here. And was it the *English* Broadcasting Corporation who commissioned this great work?

MASE: No, Sir John.

REITH: Well then? Oh this is so exciting! If that old man dying in Worcester is as much in touch with the *zeitgeist* as we are then something glorious will come out of this. [*Out*]

# SCENE 28

[*Nursing home. Violin playing of fragment*]

ELGAR: That was the end, Billy.

BILLY: You should have told me. I'd have played it differently.

ELGAR: Bloody tears. I didn't ask them to come. What kind of composer scores the end, sobs over it, but hasn't even filled in the middle? Did you look in on the dogs?

BILLY: They're both well.

ELGAR: Pining?

BILLY: Yes.

ELGAR: Good. You know Billy, I think they might let me go home soon. We'll be able to go out in the car. I have a yearning to be in one place... Damn these tears! What's up with me?

BILLY: Where's that then?

ELGAR: A bridge... and a pub... just below the bridge the river has sandbanks... the footprints of birds... sat there for many a day, Billy... We'll go in the car... Have a pint or two, a cheese sandwich...

BILLY: I look forward to that.

ELGAR: The sun will shine, Billy. The music will come from the hills. It will be worth writing down.

[*Pause*]

ELGAR: If you should bump into Vera... You'd better go now before *they* shout at us.

BILLY: Au revoir, Sir Edward.

[*Packing up*]

ELGAR: Give the dogs my love if you're passing. Tell them I'll be home soon. [*Out*]


# SCENE 29


[*Carol singing* - God Rest Ye Merry Gentlemen - *coming from another part of the nursing home*]

[*Door opening*]

THOMPSON: Like me to leave the door open so you can hear better?

ELGAR: No.

[*Door closed*]

THOMPSON: How are you?

ELGAR: Oh, all right, I suppose. Looking forward to going home.

THOMPSON: Unbutton your night-shirt, thank you. Just another week - so we can be sure that you're on an even keel. [*Pause*] Tell me; has anyone ever done any work on the ergonomics of composing music?

ELGAR: Eh?

THOMPSON: How the creative mind works - where the energy comes from, how much is consumed... all that kind of stuff. Do you know of anyone who's studied it? No one's approached you, have they?

ELGAR: They'd get a flea in their ear if they did.

THOMPSON: Why's that?

ELGAR: It would be a waste of time. Writing music is very straightforward. It comes from outside, goes through me, makes use of what I am, then moves on.

THOMPSON: You make it sound easy.

ELGAR: Is being used easy? Isn't it the most humiliating, insulting...
  [*Pause*] You keep saying how brave I am these days. I'm not. There's
  nothing to fear, you see. I'm going to be able to give the gift back, stick
  it in his hand and say: "Thanks very much, I'm sure!"

THOMPSON: There! You can button up now. Should you continue
  working on this new symphony?

ELGAR: It's not that easy. No choice really.

THOMPSON: There must be a choice somewhere.

ELGAR: Ah, there was. I had notebooks full of bits and pieces. I had
  snatches from unfinished things, quotes... all sorts... a rag-bag. In my
  mind, but lifeless, just lying there. Then they were stirred up. How
  doesn't matter. What I have to put up with now is them all swirling
  around like a snowstorm but I know from experience that they'll settle
  and that will be my Third Symphony. All I have to do is stay alive long
  enough for the storm to blow itself out and there it will be, laid out one
  morning. Finished. Ready to play. Then I can rest.

THOMPSON: So what must you do now!

ELGAR: Now? Watch, listen, catch things as they pass, wait for connections, ways through, be buoyed up by it all... Oh, I can't get anyone to
  understand. Never have!

THOMPSON: So this will go on no matter what I say?

ELGAR: It will, as you say "go on." No point in mentioning it again, is
  there?

THOMPSON: Is clarity of mind crucial?

ELGAR: What does that mean?

THOMPSON: So I know what to do. What to give you.

ELGAR: Ah, got you now. Pain and music. We'll have to sort that out as
  we go along. I'm not a superman.

THOMPSON: But we can be honest with each other?

ELGAR: Whenever possible. Remember, I'm always listening for the
  truth.

THOMPSON: Then there's a way forward.

ELGAR: It would seem so.

  [*The carolling comes nearer. A knock at the door*]

ELGAR: Go away!

BOY: We're collecting for the blind, Sir. Do you have a carol you'd like us
  to sing?

ELGAR: Any by Elgar?

BOY: Dunno, sir. We don't know who wrote them. We just sing them.

ELGAR: That's cheered me up immensely. Give him a fiver out of my wallet.

BOY: Thank you!

ELGAR: And avoid Elgar. His carols were only heathen hymns.

[*Door closes. Carol singing goes on down the corridor*]

THOMPSON: You know there may be times when I must insist that you stop working to save you so you can continue later on? Do you understand?

ELGAR: Tell *it*, not me.

THOMPSON: Has *it* got a face.

ELGAR: There have been times when I've been fooled into thinking so. Women, usually. But that was always a myth. It's not a human face.

[*Out*]

# SCENE 30

[*Nursing home*]

DOCTOR: Car is waiting, Sir Edward.

ELGAR: I said two o'clock.

DOCTOR: Everything is packed. It's a beautiful day.

[*Out*]

# SCENE 31

[*Edge in exterior atmos - birdsong*]

ELGAR: [*Fade in*] But where's my car?

DOCTOR: This gentleman came to visit just as we were getting you ready to leave. He says he'll run you home.

ELGAR: But Richard's coming for me.

DOCTOR: We rang and told him someone else would be bringing you.

[*Car door opening*]

BALDWIN: Come in, Sir Edward.

ELGAR: Do I know you?

BALDWIN: Do two old Wuster men need introductions? Stanley Baldwin. I called to wish you a happy New Year. Do you mind if I run you home?

[*Switch to car interior*]

# SCENE 32

[*1933 Rolls Royce*]
ELGAR: I'm very honoured, sir.
BALDWIN: My pleasure, Sir Edward. Perhaps you'd like to go for a drink?
ELGAR: Sounds like a very sensible idea.
BALDWIN: Where would you like to go?
ELGAR: Do you know the Talbot at Knightsford Bridge?
BALDWIN: An excellent choice.
[*Cross on car travelling to pub interior, then to exterior of the Talbot*]

# SCENE 33

ELGAR: Think you could get me down to the river bank now?
BALDWIN: Looks damn steep! The driver and I might manage the wheelchair barring accidents.
ELGAR: If you can't then we can call on the services of the strong men holding up the bar.
[*Out*]

# SCENE 34

[*Edge in river valley. Sound of carrying the wheelchair down a steep track*]
ELGAR: I'm sorry to be the cause of the leader of the Conservative Party having to stoop to manual labour. We must never let the Socialists know.
BALDWIN: [*Struggling*] When it comes to shifting national institutions we must all lend a hand. [*Under his breath*] Though an earldom would have been easier.
ELGAR: [*Laughing*] What was that?
BALDWIN: I said I was sounding wheezier and wheezier. Must give up smoking.
ELGAR: My God, you've broken out into a sweat. Don't get yourself muddy, now. Once we're on the level you can push me.
BALDWIN: We might have been better advised to do this before going into the pub.
[*Cross into*]

# SCENE 35

[*River flowing - a breeze in the trees*]

ELGAR: No birds singing. Not one. When I used to come down here thirty five, forty years ago they never stopped.

BALDWIN: It is January.

ELGAR: Yes, it's January all right. It's been January for a long time. *Gerontius* was written here. Do you know it?

BALDWIN: Not too well up on serious music, if you know what I mean. One of yours?

ELGAR: *The Dream of Gerontius* is a poem by Cardinal Newman. It tells the story of a man who thinks he is dying. He dreams that he dies and goes into the presence of God.

BALDWIN: I see.

ELGAR: Ultra-serious Catholic stuff.

BALDWIN: Hm.

ELGAR: One can't get seriouser.

BALDWIN: I didn't know you were a Catholic. Is it important to you?

ELGAR: Not now, I assure you. It was something I had to escape from. But when I was here and the river was bringing the music down, in those days I was faithful.

BALDWIN: Good spot.

ELGAR: Yes.

BALDWIN: Convenient for the pub.

ELGAR: I used to clamber up, my hand numb from the work, have a pint; then I'd go back down again. Day after day. The sun never seemed to stop shining or, if it did, I've forgotten.

[*Pause*]

BALDWIN: What's important to you now, Sir Edward?

ELGAR: Can't clamber now, only fall. Don't worry. There's nothing you can do, no matter what they've asked you, but this has given me great pleasure.

BALDWIN: I shall come back here.

ELGAR: Good. If you come at the right time you'll see kingfishers. D'you know, it's a terrible thing, but at the moment I can't remember a single bit of music that came to me here. Not a scrap. I'd read the poem many, many times, pondered over it, adapted it, broken it up... All about death, essentially.

BALDWIN: Hmm. Grim.

ELGAR: It's grim all right.

BALDWIN: Must be hard to make music out of death.

*[Breeze intensifies]*

ELGAR: Sometimes I wonder if we make music out of anything else. Why? What could possibly have interested me in such a tale? I was in my best years! In my prime! What a waste. I should be writing *Gerontius* now today.

BALDWIN: You have the symphony to keep you occupied.

ELGAR: So you know about that?

BALDWIN: Politicians keep their ears cocked for what people are expecting. This *Dream of Gerontius* went down well.

ELGAR: The old Queen was still on her throne. All the worst things hadn't yet happened. Waiters hadn't become the gentlemen. And what did I do? In full summer, with life all around me, I brought this world more music of death. Why are we like this, Mr Baldwin?

BALDWIN: Beyond me.

ELGAR: I should have been a farmer.

BALDWIN: Now you're talking. Want to come over and see my prize pigs? I've got an old Wessex Saddleback on the farm who's fathered over ten thousand piglets by my calculation.

ELGAR: Good Lord, that's going some! *[Laughs]*

BALDWIN: But all he can do is grunt.

*[BALDWIN sings softly, as best he can, the opening of* Sanctus Fortis *from* The Dream of Gerontius]

ELGAR: You do know *Gerontius*!

BALDWIN: Of course I do. Come on, we must get you home. You're shivering.

*[Hold breezy river background]*

ELGAR: *[In his head]* In those woods, by those waters, I applied myself deciduously. On the sky there were bar-lines drawn by birds. Notes floated by in the shape of twigs and, on one occasion, a dead sheep. All I ever did was copy it down, dumb. Even the instruments allocated themselves. The dark flutes, the bright trombones. There was never any other way of doing it for me. No human mind taught me music. I heard what was being played on the world's strings, winds and skins, and dutifully, obediently, entered it on paper. Where is there need to be penitent? What is my sin, unless this is all a lie and I created it in pride and rivalry? The wind in the reeds is the wind in an oboe. The mouth, the lip, the lung, is not mine. Not mine. I did no blowing, nor was the spittle that dribbled from the pipe any human saliva... Oh, dog why goddest thou my steps?

[*Cut into Rolls Royce in motion*]

ELGAR: Beautiful car.

BALDWIN: Best there is.

ELGAR: Ask him not to drive too fast. I'm not in no hurry to get home. I want to enjoy the ride. I've a feeling next time I go out in a Rolls Royce I won't be seeing much.

[*Fades*]

# SCENE 36

[*Cross on car in motion into REITH's office*]

REITH: [*Fade in*] Mase, I have news of the Elgar situation. He's back at home now, so I have employed a couple of men to go up to Worcester and find out what's going on - with discretion, of course.

MASE: I see.

REITH: The reports I'm getting back say that Elgar is doing nothing at all. As for the piano, no one's been near it but the cleaning-woman.

MASE: Oh.

REITH: And he's not writing anything. Just snoozes all the time. Total inactivity, except for playing with his dogs in the bedroom.

MASE: What do you intend to do next, Sir John?

REITH: Spur him on, somehow. This great project must not fail for lack of initiative on our part.

MASE: I wish I could come up with a suggestion, Sir John. But if the man is too weak to carry on...

REITH: Nonsense! It's nothing to do with physical infirmity. It's the state of mind that matters, Mase. We must find a way of making him want to communicate something to this day and age. Are you with me, Mase?

MASE: I think so, Sir John.

REITH: The impression I'm getting is that he doesn't want to talk to the present. So the present must talk to him.

[*Fade REITH's office*]

# SCENE 37

[*Fade in ELGAR's study. A clock. Rooks outside*]

ELGAR: How good is your shorthand?

STENOGRAPHER: A hundred and twenty, sir.

ELGAR: Mmmm - several letters to do. If I go too quickly ask me to slow down, or if I go too slowly, tell me to speed up.

STENOGRAPHER: Yes, sir.

ELGAR: What's your name?

STENOGRAPHER: Muriel, sir.

ELGAR: You're as lovely as your name, Muriel.

STENOGRAPHER: Thank you, sir. The first letter.

ELGAR: D [*Pause*] for Dear. You want me to speed up?

STENOGRAPHER: Suit yourself, sir.

ELGAR: Dear Chancellor Hitler. [*Pause*] Shall I go on?

STENOGRAPHER: That's what I'm here for, sir.

ELGAR: It behooves me to write to you on behalf of my many Jewish friends. [*Pause*] Are you all right with behooves, Muriel?

STENOGRAPHER: Yes, sir.

ELGAR: You may or may not have heard of me and my work, but I am a simple English musician who has during a long life held Germany in high esteem as the home of Beethoven, Bach, Schumann and Mendelssohn, giants in the world of music. So it has been with dismay and bewilderment that I hear what has been perpetrated against the Jews, a race full of artistic intelligence. I particularly regret the treatment you have given Mendelssohn. His statue in Leipzig has been taken down because he had a Jewish background. You may have removed this memorial, Herr Chancellor, but a man of your knowledge and experience must surely realise that Mendelssohn's reputation as a great German composer is fixed forever and cannot be done away with so easily. I therefore ask you in the interests of commonsense and decency to reconsider your policies because you will find that you are banging your head against a brick wall. Believe me to be, yours sincerely, Sir Edward Elgar Bart OM and the rest. Oh, and type it on score paper, if it will go in your roller.

STENOGRAPHER: Do you have an address, sir?

ELGAR: The Chancellery, Berlin will find him. Now... my coal merchant... Richard's ticked him off about the quality but it's had no effect... Dear... Get the wretch's name off Richard... You appear to be unresponsive to genuine, reasoned complaints, so I must warn you that should you continue to fob me off with slack instead of top-grade bituminous coal...

STENOGRAPHER: How d'you spell that, sir?

ELGAR: Got you at last! [*Laughs. Pause*] If only...

ALICE: [*On echo*] Edu, the snowdrops, the crocuses, the buds - don't miss them because your attention is all on a silly, common girl. She's laughing at you all the time.

ELGAR: [*Curtly*] That will be all.

STENOGRAPHER: Oh... I thought there was more.

ELGAR: I'm tired.

STENOGRAPHER: Very well, Sir Edward. I wonder if you'd mind... My little brother is learning the violin and he's got to do this piece by you. Would you sign the sheet-music for him? He'd be so pleased.

ELGAR: Type those letters up and give them to Richard. He will bring them in to be signed. Good bye, Muriel.

ALICE: [*On echo*] That was by far the best thing to do, my darling. One mustn't make a fool of oneself at this stage. Handel arranged for his place at Westminster Abbey and commissioned his statue well in advance. If you're writing letters it might be worth firing one off to the Dean and finding a sculptor who can be recommended.

ELGAR: I loved that girl. I loved her posture. I loved her knees. I loved the way she wrote down the symbols on her pad. I loved the way her fingers held the pencil.

ALICE: Ask Shaw for the name of a sculptor. He's well up on everything. Rodin would have done you very well. He'd have got your style. And darling, be practical: Next time ask for a plain, elderly stenographer. You'll get so much more achieved.

ELGAR: Aaaaaaaa! [*Out*]

# SCENE 38

[*Edge in ELGAR's bedroom. Rustles of paper and the sound of fire being built up in background*]

ELGAR: Damn... damn... Everything is getting out of order... The end's at the beginning, the middle's collapsed... Where's that *cantabile* piece?... cello throughout... [*Hums*] It was here a moment ago.

MOUNTFORD: [*Replacing the shovel*] I'll take the dogs out now.

ELGAR: Come on Marco, come on Mina... Get off my symphony you loafers... Go with Richard for walkies... You've got it far too hot in here.

MOUNTFORD: The fire will die down. It's very cold today and we have to keep the temperature up, Mr Thompson says.

[*Picks up the coal bucket*]

ELGAR: I wish I could come with you. One of those hard, bright blue times. Good for hunting hares. Ever followed beagles on foot, Richard?

MOUNTFORD: No.

ELGAR: Days like this I can't think of anything better. Boots well dubbined. A good stick. Hip-flask. The hounds leaping and running. A marvellous chase and kill. Then the hot-pot supper and a few songs. Paradise, Richard, paradise. I was never happier than in those days.

MOUNTFORD: We'll just walk down the road and back. Won't be long.

ELGAR: I've run all over this land after hares. They start mating about now, dancing, going mad, running around in circles, thinking they can fly. Lovely to watch them.

[*Door opening*]

ELGAR: Hey, careful, that makes a draught. You've blown my papers.

[*Door closing*]

ELGAR: [*In his head*] Oh, hell, in the fire... What piece was that? [*Laughs*] It'll never be remembered. I can't remember it. They've never heard it. Up the chimney as smoke! Into the hard, bright blue sky! Running with the hares all over Worcesterhire, up and down the hills, along the river valleys, everyone heading for the meeting of the waters. Toot-toot! Toot-toot! Breaking cover! Zig-zag, zig-zag through the bushes! Watch that smeuse, boys!

[*Papers thrown in the air*]

ELGAR: Yoicks, lightin' an' zunder! Arter 'ee, the bugger!

[*Door opening*]

CARICE: Daddy! What on earth are you doing?

ELGAR: Snowstorm on the Malverns. Tore the screaming hare asunder. The winter had been mild and she was already in young. We were hunting too late. The unborn leverets were flung into the air and the hounds snapped them up. Now they'll never run an' run an' run, those little ones, those quavers.

[*Dogs barking as they go off on their walk*]

CARICE: Don't think about things like that, Daddy.

ELGAR: I'm not. Those things are thinking about me.

[*He coughs. Silence, except for his breathing*]

CARICE: Rest now.

ELGAR: It will be written. It will be played.

CARICE: Of course it will.

ELGAR: I don't want to be remembered as a man who did not keep his word.

CARICE: No-one could ever say that about you.

ELGAR: I can hear it now.... But the drudgery of writing it down! That's what's holding me up... Someone should have developed a shorthand, or a machine. It's everywhere now. On the sheets. On the cracks in the floorboards. Every time the curtains move someone is turning over the pages of the score. I've conducted it darling. At the end the audience were thunderstruck.

CARICE: Daddy, no one is going to think any the worse of you if you can't finish it. You took on too much.

ELGAR: [*Peremptorily*] Put my papers in order. Sharpen my pencils. Then get out of here.

CARICE: Daddy... please!

ELGAR: Out! And tell that imbecile, Richard, when he gets back that I'll ring when I want him. I'm not to be disturbed when I'm working.

CARICE: Yes, Daddy.

[*Papers being gathered off the floor and bed*]

ELGAR: This is Edward Elgar you're dealing with, not some ailing layabout! Avaunt!

CARICE: Oh, Daddy, I do wish you'd listen.

ELGAR: That's all I've ever done, my darling. Listen. Listen. Listen. Until now there was plenty to hear... too much if the truth were told... but now there are gaps, silences, flat spots. That's all right. All I have to do is wait. Something will turn up.

[*Pencils sharpened*]

CARICE: You've done so much.

ELGAR: Pshaw! And what I have done will be forgotten very quickly. This is my last chance to make a lasting mark. My Third Symphony must do what the rest has failed to accomplish.

CARICE: You're not being fair to yourself. Your music is everywhere these days.

ELGAR: Like dead leaves blowing around. Compost-to-be.

[*Door opening. A sniffle*]

ELGAR: Oh, stay if you like.

CARICE: I thought you wanted to work.

ELGAR: There's nothing going on. I know that once you've shut the door I'll sit here and look at these bits and pieces like a mosaic-maker who's only got a tenth of what he needs. The other nine-tenths is somewhere else, far away. That's what makes me afraid. Where? Will I be taken to it?

[*Door closing*]

CARICE: Won't you have a word with Father Gibb?

ELGAR: Don't insult my intelligence!

CARICE: Talking to him can't do any harm.

ELGAR: None of that is any use to me. He'll serve me up the same old stuff, stuff I rejected thirty years ago. He knows nothing about what I'm going through.

CARICE: It would be a comfort.

ELGAR: Comfort! I don't want comfort, you idiot, I want the truth!

CARICE: All right, there's no need to shout.

ELGAR: Is it any wonder that I feel so lonely? All people want to do is feed you commonplaces. Ugh! [*Pause*] Hm. Perhaps you should go... something suggesting itself... Creep off, Carice.

[*Door opening*]

CARICE: Do you...

ELGAR: Ssssh! Begone! Vesuvius is about to erupt!

[*Door closing*]

ELGAR: [*In his head*] It must eclipse everything I've ever done... leave the rest standing. Yah! Break out of this prison! [*Hums*] Thirty bars here... some of it harmonically sorted. That could be played right now. The middle is coming together. Always been an end. Haven't made my mind up about the keys. Come on! Find the keys you want, you old fool!

ALICE: [*On echo*] Strange thing is, Edward, it's all perfectly true - exactly as the Church said it would be! There is a city, and a gate. Saint Peter at his post. Whether one is allowed to enter or not depends entirely upon the case one can make, plus *grace*. I was very surprised to find how accurate the priests had been in their predictions. Music is played continually and a lot of it is yours, though I do hear the Germans, of course, and the Italians now and then. You'll have no problem getting in, my darling.

ELGAR: Alice, it's not that I want you to leave me alone - I never have - but you must give me room.

ALICE: How can you compose this symphony in doubt? Doubt is an obstacle, a poison! Nothing grows out of doubt.

ELGAR: I have no doubt.

ALICE: Oo mustn't fib, now!

ELGAR: I know the power that deals with me, Chicky. Doubt doesn't come into it. Nor penitence.

ALICE: You have enough work to do writing your music. Leave these things to people who know their business. Submit to His will before you become too confused.

ELGAR: I am not confused. All I want to do is stand beneath the waterfall again.

ALICE: Oh, my poor Edu... There're stones in it.

ELGAR: If you hold your head up, they bounce off. [Pause] D'you remember the psaltery we had hanging on the landing at Birchwood? One night, full of gloom and foreboding after bad dreams, I had to get up. As I passed the psaltery it played itself. The time on the clock was 4.38 am. I have never been able to recall the tune. I need that music now. [Out]

# SCENE 39

[*REITH's office at Broadcasting House*]

MASE: But we can't wait any longer before announcing the festival programme, Sir John.

REITH: If we put his Third Symphony in that would put pressure on him, wouldn't it? He might respond. We could get a team up to Worcester to help, technicians, sound equipment, the best musical annotators, everything we need to get the music out of him. He could just lie there and hum.

MASE: It doesn't quite work like that, Sir John.

REITH: When I think of the good that symphony could do. A voice of sweet reason! Unity! Class barriers are collapsing. People are reaching out to each other across the divide. Rich and poor are getting closer as this slump grinds down all differences. And at the heart of this transformation I keep hearing wonderful music. Wonderful, stately, dignified, noble, elevated music.

MASE: [*To himself*] Oh, God.

REITH: Mase, we must go to Worcester! We must get down on our knees and plead with Elgar to finish this symphony.

MASE: Sir John, from what I've been able to gather, all he has is bits and
   pieces, very little indeed. I had a meeting with Arthur Thompson, his
   medical consultant, as per your orders, and he told me that the
   symphony is now just a dream, a game. I have to say that I always
   thought that to be the case.

REITH: Then why didn't you say so? You must learn to speak out Mase!
   [*Pause*] How could he have the gall to sign that contract? Hardly the
   action of a gentleman.

MASE: Elgar was always a musician first and foremost, Sir John.

# SCENE 40

[*ELGAR's bedroom*]

[*Edge in violin playing of slow movement section of the fragments, ending
unresolved*]

ELGAR: You get the idea?

SHAW: Um. Partially in the dark.

ELGAR: Play it again Billy.

[*The section is played*]

BILLY: Could you take it a bit further, Sir Edward?

ELGAR: Oh yes. Later on. So, you see how its coming along, Shaw? Good,
   isn't it? Quite unusual.

SHAW: As you know, I think anything you come up with is worth
   listening to. With a life-force as mighty as yours one must always expect
   something new.

ELGAR: I've learnt a few lessons. This one is going to be much simpler
   in structure than the other two. I mustn't try to be too clever.

SHAW: We went to hear your First Symphony played by the BBC Orchestra last week. What a charged atmosphere! The audience went out into
   the street afterwards ready for anything. Pity that you couldn't have
   been there.

ELGAR: Too draughty. The bit of the slow movement Billy played just
   now has to be fiery and rugged. He didn't quite get that, did you?

BILLY: Got as near as I could, Sir Edward.

ELGAR: I want it to hurt a bit... You know, disturb... [*Pause*] They gave
   the A Flat good applause?

SHAW: Loud and long.

ELGAR: How many times was Boult called back to the rostrum?

SHAW: Five or six. They wanted the whole thing played again!

ELGAR: I wish I'd been there. How did Adrian handle the Adagio?

SHAW: An herioc steadfastness of line.

ELGAR: The one who conducted that best, in his head, was Jaeger, my
  great friend, my old German Jagpot. He was dying of consumption and
  too ill to come to the first performance, but he wrote to me about what
  he had heard when he read the score. He said it was the greatest slow
  movement since Beethoven and worthy of him; which was nonsense,
  of course, but nice of him to say it.

SHAW: He was a sharp man. D'you remember that concert held in his
  memory? Packed out with composers and musicians he'd helped. All
  the hangers-on like me couldn't get in the church.

ELGAR: It's a good time to remember our German friend, Jaeger. Let us
  keep him very much in mind these dark days. Now, Billy: Play Bernard
  that bit from the Scherzo... It's here somewhere...

  [*The Adagio from the* First Symphony *backs SHAW's next speech*]

SHAW: [*In his head*] Billy can scrape at what he likes, but I'm elsewhere
  with the Adagio, and many thoughts on this disintegrating Englishman. How is it that he can move me so? He's everything that I scorn,
  that I hold in contempt. Put us side by side and there's no shred of
  similarity. He stands for everything that annoys me. The man's a snob,
  drenched in the worst kind of class-consciousness because he came
  from nothing. He idolises the worst in himself, that puffed-up sham
  squirearch, and hates what's best - his marvellous music. When he's
  dead I'll write a play about him and open it at Malvern, right in the
  middle of his territory. It will be called *Edwardian Requiem* or *The
  Organ Grinder's Gentleman.*

  [*The Adagio of the* First Symphony *crosses into the Scherzo fragment of the*
  Third Symphony *that BILLY is playing*]

ELGAR: Can you link that up in your mind with what we were talking about?

SHAW: Yes... I understand... I'm sorry. I get very ill-tempered with
  unfinished things. People are always bringing me half of a play, ten
  thousand words of a novel... I send them away with a boot up the pants
  and say: "Finish it! Then we'll see!"

ELGAR: Ah, ha, you're in a mood.

SHAW: You have too much power over me these days. I think about you
  too much. You get in the way. [*Pause*] It damages me to see you sinking.
  Edward, great Edward... I should not have come.

ELGAR: Nonsense. This has been tremendous fun. Come on, this is your financial symphony, remember? When I finish it the BBC has to fork out another thousand. Think of what I can do with that. Put it on a 50-1 chance for the Grand National! Drink the lot, perhaps... Bah! You old skinflint! I suppose you'd put it in the bloody bank. [*Angrily*] Go on, buzz off, I've had enough of you!

SHAW: I wouldn't like to part in this confusion. I'm upset in a way that I don't quite understand. Forgive me.

ELGAR: What confusion? I know none of your ideas work and all you do is pretend that I haven't got any. Mutual toleration hasn't actually got us very far, has it? And don't say you only stuck with me because of the music or I'll kill you.

SHAW: We all have our time to come into... Yours is past, mine's to come, that's all. Let us part as friends.

ELGAR: Of course. Have a super-rational time with the Nazis and Stalin and that lot. I hope your master-plan for the universe is a huge success. Amazing that it should come out of the brain of a West End Irish tinker! You're a *parvenu*, sir! Go they ways!

SHAW: Keep pegging away at that symphony.

ELGAR: Go and drown yourself. And don't come again!

[*Door opens and closes. ELGAR laughs*]

ELGAR: Now we've got rid of him, Billy, we can get back to work. There's an awkward bit of bowing that I'd like you to have a go at for me. I'm sure you can make it work. [*Pause*] Billy?

BILLY: Give me a minute, Sir Edward. I'm getting my breath back.

ELGAR: We must get on.

BILLY: That upset me with Mr Shaw back there. I didn't like the way you were talking to each other, as if nothing mattered any more.

ELGAR: Oh, take no notice of Shaw. He's just an old bent coat-hanger with moth-balls for a mind. Take up they bow of burning gold. We mun hasten! [*Laughs*]

[*Out*]

# SCENE 41

[*ELGAR's bedroom*]

ELGAR: Richard, I'm at my wits end here. [*Puts tea-cup down*] Can you handle a very delicate mission for me?

MOUNTFORD: If it's within my ability.

ELGAR: Stop fussing. Leave those things alone. [*Pause*] I've no idea whether it's in your ability or not, but you're the only one I can ask. There's a woman whom I must see. I know that she'll want to come.

MOUNTFORD: A young woman, Sir Edward?

ELGAR: No. No. She's not young. All that's gone away now. I'm free of that. Be a good chap and understand. I've known her for many, many years. Very important that I have a last meeting with her.

MOUNTFORD: What do you want me to do?

ELGAR: Ring her up - tell her that I'm in extremis. That's the only way I'll get her here.

MOUNTFORD: Is she waiting for that call?

ELGAR: She doesn't know what to think. We haven't seen each other for some time; but I've no doubt that she's standing by.

MOUNTFORD: I'd rather not have to deceive the lady in question, Sir Edward. Do I have to say that you're in extremis, as you put it?

ELGAR: I am in extremis god dammit. The pain is often excruciating.

MOUNTFORD: I know. But if I tell her you'd like to see her, wouldn't that be enough. I assume she'll know how ill you are.

ELGAR: She must know that much. What I don't understand is why she hasn't called already.

MOUNTFORD: With your permission, shall I ring and say you need to see her. Might that do the trick?

ELGAR: Hm. Not sure that she's ever understood need.

MOUNTFORD: If you rang her yourself...?

[*1930-style van heard approaching*]

ELGAR: No. We agreed not to ring each other. It was too fraught. [*Pause*] Maybe I should keep the dream? Is that the way to do it? It was all so long ago, but her beauty was not the kind that fades.

MOUNTFORD: I think I heard the baker's van. Let me know what you decide.

[*Door opening and closing. Spaniels barking, then settling down again*]

ELGAR: Quiet, children! [*In his head*] Oh, Windflower, will I ever look on you again? Will you let me die without a last sight of your loveliness? Perhaps it would break your heart to see me like this? I'd be brave. I'd find a smile. The pain hasn't conquered me. Love would flare up again. Keep me going!

[*Door opening. The dogs bark fitfully, half asleep*]

MOUNTFORD: Bread is still hot from the oven, Sir Edward. Would you like some?

ELGAR: Yes!

[*Door closing*]

ELGAR: [*In his head*] Windflower will come. Vera will come. All the women will come. They will fill this room. [*Cry of pain*] Everywhere... Chicky, Mother...

[*Door opening. Dogs stir again*]

MOUNTFORD: Is there anything better than freshly-baked bread?

ELGAR: Get the dogs out of here. Call the doctor. Get him here with his bloody needle! [*A terrible cry*]

[*The cry echoes. ALICE speaks from out of it*]

ALICE: It's time you let Father Gibb in so you can have a good talk. He doesn't want to force himself upon you, Edu, so you'll have to speak up.

ELGAR: Nothing to say to him. Nothing. Old fool doesn't know a hawk from a handsaw.

ALICE: Don't leave it too late. Things get very muzzy.

ELGAR: Not with you always around. [*Out*]


# SCENE 42

[*ELGAR's bedroom*]

DOCTOR: [*Fade in*] Do I take it that helped? You're in less pain now?

ELGAR: [*Mumbling*] Yes.. Thank you... Where.. Where're my working papers?

DOCTOR: We put them in a drawer.

ELGAR: Take them out.

DOCTOR: They'll be perfectly safe.

ELGAR: Not in a drawer... They'll be in a bloody drawer soon enough... Give them to me. Not in a drawer.

DOCTOR: I'm not exactly sure where your man put them. He just said - a drawer. He'll sort it out with you.

ELGAR: [*Strengthening*] Tell him to bring it all back!

DOCTOR: Very well, Sir Edward, but from now on you must have a nurse living in. Your man is a great help, but he cannot give you the proper care. I've arranged for someone to come tomorrow.


# SCENE 43

[*NURSE reading newspaper*]

NURSE: The German government announced in Berlin today that a ten-year non-aggression pact has been signed with Poland. Colonel Josef Beck, the Polish foreign minister, commented: "This allays any fears that we may have had over the Four-Power pact between Britain, France, Germany and Italy..."

ELGAR: The ink has come off on your pretty hands. Look.

[*Rustle of newspaper being shaken*]

NURSE: Shall I go on, sir?

ELGAR: Not with all that political stuff. It's always the same. Misery. Tell me about yourself.

NURSE: Oh, that's not very interesting.

[*Newspaper put down*]

ELGAR: I think it is. Have you taken care of a lot of dying old codgers?

NURSE: A fair number.

ELGAR: Having someone as lovely as you must have been a great mercy for them.

NURSE: I'm not lovely, Sir Edward.

ELGAR: Oh, yes you are.

NURSE: I'd better wash my hands before the doctor comes.

[*NURSE moving away*]

ELGAR: You know who I am? No, That's not what I mean. Of course you know who I am. What I am?

NURSE: I think so.

[*Clock strikes half-hour*]

ELGAR: I mean that I'm a musician.

NURSE: Yes. You compose.

ELGAR: Do you know anything of mine?

NURSE: Of course.

ELGAR: [*La-la's* Land of Hope and Glory] Heard that one? Horrible.

NURSE: Why? Everyone loves it.

ELGAR: But not me. Prop this old relic up on his pillows.

NURSE: Not until I've washed my hands. I won't be long.

[*Door opening and closing*]

ELGAR: [*In his head*] Starchy. Touch of the Amazon but underneath, a fan-dancer if ever I met one. The kind of woman to be taken to Cheltenham. Oh, I could teach her to get that brittleness out of her smile. A big hat would suit her, and hair unpinned over her shoulders... Such a strong body...

ALICE: [*On echo*] Edward!

ELGAR: You too, Chicky. Strong! Strong! How any weakness brought you down I'll never know. How I loved you, my good angel.

ALICE: At least she doesn't allow dogs in the bedroom. Treat her with respect. She has to minister to you through your ordeal. Don't make her fond of you.

[*Door opens*]

ELGAR: Where's Windflower... Vera? Where are the others? Are you the only one who's coming, Chicky?

FR. GIBB: There's only me.

Alice, don't be devious, darling.

FR. GIBB: I was asked to bring you your working papers, Sir Edward, since I was coming up...

ELGAR: I didn't ask for a priest!

FR. GIBB: Your daughter, Carice, said you had probably changed your mind by now.

[*Rustle of papers*]

FR. GIBB: My, you have been hard at it. So many notes! This is obviously a major opus. Hm, I'm not pitch-perfect but let's have a go... da-da-da-da... Complicated stuff for an old choirboy. How are you in yourself?

ELGAR: In this country a man has a right to remain silent if he's accused of anything. He doesn't have to incriminate himself.

FR. GIBB: You're not accused of anything, dear man.

ELGAR: I have always been accused of artistic pride; and by God himself. It would have been wiser of me to have kept quiet and stuck to teaching the fiddle at girls' schools.

FR. GIBB: Whoever heard of such nonsense? Your life and work have been divinely favoured.

ELGAR: You're not going to be much help to me talking like that. I'm not some old fool dying in the faith. If you want my scalp at your belt you'll have to work for it.

FR. GIBB: I'll come by tomorrow.

[*Out*]

# SCENE 44

[*ELGAR's drawing room*]

CARICE: [*Fade in*] Was he angry with me for letting you go in?

FR. GIBB: At first there was a little resistance but it seemed to go away. He talked to me. That's the main thing.

CARICE: Did you give him his symphony?

FR. GIBB: I put it on the bedside table, with the pencils, as you asked.

CARICE: I'm going to stay here now. Come when you can. We're all going to need your help. The doctor says that there will be terrible times to go through. Oh God, why does it have to be like this?

FR. GIBB: Help will come.

[*Out*]

# SCENE 45

[*Bedroom and sound of needle going down on record on a wind-up gramophone. Music starts from the end of the first movement of ELGAR's* Piano Quintet]

ELGAR: No, no. That's not right. You haven't hit it. That's too early. I only want the slow movement. Do it again. Note the spot.

[*The needle is taken off. Pause. It is lowered onto the break between the movements, then the second movement begins*]

ELGAR: That's it. Now take it off.

[*Needle being taken off with a screech*]

ELGAR: Careful now! That record of my Piano Quintet's brand new. I don't want it ruined!! [*Pause*] Open the window, Richard. There's too much condensation.

MOUNTFORD: That nurse will only close it again.

ELGAR: Well I want to see the hills. [*Pause*] Come back in half an hour. I'll need to hear the slow movement. And I won't want it botched by you being clumsy.

MOUNTFORD: Perhaps the nurse could do it better? I'm sure she'd be happy to help.

ELGAR: No. Putting the needle on the gramophone is your job.

MOUNTFORD: Your agent, Mr. Gaisberg, and Mr. Reed are still waiting to see you.

ELGAR: They know that a man must work for his living. Tell them that I'll be with them shortly. Now... the window, if you please.

[*Window being opened*]

MOUNTFORD: It's very cold, Sir Edward.

ELGAR: I don't feel it. I don't feel anything. But I can see and hear. The Malverns are clear today.

[*Rustle of paper*]

MOUNTFORD: Have you everything you need?

ELGAR: Bloody stupid question, isn't it? [*A cry*] Can't even hold the damn pencil! Tell my daughter that I've got to have someone who can take down the score at dictation. My time's running out.

MOUNTFORD: Yes, sir.

[*Door opens and closes*]

ELGAR: [*In his head*] I will lift up mine eyes unto the hills from whence cometh my help. My help cometh from the Lord which made heaven and earth. I could fugue up that second movement of the Piano Quintet, turn it round, upside down, extend it... Who'd know by the time I'd finished with it? They've all done it; Handel, Mozart... Stock-in-trade. Waste not, want not.

[*Door opening sharply*]

NURSE: What's this window doing open?

ELGAR: Yes, what are you doing open, window? Explain yourself.

[*Window being shut*]

NURSE: You'll freeze.

ELGAR: No, fry. Now the hills are fading. My own poisonous fug of corruption will send them away. And you've silenced a blackbird, which is a mortal sin.

ALICE: [*In echo*] Edu, darling, I've had a look at the place where you say you'd like to be buried...

ELGAR: Standing up, remember!

ALICE: The confluence of the Severn and the Teme. I'm afraid it's completely unsuitable. In the first place there's something there already - a large No Fishing notice - and there's a lot of soil erosion. You'd be quiet likely to be washed away in a flood. We couldn't have that.

ELGAR: I'd end up in Bristol Docks. Suit me fine.

ALICE: You must let people honour you as you deserve.

ELGAR: I've had enough of all that baloney. I want to go where the rivers meet! They can stick the No Fishing notice through my heart!

# SCENE 46

[*ELGAR's bedroom*]

BILLY: [*Fade in*] Wouldn't it be better if you told your agent... publisher... someone with authority to do it?

ELGAR: No. It must be a musician. Someone who's been through what I have.

BILLY: Then tell your daughter the same thing. I'll need a witness of some kind.

ELGAR: I'll tell Carice. But be very firm, Billy. No one must mess around with these bits and pieces of the Third Symphony. They mustn't be published or made use of in any way.

BILLY: I understand.

# SCENE 47

[*Slow movement of the piano quintet playing on the gramophone*]

ELGAR: That's enough, Fred. Take it off. Take it off.

[*The needle is taken off and the record stopped*]

GAISBERG: It's a fine recording.

ELGAR: I'm afraid it doesn't look as if there's going to be a third symphony.

GAISBERG: Don't worry.

ELGAR: I'm sorry. You've got a stake in it. I signed up with you for two years, Fred. Everything I wrote. The thing is, there is a third symphony, but I can't get it down.

GAISBERG: I understand.

ELGAR: Will Reith?

GAISBERG: He'll have to.

ELGAR: I've offered to pay the money back I've had so far.

GAISBERG: Didn't hear that. Come on, Edward. They knew the risks.

ELGAR: But the agency, Fred. You'll lose 40 per cent of all those fees. I feel that badly.

GAISBERG: That's their look-out. I'm not down here to talk about that. Leave it to the lawyers.

ELGAR: That's where we are now, Fred, lawyers and priests.

GAISBERG: Not completely. You know we're recording parts of Caractacus next week? I've had a word with the GPO and they think it could be possible to link you up directly live with the studio so you can listen, have a word with the conductor and the orchestra, give some help and advice. Would you like that?

ELGAR: *Caractacus?*

GAISBERG: Should be good. They'd really appreciate a word from the master.

ELGAR: *Caractacus* was written in place of the symphony I wanted to write for the Leeds Festival fifty years ago. Then they didn't need my symphony. English composers didn't do symphonies. They were expected to stick to cantatas. I did it for Victoria's Jubilee.

GAISBERG: If it's too sore a point would you rather leave it?

ELGAR: My mother suggested the subject. She was with me on the Malverns and she said: "Ted, can't you do something about these old hills. How about that British chieftain and the last stand he made here against the Romans?" [*Laughs*] Know what I got for *Caractacus*? One hundred pounds, and I had to provide the choral and orchestral parts. [*Pause*] You made a good choice, Fred. Yes, tell the GPO to - what was it - connect me up. [*Out*]

# SCENE 48

[*ENGINEER setting up bedroom for contact with the studio in London*]

NURSE: You mustn't keep asking Sir Edward to hold loose ends for you!

ENGINEER: Running late, sweetheart. Is there another power-point?

ELGAR: There's one on the landing. How long do I keep holding these?

NURSE: Can't you keep the cables off the bed, at least?

ELGAR: Don't be a spoilsport, nursey. These lads are working under difficult circumstances. Wiring up an old musician isn't easy. Tell Richard to bring some more chairs. I want everyone here.

NURSE: You'll get me fired. Then where will I be?

[*NURSE leaves*]

ELGAR: Lovely woman. Strikingly sudden in her rubato.

ENGINEER: If you say so, governor. I'd like to clear your bedside table, is that's all right. Now, where shall I put all these papers?

ELGAR: I'll have them under my pillow.

[*Papers being put under pillow and table cleared*]

ENGINEER: We have to get your microphone closer. Can you move further towards the edge of the bed?

ELGAR: [*Moving with great difficulty*] Is that better?

ENGINEER: Bit more.

ELGAR: All right?

ENGINEER: For the moment. We could do with more space, really. By the time we've finished that orchestra will feel as though its in the next room.

ELGAR: Which is the lavatory.

[*Out on their laughter*]

# SCENE 49

[*London studio. Sounds of orchestra listening - occasional ding of brass instrument, a furtive bit of string tuning, the scrape of a shoe*]

ELGAR: [*Over loudspeakers in the studio*] For some reason my mother, who was a poet in her own right, was very taken with the plight of Caractacus, King of Britain, and what he was up against. For myself, I saw the story as one of defeat - after all, Caractacus lost the battle on the Malverns, he was taken prisoner and shipped to Rome where he appeared before the Emperor Claudius in chains, who pardoned him because he was charming.

[*Soft laughter from the orchestra*]

ELGAR: I got into quite a lot of trouble over the final chorus, I remember. My friend, Jaeger, at Novello's, who was German-born, didn't like the tone, patriotic war-whoops and all, but I said then as I say now, England for the English... [*Whispers*] All right, Fred... I understand that you're going to start with the Triumphal March. I shall listen here very carefully for the spirit of the piece... Right... Druids stand by... Go forth, oh King! [*Chuckles*] Hill tribes, prepare to repel boarders.

# SCENE 50

[*Switch to Triumphal March from* Caractacus *being heard in ELGAR's bedroom over loudspeakers and ELGAR humming along with the music, then interference*]

REITH: [*Over loudspeakers*] Hello, Reith here. Are you hearing me?

ELGAR: Eh?

REITH: Keep humming, Sir Edward. We're set up here at Broadcasting House to record anything new that you might care to come up with.

ELGAR: I wish I'd known you were going to call.

REITH: Don't let me interrupt. All I want to say is this: Whatever's in there, let it come out. Doesn't have to be on a grand scale.

ELGAR: Terribly sorry I let you down.

REITH: We have the technological expertise, Sir Edward.

MASE: [*At REITH's shoulder, whispering*] Tell him to indicate the instrument if he can. With him the orchestration is crucial.

REITH: If you could let us know the instrument beforehand...

ELGAR: I heard. The Devil at your elbow is right, Sir John. In Elgar the orchestration is crucial. Orchestration is the crux in Elgar. It must all work crosswise for the cavalry charge.

NURSE: It would be better if you all left now.

[*Sounds of people slipping out, scrape of chairs, floorboards creaking*]

ELGAR: In Orch the Elgarisation is crooooocial. Crooooocial.

REITH: Hello! Hello! Are you there?

MASE: ...rambling.

REITH: We got all that, Sir Edward. Keep going!

NURSE: Oh leave him - leave the man alone!

[*Click. Silence. Breathing*]


# SCENE 51


[*ELGAR's bedroom*]

FR. GIBB: What is your decision, my son?

ELGAR: Bury me where the hares run and have to stop... leveret me go...

[*Laughs softly*]

FR. GIBB: Am I to proceed?

ELGAR: Mother of God...

FR. GIBB: [*Eagerly*] Yes?

ELGAR: Is a muse.

FR. GIBB: I can't follow you.

ELGAR: That's what I want. Go away.

FR. GIBB: You were born and brought up a Catholic. You are the composer of the greatest Catholic music in this country since William Byrd. I will not have you dying a pagan.

ELGAR: By the river. By the reeds. In the wind. Please.

FR. GIBB: You do not belong to yourself, my son. I act for Christianity, and the good of your soul. We must move on. I'm going to give you the Last Rites.

[*Bell tinkling*]

ELGAR: Wait... I'll do you a deal.

FR. GIBB: Sir Edward, die with dignity!

ELGAR: Oh, bosh. Who does that? I am prepared, you know. Never a great one for the age of William Byrd but I found something years ago.... copied out... We'll do it together? It's as far as I'll go.

FR. GIBB: What is it?

ELGAR: Oh, some prayer for a defunct Flemish musician. It just tickled my fancy.

FR. GIBB: I cannot compromise on this!

ELGAR: Oh, you'll be all right. Put the blame on me.

FR. GIBB: I shouldn't... Oh, all right! [*Reads*] O mors inevitablis mors
     amara, mors crudelis...

ELGAR: Oh inevitable death,
     Bitter death, cruel death...

FR. GIBB: Edward Elgar dum necasti,
     Illum nobis abstulisti

ELGAR: By slaying Edward Elgar
     You stole him from us.

FR. GIBB: Qui suam per harmoniam
     Illustravit potentiam...
     [*Outside the door eavesdropping over end of Latin*]

CARICE: I can hear it. He's accepted. He's gone back to his faith! Oh,
     Mummy will be so glad.
     [*Inside bedroom*]

ELGAR: Who by his harmony
     Gave lustre to the power...

FR. GIBB: Proptera tu musice dic:
     Requisecat in pace.
     [*Pause. A dying sigh from ELGAR. Pause*]

FR. GIBB: Now say thou with music:
     "May he rest in peace."
     [*The* Lament on the Death of Josquin des Pres *by Hieronymous Vinders
     is sung*]


THE END

# ALSO BY DAVID POWNALL

## NOVELS

*The Raining Tree War*
*African Horse*
*God Perkins*
*Light on a Honeycomb*
*Beloved Latitudes*
*The White Cutter*
*The Gardener*
*Stagg and his Mother*
*The Sphynx and the Sybarites*

## SHORT STORIES

*My Organic Uncle and Other Stories*
*The Bunch from Bananas*
(For children)

## POETRY

*Another Country*

## PLAYS

*An Audience Called Edouard*
*Motocar*
*Richard III: Part 2*
*The Dream of Chief Crazy Horse*
(For children)
*Pride and Prejudice*
(Stage adaptation)
*Beef*
*Ploughboy Monday*

## NON FICTION

*Between Ribble and Lune*